The
POMPEY HOLLOW
BOOK CLUB

A Novel

JEROME MARK ANTIL

LITTLE YORK
BOOKS
New York · NY · Dallas · TX

www.jeromemarkantil.com

TABLE OF CONTENTS

TO MY DAUGHTER

FOREWORD

If you're of a mind to wonder who Aunt Kate is in this book, you'd appreciate the legend. It came to light after the War, the year following their move to Delphi Falls, when the boy's dad took him aside and told him the family secret about Aunt Kate—in secret.

The boy was nine, maybe closer to ten, when a close friend of his, a nice old man, died. His tears for the loss of his old friend jarred his dad. It's generally thought that it was then when his dad came to realize that children born just before the Pearl Harbor attack, like his boy, had childhoods of too many lost someones. It dawned on him that their young eyes had witnessed a frightening, cruel world at war for more than five years.

"Nine-year-old boys and girls today," he concluded, "lived through a horrendous war and are sadly much older and wiser than their years for it. You've earned the right to deserve the truth. Son, Aunt Kate is not your aunt, she never was. She's your grandmother. Her real name is Catherine. It's Christmastime. I thought you would like to know the truth."

As the story goes, in 1902, Aunt Kate gave birth to a daughter, who would become the boy's mom in 1941. When her daughter was just a four-year-old girl, in 1906, Aunt Kate's husband ran off like the rotten-tomato lowlife scumbag bastard he turned out to be, abandoning them both. (Author's words; the boy's dad never uttered a curse word in his life.)

Aunt Kate's sister and her loving husband adopted the little girl so people wouldn't be saying things about a single mother with a child in 1906. Growing up in the 1940s, the boy, as were others, was led to believe the lady who was his mom's real mother was his aunt, Aunt Kate. After he knew the secret, anytime Aunt Kate visited, and read to him and tucked him in with a good-night kiss, he'd be certain to reach up in the dark, put his hand gently to the sweet old lady's velvety soft, wrinkled cheek, and whisper their secret: "Night, Grammy, I love you." That helped her sleep a little warmer on those evenings, he was certain.

Learning the truth changed the boy. It taught him it was never too early to say hello—the War already taught him it might be too late to say good-bye. This is about the boy, in his own words, the year he learned the secret. —**JMA**

Thanks, Dad.

Brother Dick and Big Mike 1941

Delphi Falls, N.Y.

CHAPTER ONE

LABOR DAY, 1948

My dad was the tallest man we knew anywhere—at six feet, six inches—even taller in his dress hat. Many called him "Big Mike." No matter when you saw him, he always wore suspenders, nice ties, and a genuinely happy smile and was ready with a twinkling in his eye to sit down to hear any tall tales about our adventures, the taller the better.

He found me staring out my new window in a trance, sitting on the edge of my bed. His head barely missed the top of the doorframe as he carried in two large bread cartons he'd borrowed from the bakery and that Mom had packed with clothes.

"Whatcha looking at, Jerry, me boy?"

He set both cartons on the bed across from mine. My name was scrawled in big crayon letters on the side of the one he lifted from the pile and placed on my bed, next to me. He pulled the flaps open to show me it was my clothes to be put away.

"Dad, I've been watching the road out by the front gate for exactly twenty-two minutes and there hasn't been one car drive by yet. Where are we, in Africa?"

He sat down on the other bed.

"You'll like the country, son, even more than Cortland. Here you can get out of the house, go exploring, without even asking. Not like the city. You'll have so many more adventures here. You'll meet a whole new set of friends, I promise. Just be patient. Give it time."

I interrupted: "Twenty-three minutes, seventeen seconds—an old beat-up truck."

"Jerry, look at your first day in a different school tomorrow as a big adventure. Make every day a new adventure. It'll be fun. We each have to write our own books in this life, son. No one will write them for us."

"The only people I met all week are carpenters, and they're all from Cortland, Dad. We're, like, in the wilderness."

Dad reflected a moment and met my challenge head on.

"You met Charlie Pitts. Well, Mr. Pitts to you. You like him. He has a little farm with a horse and buggy just down the corner and to the right, about halfway up the hill. He's going to take care of chickens for us, so we can have eggs. I think it would be a good adventure for you to walk to his farm every week and pick up the eggs. Would you like that?"

"Sure."

"Good! That's your chore starting this week. Ask your mother what day."

I turned from the window and looked in my box, recognizing my P.F. Flyer sneakers on top of the pile. Dad palmed his shirt-sleeve back and looked at his wrist watch. Seeing the time, he stood up, gazed out my window, and said:

"Son, that's Mr. Parker across the way. He's walking toward the road by the side of his house, which means he's about to call his cows in for their night milking. You've never seen that done before. Why don't you run over there, fast as you can, and watch how he does it? You can put your things away later. Don't forget to introduce yourself like I taught you, and shake his hand. Now go! Run!"

I jumped up.

"Dad, will you reset my alarm clock? I don't have a stopwatch, so I set all the hands at twelve when I started to watch the road so I could count the minutes and seconds easier."

Dad grinned. "Run!"

I ran out of the house, down the eighty or ninety yards to the front gate for the first time, turned left up the short steep curving hill on Cardner Road to where Mr. Parker was standing by the road. I introduced myself and shook his hand.

Farmer Parker, in his overalls, blue work shirt, and train engi-neer hat, put both opened hands by his mouth like a megaphone and almost yodeled up to the steep pasture hill on the other side of the road from his house and barn. It began to give me a new look on the different world I was in. He wasn't embarrassed to sing out his:

"Caho bossies! Caho bossies!"—meaning, Come home, bossies!

It was like I was at a stage play and he was on stage perform-ing or in a Saturday morning picture show. He just yodeled as if no one was watching him, until he saw the cows moving and coming down the hill. I cautiously stood behind him, being as I'd never seen a cow up close before. At least I hadn't seen one that wasn't behind a fence. I wasn't taking any chances. Twenty cows came down off the hill and through the gate, crossing the road, passing gently by and walking down his drive towards the back of the barn.

Farmer Parker turned to me, shook my hand again, and said, "Nice to meet you, Jerry, come back anytime. Right now I've got some cows to feed and milk."

He adjusted his train engineer hat, turned on his heel, and started walking down the slope of his gravel drive towards the barn.

Mrs. Parker stepped out from behind a screen door onto their gray back porch, emptied a white porcelain bowl of dish water on her rose bush, and waved hello at me just as she was walking back into the house. I waved and walked home.

When I got to my room there was a book on my pillow. My copy of the Hardy Boys' *Secret of the Old Mill,* which I must have left in the car. I pulled open the drawers on my side of the closet, stuffed clothes in, butted them closed, and stepped into the hall. I took the shortcut through Mom and Dad's room to the kitchen. The cupboards were opened—on top, over the counters, and the bottom, near the floor. Mom and Dad were emptying boxes of dishes, the toaster, waffle iron, pots, pans, bowls, soup cans, and cereal boxes, putting them away.

My oldest brother, Mike, was in the dining room with a pencil over his ear, wearing his new and white chef's apron he'd asked for and got as his high school graduation present. Dad got it at the bakery.

"Whatcha doing?" I asked.

"Taking inventory," Mike said. "Don't bother me, I'm busy."

On the table in front of him were shoe boxes filled with an assortment of strange smelly foods, spices, relishes, muddy mustards, and smushed olives. Little tins with printing on them and small glass jars with lids and labels. Junky food no normal person would give a whit about. Stuff so bad they'd never put it in big cans or pint bottles. He saved up for it all and an old Chevy, working summers. He was wrapping them to take with him to college in a couple of weeks. A new hot plate was on the table, sitting on top of its box. Probably another graduation present, I guessed, so he could stink up his dorm room, cooking. I stepped closer to check it out.

He pointed a bunch of garlic in my direction. "Don't even think about it!"

"Huh?"

"Don't touch a thing."

I couldn't stand the smells. He acted as if I would even go near this stuff.

I had to be patient. Mike hadn't been the same since his face cleared up, that's for sure, and now he had his driver's license. He thought hot dogs were disgusting and that most table food, except for maybe corn-on-the-cob, was for common people. Not for him. He said he had good taste. He'd graduated high school in June with what Mom called "honors." Dad called them "delusions."

Something about him just wasn't normal anymore. Even Mom couldn't put a finger on it, saying, "It's a stage."

Dad said, "Well I hope he gets on one"—that is, a stagecoach—"and it leaves before he makes us all nuts."

I was just a kid, what would I know, but I'd read enough of the Hardy Boys to understand what clues were, and my suspicion was Mike was becoming a gourmet, which, for all I knew, could be a strange disease with considerable inclinations.

I stood there and stared at Mike taking his inventory. He held up jars and cans like a chemist in a scary movie laboratory reading the labels. His lips mouthed the French or Italian words on them. Mike always talked about being a surgeon after college so he could discover cures, live a life of importance and elegance, not live like us—as commoners. At least that's what he said the time he caught Dick drinking milk straight out of the milk bottle and admonished, "One doesn't have to choose to BE a disgusting pig, if one doesn't want to BE one."

Dick took a last swig from the half empty bottle, handed it to Mike, and said, "To BE or not to BE ..." Then he belched and walked away.

Even though he'd grown as tall as Dad, and they both had the same first name, Mike, there was no way he was ready to go off to college alone with a hot plate. I had my reasons for believing this. From the car on Sunday, I overheard Mom talking to Father Lynch in front of our new church in Manlius, about Mike and his going off to Lemoyne College. I could swear the "gourmet" word came up, causing me to sit up straight and press my ear to an opening in the car window. Father Lynch leaned close to Mom and asked, "You don't suppose Mike has capers, do you?"

I knew it, I thought. I knew Mike had something. I quietly rolled the window down further, not drawing any attention, and not wanting to miss a word.

"I'm almost certain he does, Father," Mom confessed. "He's had them for some time now."

"Oh my," said Father Lynch. "Capers are so rare, very rare indeed, ever since the War; most difficult to get. Wish the lad luck in college, for me, Mary. My prayers are with him."

I had no idea what a caper was but that was all the proof I needed. I knew it was enough to suspect this gourmet thing was serious, maybe even rare and "incommunitcable" like diseases I heard about on Army radio.

I wasn't putting it past Mike to eat ants or grasshoppers, frogs and lizards, just like in the pictures in the *National Geographic* he kept in his room. This sort of thing is an addiction. He could open the lid of a little glass jar filled with something disgusting—take a whiff just as easily as he could warm up for his "at bat" in a Sunday baseball game at the stone quarry. It just wasn't normal.

Dad saw me staring at Mike's mess on the table; probably didn't want me to get infected.

"Son, the radio was delivered today. Go listen to your shows."

"Where's Dick?" I asked.

Dad said, "Mr. Rowe went back to Cortland in a bakery truck to bring the last load of boxes. Dick rode with him to say good-bye to his friends in our old neighborhood. They'll both be here any minute. They'll be along."

"Did you put your clothes away?" asked Mom.

"Yes ma'am."

Dad offered, "I heard NBC is rebroadcasting last night's Superman and Sergeant Preston for Labor Day because school starts tomorrow. You missed them last night. Go tune them in, son."

"Okay."

I leaned my back flat up against the dining room wall and slid along it edging around Mike, making sure nothing he was touching got on me. I made my way to the living room. Walking over to the radio I could see out the window the bakery truck coming through the front gate. Dick would be here any minute. I got down on the floor in front of the Zenith and turned its familiar old knob to "on."

It dawned on me all of a sudden how much Superman and I had in common. He came from Planet Krypton, crash landed into a field in the country when he was a kid, and grew up on a farm. I came from Cortland, a city, where last year I could walk to school. Now I was out in the country, in the middle of nowhere. I had a farm with lots of cows right across the road. Superman rode a school bus to school; now I had to take a school bus to school.

Any Superman radio fan my age knew that, like him, we were all ... faster than a speeding bullet ... more powerful than a locomotive. He could leap tall buildings, though, in a single bound ... look ... up in the sky ... it's a bird ... it's a plane ... it's Superman!

I sat waiting for the radio to warm up, watching the comforting, glowing dial on the Zenith I had relied on through the War, a familiar streak of lightning. During the War we'd listen to the news from London, Africa, or the South Pacific about bombings and killings, planes being shot down and ships being torpedoed. The only relief kids had was listening to Superman or some other radio program to help keep our minds off the atrocities of it all. Now, again, although my life may have been turned upside down all summer, at least I still had my favorite floor model radio, and I had my friend Superman on Sunday and Wednesday nights.

Maybe I could survive.

As the radio tubes warmed and brightened, their soft glow reflected off the wall behind; the scratchy hissing sounds coming through the speakers evolved to whistles and then to clear voices.

Just then Dick appeared. First his head, poking cautiously in through the front hall doorway. He peeked around, casing the joint, to see who was in the living room and if the coast was clear. He scooted towards me and, with a quick slide on the rug, sat down next to me, on the floor. With Dick I always had a sense something was up when he made an entrance like that. I was usually right.

"Where you been?" I asked.

"Cortland, with Mr. Rowe."

"Did you see anybody in the old neighborhood?"

Dick sat up and lifted his head and gave me a sheepish grin. "Yeah, I saw Patty Kelly washing her dog."

"Holy Cobako!" I gasped.

He sat there sporting the prettiest, brand-new black eye, a sort of raspberry jam, blue-grape-purple-colored shiner. I had only seen one other like it before—in a Saturday morning picture show. I was impressed. His shiner couldn't have been two hours old, still puffy around the eyelid. The white of his eyeball was a beet red. He stared at me as if he was trying to read in my expression how he looked—or just how much trouble he might be in for having it.

"What happened to you?" I asked.

The sound of my voice jolted his stare. He turned his good eye and looked at the radio dial so he could concentrate an answer better. Believable excuse-lies didn't come easy. He had to think fast. He turned back, looked at me, and tested a whispered threat using his best Jimmy Cagney murder mystery movie voice:

"Okay ... listen up. You threw a baseball when I wasn't lookin', see? And the ball cold-cocked me in the eye ... yeah ... that's it ... that's what happened. It cold-cocked me when I wasn't lookin', got it? That's the way it was, ya little squirt. Squeal and I'll pulverize ya."

Dick knew I'd help him but he also knew he wouldn't pulverize me if I didn't. He just had an image to keep up.

"Okay, okay. What happened?"

"I kissed Patty Kelly and got slugged."

Dick had a reputation for liking girls and thinking they all liked him. I imagined a gang of Patty's brothers, cousins, or even her father and mother catching Dick kissing her and taking him behind our garage in Cortland and whomping up on him. Mom wouldn't have minded Mrs. Kelly pounding him—Patty was Dick's age but only half his size and really shy.

"Patty's boyfriend caught you! Did Bobby Grumman see you, and tell? It was her Dad, wasn't it? What happened?" I begged.

Dick tightened his lips and edged them over to the side of his face with the good eye, in a devilish smirk. "Patty slugged me."

I stopped breathing. My imagination whirred.

Then I fell over sideways, tipping like a fallen tree, to the floor with a thud, laughing, holding my sides, gasping for air.

Dick was twelve, the smartest kid in the whole family—with a genius IQ. His problems started when someone told him how smart he was when he was little and ever since he's managed to do something really stupid, with regularity, to get into some scrape or trouble constantly. Seems ever since they told him his actual IQ and what it meant, he either thought everything he did was okay, because he was so smart (his brain could never be wrong), or he couldn't help himself because his brain was faster than he was and his body couldn't keep up. Here I was, my first day in the country, and I already had to lie for him, again, or else. I spent more time in the Confessional confessing my lies about Dick's sins than I did my own sins.

The Superman music opening began, so we both sat up to listen.

"Why'd we move from Cortland to Delphi Falls?" I asked during a commercial.

"I guess because we have more kids than we had rooms in the house in Cortland, and Mom and Dad wanted us to grow up in the country. Two bathrooms; I don't know; lots of reasons."

He mumbled something intelligent about the War being over, the Iron Curtain in Russia, the Atomic bomb, and Air Raids.

I thought: Why?

"We moved right in front of a seventy- or eighty-foot water falls. It's like we're in the woods," I said.

The falls bothered me because I never imagined water could make so much noise.

"I think I'm going to hate the country," I said under my breath. "I miss my friends."

"I got it worse than you," mumbled Dick. "I'm twelve; what are you, seven? Eight? Nine? I knew my friends longer than you knew any of your friends."

Dick made absolutely no sense whatsoever, again. I told him to keep quiet.

Just as the runaway train came down around the side of the mountain, Superman, seeing this from two hundred miles away, flew in and lifted the car stuck at the crossing off the railroad track just in the nick of time and saved the family and their dog. Listening to Superman was always the good part of my week.

Later, as I lay in bed, I looked back over my head, out the window of my new room with no curtains, through the glare of the front porch light at the stars in the distance and thought about Farmer Parker's yodeling and the cows and how gentle they seemed, walking by.

The next day I had to get on a school bus, which I'd never done before, ride to a school I'd never seen before, and meet a teacher I didn't even know. That's all I remembered thinking about before I fell asleep.

Walking behind Dick down our long dirt driveway, I repeated to myself, with every step I took to the front gate, "This is an adventure. This is an adventure. This is an adventure."

Mr. Skelton, the driver of the big yellow school bus, wore a hat just like Babe Ruth wore in the book we had about the Great Bambino, just like the hat I wore in Cortland when I had to wear my knickers. Mr. Skelton said, "Hello," when the bus door opened. He seemed nice enough, but gave the impression that part of his job was not smiling—especially after he'd seen Dick's shiner. He'd squint his eyes tight, curling his forehead up, wrinkling his bushy eyebrows as he looked up through the mirror and back at the kids to make sure nobody was getting into trouble on the bus. His eyes followed Dick through his mirror all the way to the back of the bus, remembering exactly where he sat down.

I sat in the first empty seat behind Mr. Skelton.

I looked attentively out the bus window at what we passed by. Nearly everything I saw was new to me. There were big red barns with tall silos. There were cows grazing in large green pastures; some were brown, but most had large, black and white spots on them like Farmer Parker's. At one stop, Dale Barber got on, made me his instant friend with a big grin, and sat right down next to me. Dale had wavy brown hair and a few freckles on his nose and smiley eyes. He liked to talk and tell jokes. I soon found out he was in my grade. Dale told me who lived in every house we passed by; if there were kids who lived there, what grades they were in; how many cows were in each barn; how many heifers they had; if their bull had a ring through its nose or not.

"You should walk over and meet the Parkers, across the way from your house. He's a nice man. His dog's called Buddy and he don't bite," he said.

"I already met them, last night," I said.

"Well there ya go," said Dale, pleased with my spirit of adventure.

Kids got on the bus in the middle of the town of Delphi Falls. Dale told me who they were as they passed by. One, in our grade, was welcomed to sit with us through the tour, scrunching me to the window.

Dale's tour continued.

"That's where the Cooks live. There's a ton of Cooks, every one of them are good at sports. This hill we're going up would make good sledding in the winter if we were allowed. We have a toboggan. Too many milk and farm trucks, though. Best sledding is at the Penoyer place. One of 'em's in our grade."

Dale pointed a finger.

"That's the Dwyer place. See that barn over there? They are big farmers, came with the pilgrims, I think. That boy behind us back there with the red cap on? That's Ray Randall, he's a good baseball pitcher. The farm up on the corner we're going to turn at up there is where the Conways live. Lots of land, lots of cows and corn. Big farm."

Dale went on and on.

He had a way about him. He could find the best in everyone and everything. His hair was thick locks in need of a trim but neatly combed. He said his nickname at home was "Bub" but I could call him Barber.

I couldn't help looking over at Linda Oats with her red hair, freckles, and blue eyes. She sat on the seat across the aisle. She was very pretty. She was older and probably a Presbyterian, with my luck. The rest of the kids getting on the bus were bigger and sat towards the back.

By the time we were pulling into Fabius, Barber had me pretty well convinced he knew just about everything important there was to know about the country. When we arrived at the school, I didn't know where to go, so I just naturally followed Barber.

He stopped short, causing me to bump into him.

"Oh, geez," he said. "I forgot which way we're supposed to go."

We ended up in Mr. Mobley's office asking directions. Mr. Mobley had golden hair and was smiling as we walked into the principal's office, a post for which it was very strange for me to see a man.

At St. Mary's, where I had just moved from, all the teachers and people who walked around the halls looking important were nuns. We called them "Sisters," ladies who never married. They wore black veils over their heads, and dresses to the floor, and had rosary-bead belts.

"What's your name, son?" asked Mr. Mobley.

"Jerome Mark Antil," I said above all the noise.

"Come along, boys. Let's find your classroom."

Mr. Mobley walked us through the busy first-day-of-school halls to our classroom, just a few doors from his office. When he opened the door to the back of the classroom, I knew this was it, do or die.

Every kid in there was about to spend a good part of the next decade with me.

"Mrs. Huffernink," he announced, "here's a special delivery for you on this first day of school."

Twenty-eight kids turned around in their seats.

"I believe you know this lad, Mr. Barber. I would like to introduce you to Mr. Antil. Jeremiah Mark is a new pupil here. His family moved to Delphi Falls from Cortland."

"Huh?" I grunted at his mispronunciation.

Mrs. Huffernink wore wire-rimmed spectacles. Her hair rolled around the top of her head like the snakes we'd make from clay we got for Christmas. Two pencils stuck out on the side like tenpenny nails. She said, "Everyone, please say 'good morning' to Jeremiah Mark."

"GOOD MORNING, JEREMIAH MARK," yelled the kids.

I didn't say anything.

She raised her head up almost backward, looking under the bottoms of her spectacles, walked over, placed her hand gently on the back of my neck, and steered me to an empty desk.

"This will be your desk until we get settled, Jeremiah."

I had lost sight of Barber somewhere in the crowded room. I wasn't near his desk. My hand felt the set of initials carved in my desktop as I sat down behind a boy who turned around and grinned at me with two missing teeth. It was almost as if he knew that he would grow up to be mayor or something and was counting on my vote. He had enough curly hair for several people, and seemed an agreeable sort.

At home we always called the bathroom a "bathroom." Sometimes Mike called it a "John," and at times my oldest aunts, Mary and Dorothy, referred to it as the "potty," but, all in all, it pretty much was a bathroom. That was clear. For some strange reason, probably known only to the Board of Education and some people in too many meetings, different schools in the forties chose to call their bathrooms by different names.

At St. Mary's, the bathroom was called a lavatory—and the time I had the accident and peed while sitting in the sandbox in kindergarten, that was called a sandbox, not a lavatory.

Maybe it was a Catholic school thing. Lavatories didn't have bathtubs in them, so perhaps it would be a lie to call them bathrooms.

I was in Mrs. Huffernink's grade precisely two minutes when I "had to go." Not being certain of the procedure in this new environment, I cautiously raised my arm, just as I would have at St. Mary's, to see whether that would work.

"Yes, Jeremiah?"

Except for the name, so far, so good!

"Sister, may I go to the lavatory, please?"

With what appeared to be downright impudence, my blurt of an old habit, "Sister," and the sound of that other word, lavatory, caused all motion and noise to stop in the room. Every kid turned their heads in my direction, mouths opened, wondering what language I was speaking. The Mayor, in the desk in front of me, raised his arm, and without waiting, shouted, "Can I move to another desk, Mrs. Huffernink?"

After the stunned silence obviously caused by the alien from another planet's language and the audacity of his calling Mrs. Huffernink his sister, everyone began laughing, rumbling amongst themselves various secret messages, like "Hurry to the cafeteria at lunch hour so we can fill a table so he can't sit with us." The stirring from the very same group who, just minutes before, had yelled, "Good Morning, Jeremiah," like they meant it, was taking on a whole "Stations-of-the-Cross" crucifixion tone. I could feel the crowd turning on me.

Mrs. Huffernink gave an understanding smile and said, "Go to the basement, Jeremiah, go to the basement. You may be excused."

I got up from my desk, went out into the hall, leaving the snickering, and looked around for stairs to the basement. I was told that my grandmother in Minnesota had a bathroom outdoors they called an outhouse. Even Barber was kind enough to point out a few of those (outhouses) on the bus ride to school, but I never heard of a bathroom in the basement. I went down the only stairs I could find and saw three big doors at the bottom. One door opened to an empty gymnasium, so I knew that wasn't it. The next was to a room filled with musical instruments, so that wasn't it, but I did like the looks of the big horn in the back of the room that I found out later was a tuba. I opened the last door and looked in to see a big furnace. I could see the warm light glowing from the side of it, so I assumed it had coal burning in it. City kids would know these things. For sure this was the basement because furnaces were in basements.

A man in coveralls with a push broom in his hand turned and said, "Son, why aren't you in class?"

"Mister, I'm looking for the lavatory in the basement because I have to go to the bathroom, and Mrs. Huffernink told me to go to the basement."

Another man was with him. I have no idea what they said to each other, but the man in coveralls shook his head and I had the sense he was laughing at me or that word again. My patience was pushed to the limit.

"Son, we call bathrooms a 'basement' here. People with out-houses have potty chairs in their cellars or basements to use in lightning storms or during blizzards when they can't get outside. That's why we call bathrooms a 'basement' here. Who's your teacher again?"

I thought, Where am I, in Poland? It was the only foreign country that came to mind.

When I repeated "Mrs. Huffernink," he told me there was a "basement"—he paused in mid-sentence, turned to his cow-orker, and rearticulated in a stage-aside mocking of the King's English, "A bawtharrrrooom"—right next door to Mr. Mobley's office, and then he asked if I knew where that was.

I went back up the stairs, down the hall, and made it to the "basement" just in the nick of time. Returning to my room, I paused outside the door and gave some thought as to how far it may be if I were to leave and walk home and make my getaway now, and if I could ever find my house in the woods, if I did. I pushed open the door. As I expected, every head turned and fol-lowed me around to my desk. I sat down. The Mayor was still in front of me, but cowering up against his desktop.

Mrs. Huffernink stopped reading. "Jeremiah, you want to come here a moment, please?"

For some reason, I felt like my brother Dick, certain that I was about to go on trial and have to stand in the corner or be expelled from school. Maybe I was in trouble for taking too long. I got up and walked to the front of the room by her desk.

I would have easily settled for any of that, for it was worse. My new teacher had noticed, under her glasses, my pants fly was unbuttoned. After putting the pencil back into her hair nest, and looking away, she proceeded to point at my buttons.

"I think you forgot something, Jeremiah."

"My name is Jerome, not Jeremiah, Mrs. Huffernink."

"I see, dear. Jerome it is."

She looked up at the ceiling and waited while I fastened them, my back to the whole class. All the boys got buggy-eyed, glad it wasn't them standing up there on display for this humiliation. The girls mostly put their hands over their mouths and giggled.

"Leave him alone, you guys!" said a girl in the front row.

It did seem to break the ice, and made me look almost human. On the way back to my seat I got a couple of invites to sit at tables at lunch. I glanced over at the girl in front who had spoken up for me. She sat at her desk with her hands clasped. Catching my eye, she pushed out her lower lip and puffed away a curl hanging over her eye, and smiled.

After the lunch bell rang, heading to the cafeteria, I found myself walking down the hall next to a kid from the next row over with big thick glasses and a comb sticking out from his back pocket. He was Bobby Holbrook. I couldn't help watching him lift his paper lunch sack up close to his face, open it, peek in, and then twist the top closed tight again. The paper sack looked worn, oil-stained, and wrinkled from many school lunch trips from home. I could sense his disappointment from looking in the lunch sack.

"How many kids you got at your house?" he asked.

"Tons of aunts and uncles and cousins at holidays, but me and Dick mostly. My brother Mike's leaving for college next week."

"We got eleven," Holbrook said, "plus two cousins living with us who lost their parents in the War. In France, I think."

"Your mom pack you lunch every day?" I asked. "What'd she make?"

He stalled answering and kept walking.

"What'd she make?" I repeated.

"Sandwich and an apple," he said. "I never get all that hungry at lunch."

I knew better. Any kid who lived through the War would know better. The rumpled lunch bag and his having to peek in it and his big family were the giveaways. My guess was he hadn't even had breakfast. Either that or the eleven kids took turns eating a good lunch.

Most American kids born in the early 1940s could tell when other kids were rehearsed on things they would say to keep from being embarrassed or sad. We had keen sensitivity about these things. Like those not having enough to eat, or those losing a brother or a parent in the War. We all had one thing in common: we knew what it was like to live most of our lives with an entire world at War. We knew how to look after each other when grown-ups couldn't always be around. That plus five years of scrimping, sacrifice, food rationing, and sharing.

I asked, "Sandwich? What kind of sandwich? I like sandwiches better than almost anything."

"Ketchup," he said, under his breath. Holbrook shifted his eyes around hoping no one had heard him.

I knew there was no such thing as a ketchup sandwich for a real lunch. Kids whose families had hard times sometimes got ketchup or honey sandwiches to make them feel like everyone else. Dad told me poor kids in the south sometimes got molasses sandwiches.

"My favorite," I mumbled.

While we were walking, I dug into my right pocket, pulled out my lunch quarter, reached around under my left arm, and poked it to the side of his ribs.

"Wanna trade?"

He looked down at the quarter and then over at me.

"For real," I said, looking straight into his eyes. "I love ketchup."

He gave me a look that let me know he knew he could trust me. We made the trade, as we would go on to do every day from that day forward for all of our school years together. He would have done the same for me.

It was then when Holbrook and I started laughing and talking. He told me his dad was a part-time brakeman for the railroad, and they lived on Berry Road. He said his dad was buying the house from a farmer for seven hundred dollars, and they had no hot water but they had a waterfall in the creek behind it that went by their land, too. We both found ourselves walking behind Dale Barber, down the hall to the cafeteria.

"Who's the girl who spoke up in class, the one in the front row?" I asked.

"Mary Crane. She lives near me." He pointed with his finger. "That's her, down by the cafeteria door looking at the bulletin board. Maybe we can sit with her."

Mary turned and caught Holbrook's eye and waited for us. She introduced herself to me.

"I already know Bob. We ride on the same bus. Want to sit together?"

Barber joined us and we found a table and talked all through lunch. Holbrook was enjoying his hot meal so much I could tell he hadn't had breakfast. While I was opening the lunch bag I traded my quarter for, Mary came up from behind, reached around me, and slid a small bottle of milk near my lunch sack for me. She cupped her hand over her mouth and whispered in my ear, "I saw what you did."

Mary lived not too far from the Holbrooks and she knew how many kids they had and how hard their father worked.

She walked around to the other side of the table, sat down, and smiled at me through some loose strands of her hair.

We all talked like we had known each other for the longest time, while most of the other kids had run out to the playground after eating. My new set of friends assured me that I would grow to like the country, in time.

Mary agreed. "We moved here this summer from Manlius. I had to live with my grandmother before that, in Syracuse, after Dad went off to War when I was three. The city was scary. When he came back home wearing a uniform after the War, I cried and hid under the bed. I didn't even recognize him. Now, in the country, I deliver newspapers on my road early in the morning to earn extra money. My dad drives me around before he goes to work. He loves driving his new Ford. He'll drive me anywhere I need to go."

"Money for college?" I asked.

"Just money," she said. "For things we may need. Maybe for college, too."

"What's your dad do?" I asked.

"He's a blacksmith. Works on cars. He worked on army tanks in the War. He can fix almost anything that needs fixing. What's your dad do?"

"He works in a bakery."

Dale Barber added, "I know a boy, Randy, whose dad can't tell him what he did in the War because of the secrets. But you can ride with him on his milk truck, if you want. He hauls milk cans from farms to the dairy. He rides with him on Saturdays and Sundays, if you ever want to go. Let me know."

Lunch in the cafeteria this day made it a good day.

Finally, the bell rang and school let out. For the whole first week of school we had to line up and walk to the buses together. Mr. Skelton was still sitting on the bus.

This was all so new to me. I wondered if he sat there all day, waiting for us, or if he got to go home, or go for a walk during the day.

The ride home was entertaining because I got to sit with Dale Barber and learned from him about everything on the other side of the road. I saw that he lived on a big farm with a lot of barns, silos, and good stuff like animals and tractors and trucks and machines. I also saw Linda Oats get off on the corner of our road. What could have been better than having the prettiest girl on the bus live on the very same road I did?

After the bus stopped at our house, Dick and I got off. We stood there a minute, looked around, and took it all in. This was our first long walk from a school bus up the long dirt driveway to our house. We studied everything around us in both fear and wonderment.

The tall trees that climbed up into the steep woods, the towering cliffs, the creek trickling down through the center, behind the small barn and big garage barn that stood side by side, and

the house that once was an old dance pavilion—it was all still
new to us, and still intimidating.

"I'm going to check out the barn and see if the old dented-up
popsicle cart is worth fixing," said Dick.

He had seen a popsicle tricycle-cart at the used bicycle shop
in Cortland. It had been backed into by a milk delivery truck
and smashed against a brick wall. He traded his Log Cabin Syrup
coin bank can filled with Indian Head pennies for it and talked
Mr. Rowe into hauling it up with the moving boxes.

The minute I heard him say he wondered if it could be fixed,
I had an idea, but I didn't say anything. I was about to figure a
way to give his popsicle tricycle-cart to Mary Crane for her dad to
fix so she could make some extra money with it selling ice cream
and popsicles. I knew she was going to be a best friend. I thought
about her buying me the milk at lunch with her own money.
Dick owed me for the black eye I fibbed about for him. I just had
to figure out a way to make his popsicle cart disappear and show
up at Mary's without him having a brain hemorrhage.

The waterfall behind our house was the Delphi Falls, but the
actual town of Delphi Falls was a mile away, which made no sense
to me. But I had no time to think about it. I was still recounting
the Superman episode from the night before, when he saved
the family from the high-speed bone-crushing oncoming train.
Today Superman was going to go swimming, out back, under the
falls, where there was a good swimming hole.

I was getting undressed when I saw out my window Dick walking from the swings to the barn garage. I knew Dad was at work
and Mom wasn't at home, so I thought, Why not?

Thinking was something I would always try to do regardless
of how much trouble I seemed to get into. I would think as a
precaution, in case someone asked, "What were you thinking?"

But right then I had more important things on my mind.
Superman, disguised as Jerry Antil, was going to check out the
water falls, and I thought, If I was going as Superman, I was faster
than a speeding bullet, and if I was faster than a speeding bullet,
no one could see me … And if no one could see me, and nobody
was home anyway, I probably didn't have to wear anything at all.
Nada. Nothing. Naked as a jaybird.

It all made perfectly good sense to me.

Out I ran, like a flash—truly faster than a speeding bullet. I was a sonic streaky blur, from my room, through the house, and the entire distance to the waterfall. It was so cool; my feet barely touched the ground.

Under the waterfalls I could hardly hear myself think, with the water crashing down more than seventy feet into a swimming hole below. On the tall shale cliff by the creek, I found fossils in the stones from prehistoric times. In the creek, I could see minnows and tiny crawfish going under the rocks. I would watch the water start at the top of the falls and keep an eye on it all the way down, until it splashed in the water below.

When it was near time to go back to the house, I crossed over the creek—very carefully, so as not to slip or stub my toes on rocks—and as I got to the other side, I knew my Superman powers would take over again, so I could get back to my room unseen.

Off I shot, like a rocket … the house was instantly appearing closer and closer … and I saw with my x-ray vision that the back door to the living room was open.

Funny, I didn't remember leaving it opened.

Oh, well, not to worry—I was a bullet speeding through the air, and I got closer, and the closer I got, the more I convinced myself I could make the living room with one big single leap, no steps, and off I went—up, up, and away!

I sailed through the air, through the open doorway, and landed on both feet perfectly, coming to a sudden stop, balancing myself upright just a few feet inside the door, on the living room rug.

"Why hello, Jerome," said Mrs. Huffernink, looking over her spectacles this time. "Your mother was nice enough to invite me over for a visit and a cup of tea."

I stood there frozen … stark butt-naked, looking stupid.

"Aren't you chilly, dear?" asked my mom. Her tea was spilling out from her cup, onto the coffee table now.

Mrs. Huffernink handed her a napkin.

I didn't say a word. I actually think I went blind for a moment. I turned around and walked across the living room, down the hall, and into my room, where I collapsed forward on my bed.

This was only my first day at school, in the country, I thought.

I covered my head with my pillow, my mind going a complete blank, again. Lesson one: it's a basement, not a lavatory. Lesson two: button my fly. Lesson three: she's Mrs., not Sister. Lesson four: Superman must wear swim trunks.

How was a boy to know that listening to him on the radio?

CHAPTER TWO

HAVE NO FEARS, ADVENTURE NEARS

I was telling my dad about Holbrook's ketchup sandwich, how big and poor his family was and how it reminded me of the War, again, just as though it was still going on. I told him how Mary Crane cried and hid under her bed when her dad came home in uniform and how he now drove her early in the morning before he went to work so she could deliver papers on their road to have extra money. I told him about the boy, Randy, whose dad couldn't even talk about the War because of the secrets. I could tell by his eyes, Dad understood everything I was feeling.

That evening, as I knelt on new linoleum, leaned on my new (to me) bed, it seemed fitting to make my reflections the only way I knew how—my bedtime prayers. The family seemed settled into a new routine, a new culture, but my memories of Cortland still kept churning up for some reason. The painful part was I wasn't sure why.

"Now I lay me down to sleep, I pray the Lord my soul to keep. If I should die before I wake, I pray the Lord my soul to take."

I had become used to the War, witnessing its five-year entirety from the year of my birth. I still wasn't used to the "country" I knew little about; the edge of a steep hill next to a house I'd never seen before late this summer; the woods that had sixty-foot trees at the bottom of it that looked like three-hundred-foot trees at the top of the hill; the seventy-foot waterfall behind our house thundering constantly, like it was alive and wanted to bust free from the rock and boulders it plummeted over all day and night, and down the creek by the cliff on the other side of a one-story house I still could get lost in.

I liked the kids I was meeting, Holbrook and the others, Dale Barber, Mary Crane. I liked Mr. Pitts's place, where I went and got eggs, and Farmer Parker's, where I watched the cows, but my thoughts were clouded with a "homesickness" that came over me from time to time, thinking I was missing a part of me because of our move. I missed the Cortland part of me that saw the beginning, middle, and end of the War that affected every single family, every single neighbor—and brought us all together. I remembered watching Mom weeping while we listened to President Roosevelt's funeral on the Zenith radio. I was confused by the new empty, detached feeling I had from time to time.

Suddenly, in the dark ... a hand touched my shoulder.

"Psssssst ... Jerry ... Pssssssst! Want to go fishing?"

It was Dad, waking me up to go fishing with him. He'd never taken me fishing alone when we lived in the city. The whole family would go together to Little York Lake on Sundays to picnic and fish, and we'd listen to Walter Winchell's radio broadcast or to "Stop the Music" on the way home. None of the lights were on in the house, and no one was awake, so I knew this would mean I'd get to ride with Dad in the car, which was great, because he knew how to have one big adventure after another. He had his work suit and tie on, which I didn't understand. I sat right up, got dressed, and walked through the dark to the car. He didn't want to wake anyone, so he started the car with the lights off, backed around, and drove down the driveway toward the gate. He didn't turn them on until we were near the road.

See what I mean? I thought. How many people could have done that without backing into the swings or swiping the side of the barn garage or dumping the car into the creek? Just my dad! That alone was an adventure, and we weren't even out of our driveway yet!

"Where're we going, Dad?"

I only asked because of his dress clothes, and wasn't sure if it was night or morning, but it was fun to be up this late or this early—whichever it was—with my dad, and knowing inside every house we drove by, everyone was asleep and missing out on everything.

"How's school, son?"

"It's okay. Mr. Mobley thinks my name is Jeremiah Mark."

Dad smiled. "I'm impressed. Not even a week and you already have two names, just like Superman and Clark Kent."

I sat up a little taller.

"We're going to Little York Lake and catch sunfish or some perch—but first, we'll go to Bucky's Diner in Cortland and get some breakfast. Later I have to make stops at grocery stores in Auburn, Seneca Falls, and Fayetteville before we go home. I thought you'd like the ride."

Holy cow! I loved Bucky's Diner because it was open all night and Dad and Bucky were good friends. Bucky always had a big white apron wrapped all around him which almost reached the floor like a dress, and a white string tied around his waist to hold it up. He wore a paper hat that looked like an army hat, and it said "New York State Fair" on it.

Dad worked at a bakery in Homer, which was right next to Cortland where we used to live, and he always liked to stop at grocery stores to see if the bread was straight on the shelves, for the customers to see it—and wait just a minute …

"Cortland!?" I asked.

It just dawned on me what he'd said. I hadn't been in Cortland since we moved to Delphi Falls. I had forgotten how far we drove to Delphi Falls before Labor Day. It seemed like hours.

"Is Cortland far away?"

"Thirty-five minutes."

"Is that all, Dad? For real?"

"Oh just about as long as it takes to listen to your Superman radio program," he said. "I had a feeling you'd like to see Cortland again."

"I thought we moved to China, like a million miles away, and it was close by all the time?"

It wasn't long before we were driving through Fabius, passing the school and heading out through the other side of town.

"Where's this road go, Dad?"

"Tully, and then we go south to Homer on 11. Pretend you're on a steamship freighter, Jerry me boy—sailing you from one port adventure to the next—while you explore the world, protecting it from evildoers and the enemies of mankind."

"Like Hitler and Mussolini," I mumbled.

Dad grinned.

Dad was great. While he was encouraging me to become the Superman we both suspected was inside me, I saw in the distance a country road sign tilting to the left. I kept my eyes on it trying to make it out.

When I could I shouted: "Berry Road. Dad, that's Berry Road. That's where Holbrook lives."

Slowing the car down, Dad said, "Well let's go have a look. It can't be that long of a road. We'll drive it up and back. What clues do you have about his house, Jerry?"

I was amazed. Dad turned on Berry Road just as easy as he made it around the swings and the barn at home. He didn't even have to think about it. He was great!

"He's near a creek. That's all I know."

"That's a good clue, son, maybe all we need. Where there's a creek, there should be a bridge. Keep a look out for a small bridge, just like the one by our house."

A couple miles up, we drove up and over a small bluff where there was a curve in the road.

"There's a bridge, Dad. There's a bridge."

It was a little concrete bridge, two or three feet high, the width of the creek on both sides of the road.

"Then that white house there by that maple tree could be the Holbrooks'," Dad said. "We'll turn around and head to Cortland, but maybe now you know. Ask him on Monday. Ask him if they have a white two-story house with blue shingles."

We could see a car up ahead with its interior lights on, driving slowly, near the side of the road, almost like it had a flat tire. I could see someone in the backseat. Then I saw an arm flip out the rear window and a rolled-up newspaper flew high before landing on a lawn.

"Up ahead, is that a Ford?" I asked.

"It is a Ford, why?"

"Can we get close, I wanna see who that is. They're delivering papers. It might be Mary Crane and her dad."

Another rolled up newspaper burst from the arm leaning out the opened rear window, even higher than the last one, and landed in the middle of another lawn.

"If that's Mary, she has a good arm," said Dad. "She'd be a dandy outfielder."

Dad slowed the car, pulled around next to the Ford. I rolled down my window.

"That's her. That's Mary Crane. That's her for sure in the backseat, delivering her newspapers."

Dad tooted the horn a short quick friendly toot and waved at Mr. Crane, who smiled and waved back. I waved at Mary. She caught my eye and waved back with a grin as Dad slowed down, pulled into a driveway, and backed around so we could get on our way again.

"Her dad drives her every morning."

"I remember you telling me. Nice girl."

What an adventure we were having, and it wasn't even daylight.

In Cortland, we drove to the side of Bucky's Diner and parked. I felt like I had traveled around the world. I would have never dreamed I would see it again since we moved. When we walked in, I sat on my favorite counter stool like I always had when we went there before. I made my compulsory two or three spins around on it, pushing off from the counter every time I circled around. Bucky was in his apron and hat just as I remembered him. Then, like always when we went to Bucky's, Dad took a shiny quarter out of his pocket and with his thumb flipped it way up in the air so it blurred it was spun so fast through the air, high enough nearly to touch the ceiling.

"Call it, Bucky!" he shouted, not taking his eyes off the flying quarter on its descent.

The game they played was if Bucky called heads or tails, and if the coin landed the way Bucky called it, Dad would give him the quarter for his coffee. Win or lose, Bucky would put both his hands on the counter, jump his legs up sideways, and click his heels together in the air. If Bucky didn't call it right, Dad's coffee was free. It was fun, and everyone in the diner would gather around and watch. I knew coffee was only a dime, and one time I asked Dad if he felt bad losing a quarter if he lost. He said no, he did it so that if Bucky lost, he could make up for the free coffee the next time by winning a quarter. Dad was nice like that.

"We need two egg and bacon sandwiches on white, wrapped in wax paper if you can, Bucky," said Dad. "Jerry and I are going to go empty the sunfish and perch out of Little York Lake before the sun comes up. We want to catch them napping."

"How 'bout I wrap up a piece of fresh apple pie to keep the boy awake?" asked Bucky.

Dad winked at him like that would be nice, and after he took the last sip from his coffee, Bucky handed him a paper sack and we went out to the car. It was still dark outside.

I was getting pretty good about putting a worm on a hook so it would stay, in the daylight, but it was way too dark, and way too early in the morning to see what I was doing. Dad hooked some of the worms for me. We sat on the end of the wooden dock with our legs hanging over for about an hour. I caught three sunfish that weren't very big, and Dad caught one bullhead.

Dad lifted the stringer out of the water with the four fish dangling on it.

"What do you say about our putting these fish back in the lake to grow a bit more?" he asked. "We know just where they live, so we will catch them again when they're bigger and can make a nice meal."

Made perfect sense to me, and after all, just going fishing alone with my dad was great!

Before we ate our sandwiches, he held me by my legs and the back of my belt so I could reach down into the lake and rinse my hands off good. He rinsed his, too, to get the worm guts and smell off them.

We took the poles and everything back to the car just as the sun was starting to come out. Dad drove into Homer and around the back of the bakery, where everyone was working and hurrying about, walking up and down the stairs, and bakery trucks parked everywhere were being loaded up with cartons of warm bread before the drivers took them out. It was then I learned why Dad wore his work suit and tie all the time: because bakers had to deliver bread all over, and since they always wanted to deliver it fresh to all the stores, the bakery had to run twenty-four hours a day. Everyone in the bakery we walked by would ask which boy I was (they could never keep us straight), and they would pat me on the head and tell me how much I had grown. It was nice to see nobody had forgotten us just because we'd moved.

Dad went inside the bakery office area, poured a cup of coffee for himself, and made a hot chocolate to go with my piece of apple pie.

"Let me do some business," he said, "and then we'll go."

I needed time to eat my pie, so I was okay with that—and besides, the sun was just coming out and I had had three adventures with my dad already!

After his business, we went down the back stairs to the car. He told me to crawl into the backseat and get some sleep because he was going to drive to Auburn and then to Seneca Falls to look at grocery stores before we went home. I could lie down in the backseat and fit perfectly. Dad turned the radio on and I heard the music or the talking in the backseat as he turned the dial for the best reception from town to town.

When I woke up the sun was bright, and the car wasn't moving. I sat up, rubbed my eyes, trying to remember what I was doing in the backseat of the car, and saw we were parked in front of a grocery store somewhere in the country. There were no houses or farms anywhere around. I opened the door, got out, and went inside. I walked around one aisle by the vegetables, but didn't see my dad. I turned a corner in the store by a pile of acorn squash ... and still no Dad. A comic book stand and a Superman comic caught my eye. I hadn't seen it before so I paged through it a little while. After I was done, I set it back on the rack, walked around the store, looking for Dad, and when I couldn't find him, I decided to go back to the car and wait there. He was probably doing business. I found the front door and walked outside.

The car was gone.

"This can't be good," I thought, as I seemed to think more and more in those days since our move to the country.

I rushed back into the store and up to the front counter. The man behind the counter was putting cartons of cigarettes up on a shelf behind him, and he had his glasses pushed up over his forehead, on the top of his head.

"Where's my dad?"

"Who are you, son?"

"I'm Jerry. Where's my dad—Mike?"

The man smiled, told me right off he knew Big Mike, and started to talk to me. I told him I'd been asleep in the backseat and had come into the store to find him, and when I went back out, he was gone.

"Don't worry, little guy," the man chuckled. "Your dad will see he lost his boy as soon as he looks in the backseat, and he will turn that car around on a dime and come back right away, in a big hurry … I promise."

Well, this made me feel better, but I did think about crying.

What if he forgot he brought me this morning to the middle of nowhere, and just drove to all those places he was going to and never remembered me, and then I was here forever? It was a regular occurrence when either Mom or Dad, sitting at the supper table, looking at one of us, straight in the eye, would pause, in mid-sentence, and have to gather their thoughts—to recollect what our names were. One time Dad looked at me as if he was thinking, "I know your name. I remember driving you home from the hospital." I would have nightmares about being left in a store and my parents not remembering my name until a letter came, addressed to me, from the Army draft board.

The man came outside with me, handed me an orange popsicle, sat down on the stoop, and pulled his glasses down so he could help me take the frozen wrapper off.

"I'll wait here with you, Jerry, because I just know your dad will be along any minute now."

It took a lot to keep from crying, but the popsicle helped, and the man sitting there with me helped, too. I didn't feel all alone.

I'd have been okay being dumped in Cortland where I knew things, but this was the wilderness.

Off in the distance we could begin to see some dust billowing up in the air from the road.

"Well, lookie at what we have here," said the man with a smile. "It sure 'nuff looks like Big Mike heading this way."

We could see a tiny light-green car coming this way, from down the road.

"Dad's Oldsmobile is light green," I said to the man.

Please, God, let that be my dad, I said to myself—I'll clean my room and do all the good things I'm always supposed to do.

The light-green car got bigger and bigger, and soon a big long arm stretched out its window, straight up in the air, and waved at us as the car got closer and closer, slowed down, and turned into the store's parking area. It sure was my dad—and that's when I started to cry. Not because I was sad or scared, but because I was happy. Happy to see Dad didn't forget me.

He got out of the car, walked around, and rubbed my head, laughing a big laugh.

"Thank Mr. Morgan for watching you, Jerry, me boy. I discovered you weren't in the backseat when I wanted you to wake up and sing a song with me."

Put another nickel in … in the nickelodeon … all I want is loving you and music … music … music …

That was one of Dad's favorite songs, which Theresa Brewer sang on the radio. So we sang it together loud so we could hear because we had the car windows open.

This time I sat in the front seat, wondering what Jeremiah Mark's next adventure would be.

CHAPTER THREE

A LIFETIME ADVENTURE PASS!

My thirst for adventure started at sunup this Saturday, negotiating with gourmet Mike on the possible advantages of his getting out of bed and driving me to the picture show I discovered up in Cazenovia. He was leaving for college the next day.

John Wayne was in a movie showing there. Not only would they have a Superman serial, but at noon they had the movie, *She Wore A Yellow Ribbon*, which I'd heard on the radio had a lot of Indians, a horse Calvary, and was otherwise spectacular, in Technicolor.

Passion, to me, was watching that 1870 Indian scout galloping in such flight that nary a hoof appeared to touch the ground, as he outran arrow after blistering arrow, the brim of his cavalry hat pushing flat back against his head in the wind. Passion was the cavalry lieutenant, with the daring to tell the other lieutenant to remove his uniform blouse (worn over the shirt) so they could duke it out over a girl they both loved, the one with the yellow ribbon in her hair, so pretty they wrote her a song.

Nobody had televisions—they were hardly invented yet, and nobody could afford them if they were, so if we had the fifteen cents it took to get in, we would go to the picture show on Saturday mornings and stay until someone came and dragged us out.

I negotiated with Mike, who was not yet fully awake: "If you drive me it would give you an excuse to maybe go see a *la-tee-da* girl in Cazenovia before you go to college." I was tempting him. I was counting on a lure bigger than popcorn for breakfast, to give me an edge. Scratching his head and yawning, Mike rolled over and just happened to remember a girl he might be able to call, who hadn't left for college yet.

"Tell you what," he said, relenting. "I'll drop you off at the picture show. Then I'll walk next door to the Lincklaen House hotel and sit in the restaurant with a girl I know. I think I'll get a malted ice cream milkshake, with an egg in it, maybe a raisin Danish. We'll see. I'll wait with her there until the movie lets out."

I backed away from his bed, stood there with my mouth open, stupefied: "An egg?"

"Yes."

"Raw?"

"Yeah."

"You crack a raw egg in ice cream?"

"Of course; maybe two."

"You put slimy raw eggs in an ice cream milkshake, then drink it?"

"Two teaspoons of malt, too."

The concept sent an axe to the pit of my stomach, but I knew with anymore talk about raw eggs and malt-whatever with ice cream, I might lose more than my ride to Cazenovia.

"Malt with an egg is a delicacy for the palate—healthful, too," Mike affirmed proudly, sitting up. "Get in the car, let's go."

Agh! I thought. There was no hope for him. But I was desperate. I backed quickly out of his room, breathed some clean air in the hallway, ran out, and got in his car.

The movie was everything the man on the radio said it would be. The music was great. I could sing the song by heart. I remembered every scene, especially when John Wayne talked to the Indian chief about them being too old for war, why they should all be friends, that war was no good; the part when his men gave him a pocket watch because they loved him, and he started to cry looking for his glasses to read what they had engraved on it; the part when the doctor and the wife of the commander had to operate on a man in a wagon, on the trail, so he wouldn't die, and they slowed the wagons down so they didn't bounce around too much.

I memorized the whole movie—which I should have, I guess, because Mike forgot me. Without even realizing it, I sat through the same movie over and over for most of the day.

Then someone tapped me on the shoulder. When I turned my head around, it was my dad.

"Ready to go home, son?" he asked.

I turned around in my seat and stared up at him in a daze, wondering why he was there. I got up and walked out with him. My eyes glazed over while they adjusted to the daylight, now nearing sunset. I thought maybe I was dreaming. I walked cautiously as I squinted my eyes open just enough to see if I was still on the sidewalk.

"Where's Mike?" I asked.

Dad said, "Mike came home hours ago. When I got home, I asked him where you were or where Dick was. He said Dick was with your mother, and that's when he remembered he forgot you were with him, and he had left you in Cazenovia."

I stopped walking. Now I opened my eyes and looked up and stared at Dad. He stopped walking and stared down at me.

"He forgot me? He left me alone in Cazenovia? I'm a child! How could he forget me?"

This forgetting me was getting old, I thought. When Dad opened the car door for me to climb in, I turned to him again and asked, "What is it with people forgetting me everywhere?"

Dad smiled, and told me some of the greatest adventures in the world happened when we did something alone, and then we knew we had a great sense of accomplishment. He told me being alone wasn't always bad.

Kids had big unspoken superstitions that would last for years, and they would get even bigger as we got older. When we lived in Cortland, I'd get left at the shoe shine parlor sometimes when Dad started walking down the sidewalk reading the morning newspaper, or at Leonard's coffee shop once until Dad remembered me when he got in his car to drive home. Dick was left behind so often, and be found by friends who would keep him until someone came to get him, that he learned how to shuffle and deal a double-down bridge game by the time he was five. I'd usually just cry.

Dad asked me, "Did John Wayne do anything alone in the movie?"

I told him yes, near the end of the movie, Captain Brittles (that was him) started to ride alone, to California, but he had his horse.

"Does Superman ever do anything alone?"

"Sure, all the time; nobody can keep up with him."

"You like watching Farmer Parker, across the road, call in his cows for milking all alone. He has no one to help him," he added.

"Mary Crane got her own paper route. Her dad drives her, but it's her route; she does the work rolling the papers and throwing them and collecting the money."

Dad pulled the car over to the side of the road, brought it to a stop, and put it in park. He looked over at me and said, "How would you like to go on the best adventure any boy your age could ever possibly go on?"

I said, "Sure."

He smiled, turned forward, put the car in drive, and drove back on the road. "Tomorrow, Jerry, me boy, you're going to have an adventure of a lifetime. I'm going to show you that being alone is only a state of mind. When you need them, your friends will always be there for you."

I didn't know what it was, and I didn't even ask, because I knew when my dad said it would be a great adventure—I trusted him more than almost anybody.

When we got back to the house, I looked around to find Mike, and saw him in the den where all the books were. He was packing to leave for college. I walked in where he was sitting, stacking his college books. I kicked him in the shin.

"That's for forgetting me in Cazenovia," I said as I walked away.

He didn't say a word. He knew he had it coming for forgetting me. I went to the kitchen to make a peanut butter sandwich.

The next morning Dad woke me early. He told Mom that he and I would be spending the morning together, and we would not be going to church in Manlius with all the others. We drove, instead, to St. Mary's in Cortland, where I was baptized and had my First Communion, and we went to Mass. Afterwards, we went to Bucky's Diner—Dad flipped the quarter high into the air again, and Bucky won, and clicked his heels and everyone cheered. I had a hot chocolate while waiting for breakfast, and Dad put a nickel in the coin-operated phone—ding—and started talking to someone.

"What time does it take off," he was asking, "and what time does it land?" Then he said "thank you" and hung up the phone.

He winked at Bucky and told him I was going on a great adventure this morning. We had to be at the airfield in thirty minutes, but we had plenty of time, so I could take my time and finish my breakfast. I didn't have any idea what an airfield was, and I didn't care. I was going to have an adventure.

When Dad drove into the airfield, I figured it out. There were four airplanes there. Three were small planes, and one silver plane was bigger. It said "Flagship" on its side. He said the bigger one was a DC-3, a passenger airplane. I knew there were Army airplanes in the War they called bombers, which flew low over our house, and I knew about fighter planes, but I had never seen an airplane that just carried people.

Dad walked me inside the building and gave the man at the counter some money for a ticket. We walked out to the DC-3, and he handed me the ticket.

I looked up at him.

"Are you going with me?"

"Son, this is your great big adventure, all alone. You're going to get in this airplane—you've never been in an airplane—and you're going to fly alone to Watertown. When you land, someone will be there to meet you right when you get off the plane and hear all about your adventure. The airplane leaves in twenty-eight minutes. Have fun, son."

I looked him in the eye. "Are you sure, Dad?"

"I promise, son. You're practically a decade old. You need a big adventure all alone."

My dad was so right. Sometimes I felt like I almost had to run away or something, jump a steam freighter or do some adventure, because I was getting tired of just seeing other people do it in the movies. It gets embarrassing when you sit in a classroom and think getting away from it all was standing up and walking over to use the pencil sharpener.

He put his hand out for me to shake, like a grownup, and then told me to get on the plane and have a good adventure.

"Mind what they tell you," he said as he walked away and got into his car and drove off.

I climbed the steps into the plane. When I got in, the whole aisle was tilted, so I had to walk uphill to get to a seat. I was the only one there except the pilot and the stewardess.

A stewardess was a lady in a uniform and hat who made sure I was comfortable and had plenty of milk to drink, at least that's what she told me.

The pilot let me come up to his cabin and look at all the instruments and feel the steering wheel. The stewardess then had me sit in the front seat and buckle a seatbelt, which I had never seen before, so she buckled it for me. I looked at the ticket in my hand. It said "$12" and "Watertown." I didn't even know where that was—and I didn't much care.

I'll never forget the loud roar of the propeller engine I could see out of my window when it started going around, and the giant puff of smoke belching out of it as it turned so fast it became a blur. Then I could feel the plane starting to move. I watched us turning around, almost in a full circle, before we started moving forward, bumping up and down on the grass field, as it moved towards a long cement place. Then the plane started to move faster and faster, and the faster it went, my back pushed deeper and deeper into the seat back—faster and faster we went. I grabbed the seat arms, one in each hand, and looked out the window at things speeding by. All of a sudden, my heart leapt into my throat. I saw the ground move from under us as the plane jumped up, and I could feel myself getting lighter like on a ride at the county fair. We started to fly, and the plane wasn't tilted anymore, the floor was level, like in a house. We were up in the air, and the trees and barns and buildings below us were getting smaller and smaller. The cars I could see below looked like ants on the ground. It was amazing.

Now I knew what it was really like to be a bird—or better yet, Superman. After a while, the stewardess told me we were getting ready to land in Watertown. I could hardly wait to tell everybody about my plane ride adventure. It was like a flying carpet, seeing a cloud go by, and the houses and farms below got bigger and bigger as we came down. Imagine being taller than a tree. I could see the ground coming closer and closer, and then I could feel the plane land on the ground with a bump, and the propellers make a lot of noise until we came to a stop. The floor was tilted again. When the door opened, and I was told I could leave, I walked to it and stepped out. There, right at the side of the field, was my dad, waving! Wow! He beat the airplane, and was there—just like he promised—when I needed someone; my friends would always be there for me. What an adventure! I would never forget it as long as I lived. In one weekend I got to see my favorite movie ever and memorize the song—"Round her neck she wore a yellow ribbon … she wore it for her lover who was far, far away … far away … far away … she wore it for her lover who was far, far away …"—and I got to go on an adventure all alone. I would never be afraid of being alone or of any adventure ever again!

CHAPTER FOUR

CEMETERY SECRETS

The screen door slammed behind me as I yelled: "Dick?"
No response.
"Dick!"
No response.
"Where's Dick, Mom?"
No response.
"Mom?"
Mom's voice muffled from her and Dad's bedroom: "I'm vacuuming! Get the dust mop, dear. Dust mop your room—under your bed. Pick up all your clothes. Your dad called. He's bringing Aunt Kate"—my grandmother from Cortland you heard about already—"for supper and to stay over. I want your room picked up; we may need the extra bed in it tonight, dear."

"Where's Dick?"

"Get yourself a snack. There's peanut butter in the cereal cabinet, grapes in a bowl by the sink. Drink some juice. Your father dropped Dick off at David Duba's house this morning. He'll pick him up when he comes back from the bakery, later."

Duba lived in Fabius. His dad had a big chicken barn with hundreds of chickens. They sold chickens and eggs. By now Dick and Duba were really good friends, both with glasses. Dick's were thicker. If Dick had the higher IQ you couldn't tell, they both got into the same trouble. David had better grades in school, but Dick could probably tell you what was in an encyclopedia before he looked. If Dick ever picked up a book it was rare, but when he did he would read it from cover to cover in one sitting and give his teachers fits all year by knowing all the lectures without ever opening the book again. He and Duba were thirteen, always together, mostly talking about girls or about how they were going to drag race when they got cars of their own. Dick tried to impress girls by saying he could drive Dad's Oldsmobile anytime he wanted, which he couldn't. Duba would do the same—tell girls he could get his dad's Lincoln anytime, which he couldn't, either. Sometimes Dad and Mr. Duba would take them out on back roads to let them practice driving. They both knew how to drive well. It seemed a lot of kids in the country, by twelve or thirteen, knew how to drive. Farm kids needed to know and many had special driving permits and could drive on the road with tractors, implements, or farm trucks, hauling things or making deliveries. At ten, Dale Barber would drive his dad's Packard around the farm.

Mom walked into the dining room and said, "Oh dear, I asked Dick to carry these boxes to the barn garage and put them on a shelf for me. I don't know what I'm going to do with that boy. I have a PTA meeting to go to. I'll be gone an hour. Please take them out before you go over to the Parker's? Are you going there?"

"Yes, ma'am."

The day turned into a sunny spring afternoon. After toting the things to the barn garage, I headed over to Farmer Parker's to do what I loved to do—watch him call his cows in off the tall side hill pasture for their late afternoon milking.

"Caho bossies! Caho bossies! Caho bossies!" Farmer Parker yodeled in a strong, low voice—raising it when he said "bossies" almost like he was singing.

Farmer Parker wore his bib overalls everywhere, like Mr. Pitts and others I've seen, but unlike them, he wore a train engineer hat, which appeared to match his overalls with the small stripes. Farmer Parker didn't chew tobacco like some. Charlie, up at Shea's store in Fabius, said that sometimes people chewed tobacco to help stop the pains of toothaches. Farmer Parker had store-bought uppers, probably no toothaches.

As soon as Buddy, his Border collie, heard him sing out, the dog knew it was time to go to work. He jumped up from a deep sleep and, without so much as a stretch or a yawn, sprang off the porch, crossed the yard, over the road, up through the opened barbed-wire gate of the side pasture, straight up the steep hill to do what he did every afternoon—help bring the cows down for milking.

"Caho bossies!" shouted Farmer Parker. "Caho bossies! Caho bossies!"

Looking up at the hilltop, we could see the heads of cows begin to bob up and down, up and down, from one side to the other for stride and balance, in a gentle motion, as they ambled down the hillside, one right behind another. They were Holstein cows, which looked like they had big, black and white jigsaw puzzle pieces on their sides.

The dog would run from one side of the cows around behind them to the other side, not making a sound, just keeping them moving, pointing them in the right direction, down their well-worn cow path, in no particular hurry.

Farmer Parker would say, "These are milk cows, for milking. They aren't beef cattle, for stampeding. They're my ladies, and you can't hurry ladies."

The cows followed the single, dusty, worn cow path twice on most spring and summer days, winding gently down the hill, one behind the other, circling around the bushes and trees, down and out through the opened gate.

When the cows stepped onto the road, close enough to touch, Farmer Parker would lower his voice and talk right to them, like he was saying, "Hello ladies, and did you have a good day, today?"

"Ca bosseee," he would say, "ca bosseee."

They walked down the sloping driveway around to the back of the barn and in through sliding doors, passing by either side of a long green wagon parked in front of the door.

The bottom floor of the barn, where the milking was done, was concrete. There were whitewashed wooden milking stanchions lined up along both sides of the room, ten on each side. Watching, I learned how each cow seemed to know exactly where to go, once inside the barn. All twenty of them walked to their own spot where their milking stanchions were, carefully stepped up on the milking platform, over the gutter trough, and put their heads through the neck sections where their feed bowls were waiting for them. Farmer Parker would walk in front of each one of them, down a narrow pathway between the inside barn wall and the row of milk stanchions, close the stanchion and flip a bolt, holding it secure, so they couldn't pull their heads back out to leave the barn, until they were milked. He'd pour a full scoop of sweet feed in each bowl and move on to the next. Then, one by one, Farmer Parker would bring a milking machine to milk them. After he moved the machine to another cow, he would "strip" the previous cow by hand using a three-legged stool to sit on and a shiny bucket, making certain he got all of the milk. Leaving milk in a cow could be painful for a cow over time. A dusty radio with cobwebs sat high on a shelf—turned on, so his "ladies" could listen to music. Cows were smart, and because of them, we had milk to drink, ice cream, and cheese.

On both sides of the room, just behind the cows, and a step down, there was a long gutter trough built in the floor, about twelve inches wide and eight inches deep. It went behind the cows, the full length of the milking platform. If a cow had to do number one or number two, it would fall into the trough, behind them. Later, when the cows were let back out of the barn after milking, Farmer Parker would shovel all that—they called it manure—into his green manure wagon and take it to the fields, as fertilizer.

As I always had, I thanked Farmer Parker for letting me help bring the cows in, but this time I asked if I could ride with him on his manure wagon sometime.

He asked, "The spreader?"

I asked, "Is that what you call it? Is that anything like when Huck Finn tells his stretchers?"

"Same principle," he chuckled. "It all gets spread around pretty good, that's for sure. If you can be here early in the morning—and I mean early—I'll take you out on it."

"You bet I can," I said, and then I waved, and left for home.

As I walked towards home, I could see Mike's Chevy driving up the road. He was coming from college, in Syracuse, which was strange. He typically didn't come home, except sometimes on weekends if he needed money, or if he was going to play baseball at the stone quarry on Oran Delphi Road. Maybe this time they couldn't stand smelling his cans and bottles and they threw him out. His Chevy slowed down as it turned into our driveway. Walking alongside, I stuck my head in the passenger window to say, "Hey. Did you come for some real food?

Mike smiled. "I forgot two books I need. I'm going right back."

There was a large carton on the front seat on the passenger side.

"What's in the box?" I asked.

He reached over, pulled the lid back, and showed me a fluffy white and gray rabbit with floppy ears.

"My professor asked me to take care of it so his daughter wouldn't find out. He had to go to a conference in Albany for a week. He wants it taken care of while he's gone."

"You like college?" I asked.

"Bio-lab experiments are hard," said Mike.

"What's a bio-lab?"

"We study living matter; living things."

Suddenly it dawned on me. I'd heard, when they said "experiment" in a biology lab, it meant curtains for an animal they were studying. I knew the older kids at our school studied dead frogs and things like that, because I had seen them on the school bus, in pickle jars—frogs, not kids.

Well, pickled frogs were one thing—at least they always seemed to have a smile on their faces, and at least they came already pickled in a jar. This was a live bunny rabbit, that liked its neck scratched when I reached in through the car window. I had to find out what he meant when he said "take care of it so his daughter wouldn't find out about it."

I had to think … fast!

With the best detective questioning technique I could muster, I had to find out what experiment Mike was working on and exactly when the professor was coming back. That's exactly how the Hardy Boys, boy detectives, would have done it.

"What experiment are you doing?"

"Reproduction," Mike said. "My assignment is to study a male mammal and dissect a specimen. I have a choice of animals."

"Is the rabbit male?"

"Yeah."

He jumped out of the car and ran into the house.

I scratched the bunny's neck and thought. First off, I didn't know what mammal meant, and second off, I didn't know what a specimen was, so I was totally in the dark, as usual. Nobody ever told me anything. But I did know what dissect meant.

When Mike came out of the house with his two books and got into his car, I asked him what male had to do with it, because I knew it either meant Mr. Johnson, our mailman, or something about being a boy.

"We're studying the male reproductive system."

"Huh?" I said, in a startled voice, confused about what he said.

The car edged forward as he lifted his foot from the clutch.

I didn't know if I should run and tell Mom that Mike had gone completely nuts now, or just go think about it. It was clear to me: Mike was becoming weirder, being away from home. I think this gourmet fever he had was bringing him to a point of murder. I needed one more clue. I needed to know when the professor was coming back.

"How long will you have the rabbit?"

"All week. His daughter can't find out. I'll bring it here next Saturday when I come for the book Mom ordered for me, so you can see it and give it a carrot one last time, if you want, before the professor gets back on Sunday. Okay? After that it'll be too late."

Curtains! I thought. My jaw dropped open in astonishment with how cold-blooded Mike had become.

"Stand back!" he insisted, and drove away.

I ran in the house to the book den and pulled the big diction-ary down to look up the word "reproductive." Over a bookshelf,

I could see Mom in the living room talking with Mrs. Westwood, the fifth-grade teacher.

"How do you spell 'reproductive?'" I shouted at either one of them, interrupting their conversation with my sense of urgency.

"Tell me when you have a pencil," shouted Mom—never denying a youth an education of any kind. When I told her I was ready, she shouted, "R-E-P-R-O-D-U-C-T-I-V-E."

Mom and Mrs. Westwood looked at each other, shrugged their shoulders, and went on drinking their tea and talking. I think I could hear one of them say, "Heaven only knows."

The dictionary was no help at all. It just said reproduction was stuff about making babies. No help at all. Mike obviously didn't know what he was talking about. A male couldn't have a baby, even I knew that.

I ran into Mom and Dad's room, picked up the telephone, and waited for the operator. A voice came on: "Operator."

"Operator, I need to call Bobby Holbrook."

"Let me get him for you. What's the number?"

"I don't know."

"Oh dear. I would need a number."

"I don't know it."

"Are you an Antil? Which one are you?"

"I'm Jerry."

"Hello, Jerry. I'm Myrtie. Nice to meet you. You don't have to call me operator, or ma'am. Just call me Myrtie, okay?"

"Okay."

"Do you know what road they live on, dear? The Holbrooks?"

"Berry Road. It's near Fabius, I think."

"That's out of my area. If you give me just a minute, I can call an operator friend of mine in that area and ask around?"

"I can wait, thank you."

"I'll be right back, dear."

All I could think about was the floppy ears on the rabbit Mike was going to dissect and murder. Myrtie came back on the line.

"Jerry, the Holbrook house doesn't seem to have a telephone. Would you say this is an emergency, hon?"

"Oh yes. It's life and death."

"My goodness. Well, let me read some names on Berry Road. Maybe you can recognize one of them and I could connect you so they can maybe get a message to your friend. How will that be?"

"That would be great. Thanks, Myrtie."

"How about Smith, do you know the Smiths?"

"No."

"Recognize the name Doxtator?"

"No."

"Do you know the name Paddock?"

"Not sure."

"Kellish, how about Kellish?"

"I know Tommy Kellish. He's in my grade."

"I'll ring them, then. Let's hope it's his house and they live close to the Holbrooks. Good luck, Jerry. I'll listen to see if you connect. If it's not his number, pick up again and we'll try something else."

"Thank you, Myrtie."

"You're welcome, sweetheart. Don't be a stranger."

"Hello?"

"Tommy?"

"This is Tommy."

"This is Jerry."

"Oh, hi."

"Do you live near Bobby Holbrook?"

"Yeah, next house up."

"Tommy, can you find out if Holbrook could meet me, somewhere soon, about something important? If he can, would you call me back and tell me? He doesn't have a phone."

"I know," said Tommy.

Then I thought about it …

"No," I said, "better than that, if Holbrook tells you when he can meet, could you call Dale Barber and tell him, so he can meet with us, too? Then will you ask Dale to call me and tell me when and where to meet? That will all be easier."

Tommy said, "Sure, but it'll have to be later on, because I have to drive the tractor over to our neighbor on the other side, who needs to use it tonight and tomorrow to pull tree stumps."

"That's okay. That will give me time to look through my Hardy Boys mystery book to see if there are any ideas in it that could help."

"This sounds serious," said Tommy.

"It's my brother, Mike. He's a gourmet. Some kind of reproductive thing he needs for college. He's going to get it from a rabbit that will get murdered."

"That is serious," said Tommy.

Neither one of us had any idea what we were talking about.

It was amazing how much I could learn from someone when I used my Hardy Boys, boy detectives, questioning techniques.

Dad brought Dick and our Aunt Kate home and walked into the house just as Mom called us to supper. Dick and I sat on one side of the table, Aunt Kate, as our guest, on the other side of the table, with her cane leaning on the arm of her chair. Mom was in the kitchen, getting bowls of food. Aunt Kate stayed with us during the week sometimes. Dad carried a platter in and sat down at his spot at the head of the table. Mom came in and sat down.

Aunt Kate took forever saying grace and praying to all the saints in heaven who looked over everyone and asked the Lord to bless Dad for driving so safely all the way from Cortland and she asked the Lord to look over Dick. (She knew the nuns in Cortland that used to teach Dick.)

When she was done and said, "Amen," Mom blessed herself and lifted her salad fork as I blurted: "I saw Mike today. He said he's studying reproductive thingies in a bio-something so he's going to massacre a rabbit in his laboratory to get one … you know … a thingy!"

Mom's fingers fell limp, letting the salad fork fall out of her hand, dropping onto her plate with a clang.

Dad pursed his lips, holding back a grin, and knew enough to just sit back and keep quiet. He just watched and waited for it all to unfold.

Aunt Kate scooted around in her chair thinking the clang of the fork meant there might have been hot food spilled.

Dick very slowly turned his head sideways, leaned over, tilted it over me, and stared down, like he was looking at me through a microscope in a General Science class.

Mom asked, "What in heaven's name are you talking about, Jerry?"

Dick pushed his glasses up over his forehead, resting them on the top of his head like the goggles of a World War I flying ace and continued to stare down at me. I locked eyes with him and stared back up, as if to say, So what if you're older, taller, and smarter, you don't scare me. Staring Dick down, I said to Mom, "Mike told me he needs a reproductive thingy, so he has to murder the rabbit he has before the professor gets back just so his daughter won't find out about it and try to stop him. He wants me to give the rabbit its last carrot, before he—you know."

Mom's eyes glazed over as she stared at Dad, kind of like she was wondering if maybe there was a mix-up of babies at the hospital, as if I wasn't really her child. Not knowing what to say, she closed her eyes and shook her head back and forth a few times, like maybe she could shake this nightmare out of her brain.

Even though I knew he probably couldn't see me without his glasses, Dick was still staring down at me.

"What!?" I yelled up at him.

Dick blurted, "You're dumb as a stick, you know that?"

I wasn't going to argue with him, because I had had an exhausting day, and to be quite frank, I was getting myself confused with this whole mess. He did have a point.

Mom bristled, set her fork back down, and said, "Richard, come over here, this instant."

Dick flopped his glasses back down, pushed his seat back, stood up, and walked over to Mom, never taking his eyes off me, like he was waiting for something to crawl out of one of my ears.

Mom turned her chair and leaned her face into his. "What did I teach you about impertinence?"

"You told me to look it up," he answered.

"Apparently you haven't. Now I suggest you go to your room and look it up—and then have supper, alone, in the kitchen, after you have learned it. March!"

With two fingers, Mom delicately lifted her favorite salad fork again. Her salad fork was one of her few remaining remnants and memories of her past city life in Cortland, like the afternoon teas, her bridge clubs, quiet socials—the city life she once enjoyed before we moved in front of a waterfall in the woods.

"Jerry," she said, "when you're older, we'll teach you about animal reproduction. But for now, I am certain you completely misunderstood your brother. Eat your vegetables, dear."

"But he's going to murder a rabbit, Mom," I pleaded.

"Sometimes science has to make sacrifices for medicine, so human lives can be saved," she said.

None of this made any sense to me. The phone rang, which was a good thing.

It was Dale Barber.

"Meet us in the morning at the Delphi Falls cemetery," he said.

"I don't know where that is," I said.

"Get a piece of paper so you can make a map."

I set the phone down, ran into the kitchen, and saw a big piece of butcher paper lying on the counter that once was wrapped around some liverwurst. I grabbed it and ran back to the phone in Mom and Dad's room.

"Ready," I said to Dale.

"Go through Farmer Parker's place, go out behind his barn, down his back pasture, cross the creek, and go up his back hill to the top. Go straight over the big hay field up there, then down the northwest corner of the field. Holbrook and me will be in the center of the cemetery. Draw a good map so you don't get lost. Northwest will be the farthest corner on the right.

"Make it early," he added, "I have chores to do after I get back home."

"I'll be there," I said. "I'm riding on Farmer Parker's manure spreader in the morning, and that will be on top of that hayfield, behind the cemetery, I think."

I put the butcher paper on my bed, went back into the dining room, finished my supper, pushed my chair in to the table, carried my dishes to the kitchen, and headed to my room to set my alarm clock and finish drawing my map.

I stopped in Dick's room and asked him to tell me about the reproduction stuff. He gave me a look, trying to remember how old I was, and told me Mom would pound him if he did, so I should just go to bed.

It was still dark when the alarm clock rang. I got out of bed, looked out my window to see Farmer Parker's house lights already on across the way. I dressed quickly, folding the map down so it fit in my pocket. In the kitchen I ate some shredded wheat in the dark. I hated the taste, but I liked reading the Indian stories on the divider cards in the box. Stories like what to do on the trail by your campfire, so you wouldn't get bitten by rattlesnakes while you slept.

I left the house and walked through the gate over to Farmer Parker's. The small side barn door light was on, so I went down to it. I could see my breath in the morning air. Inside the barn, Buddy was curled up on a workbench, asleep. The radio was playing music and the early-morning farm reports. Farmer Parker was busy milking. He lifted his head to say hello. Every time he "stripped" a cow, by hand, filling a shiny bucket with the last of her milk, he'd pour it through a cloth filter into big milk cans. The filter he poured it through was to catch flies or anything that may have gotten into the bucket by accident. When the cans were full, he'd stomp a lid down on the top of them and put them outside, on a rack, to wait for Mr. Vaas to come by in his truck and haul them to the dairy.

The lids were curved down at the sides, wider than the neck of the big milk can. This way they acted like an umbrella and would keep the rain out of the milk.

While he was busy milking, I walked out through the opening of the two big sliding doors that led out to where the spreader was sitting, to take my first look at it, close up. It was a green wooden wagon with short sides, built like a long box, on four tall metal wheels with long metal spokes. At the back of the wagon was a swirly-looking, egg-beater-like wheel that had long, pitchfork prongs attached to it. I imagined the swirly wheel going around and around, the wire forks catching hold of the manure as it slid back on the chain belt I could see on the floor of the box. The chain belt probably moved when the wheels went around. Then the swirly wheels would spike the manure, pitch it out the back, and off the wagon onto the field he was fertilizing. Two large workhorses, Sarge and Sally, were already hitched up to the wagon, waiting. I rubbed their soft velvety noses, said good morning to them, one at a time. I could see their breath in the cold morning air. Farmer Parker had told me once that he was going to keep his horses as long as they were able to do the work, and then get himself a Ford tractor. He said Sarge and Sally could practically run the farm without him. I wasn't sure what happened next, so I decided to watch and learn, like my dad would tell me. I went back inside the barn where it was warmer, sliding the doors closed behind me.

Farmer Parker was hosing off his milking equipment, putting it away. He asked if I wanted to help.

"You bet," I said.

"Go up the drive, cross the road, open the side hill gate wide. It's the same one as last night. Make sure to pull it all the way back, so the ladies don't step on the barbed wire and spook. I'll let them out when you're ready."

I ran outside, up the drive, crossed the road over to the gate, and did just what he said. I could hear the barn doors slide open, saw the bright yellow light from inside the barn light up the dark ground behind the barn where the horses and the manure spreader were standing. All twenty cows, and the heifer following them, started coming out slowly, around the barn, around the spreader, up the drive towards me. Their heads were bouncing up and down, up and down, this way and that way, up and down.

They crossed over the road, right in front of me, and I talked to them: "Ca bosseees, ca bosseees, ca bosseees"—just like I'd heard Farmer Parker say a million times.

They looked friendly enough. I could see them watching me as they went by, as if they were talking to each other.

I don't remember seeing you at the gate before, young man.

That's the Antil boy from across the way—my, how he's grown.

They didn't stop, or even slow down. All they wanted was to stretch their legs, climb the hill, and graze in a nice sunny green pasture all day.

"Ca bosseees, ca bosseees," I said.

I just liked saying it.

"Is that all of them?" I shouted to Farmer Parker.

"Lock her up," he answered.

I closed the wire gate, making sure I did it good. Buddy was standing there waiting for me, and together we walked back down to the barn with him wagging his tail. Farmer Parker already had the spreader backed all the way into the barn and was shoveling manure into it. He would shovel it into the wagon from the gutter trough on both sides for the length of the spreader. Then he would say, "Pull up, Sarge!" and the horses would start to move forward, until he shouted, "Whoa, Sarge!" and they would stop. He would shovel some more from both sides and repeat the process.

By the time he was finished shoveling, the wagon was outside again, filled with manure. The gutters behind the milking stanchions inside were empty. He hung the shovel on two pegs on the wall and told me to jump up on the wagon and sit on the foot rest. There was only one seat, in the middle of the front part of the wagon—where he would sit. The foot rest below the seat was the width of the wagon—like a bench—so I fit on it, hanging my legs off with room to spare. He closed the barn doors, climbed up into the driver's seat, untied the leather reins from a handle on the front of the wagon, and said, "Giddyap, Sarge, let's go!"

The leather, buckles, and chains of the halters, collars, and gear the horses were wearing started to creak and jingle as the horses leaned forward to get the wheels rolling. They started walking on Farmer Parker's command, pulling us around the barn and behind it, across the driveway, towards the gate of the rear pasture. The cows, by now, were all near the top of the side pasture, and wouldn't need tending until the milking that night. Farmer Parker had me jump off and open the back gate so he could pull the wagon through it.

Riding the wagon down the dirt wagon tracks in Farmer Parker's back pasture was like being in a cowboy movie, on a buckboard. The occasional snorting of the horses, the twirling of their ears with each step, the sounds of their hooves, leather harnesses, and chains seemed to make the simple wooden wagon come to life. We crossed the creek over the small wooden bridge.

Clunk, clunk, clunk, clunk, clunk.

With snorts and heaves, Sarge and Sally pulled us up the big, long back hill, higher and higher, until we were at the top. The level hay field lay in front of us. I looked around at the manure on the wagon; steam was billowing off it in the brisk morning air. We were now on top of the highest hill in the area. Way down behind us, in the distance, I could see Farmer Parker's house and barn. Across the road from it was my house, the waterfalls, and the woods on both sides.

When we got inside the gate, the horses seemed to know where to go. They pulled the wagon across the hay field, towards the place he wanted to start. I could tell what part of the field had already been fertilized and what part hadn't. Each day, Farmer Parker would start where he had left off the day before, and eventually all of the field would be fertilized.

I remembered I had to ask him something.

I took the big folded piece of butcher paper out of my pocket, unfolded it until it covered my lap and then some. It was the map I'd drawn with a black crayon the night before, when Barber told me where the Delphi Falls cemetery was for our meeting. I spread it out on my knees to get the creases out best I could. Then I raised it up proudly and asked Farmer Parker to tell me specifically where on it I had to go to meet the boys, after we were done spreading. He pulled on the reins, told Sarge and Sally to turn. The wagon started to line up with the area he wanted to fertilize. When we got over the exact spot, he pulled back on the metal lever he was resting his left arm on. The chain belt on the floor of the wagon started to turn and make noise. The load shifted backwards, very slowly. The swirly spiked wheels at the back of the wagon began to spin like propellers and toss the manure it caught in its forks, way up in the air, all around the field behind us.

He pointed across the field. "See that sugar maple, over yonder, the big one, next to that four-year-old elm?"

"Yes," I said.

"Go between them, then down to the bottom of the hill. You will be in the cemetery, right where you want to be."

I was about to tell him thanks, when a gust of wind blew past, up from the ground, and jerked the map out of my hands. It sailed way up into the air in circles, like a kite out of control, like a tornado I saw in a library book at school. It flew away, up and behind us.

All of a sudden, this map, which held the directions to what would surely become a legendary first meeting at the Delphi Falls cemetery—a map that only yesterday had been wrapped around some liverwurst for Saturday's sandwiches—became more valuable to me than the only map to the Lost Treasures of the Incas.

I jumped off and started around the side of the wagon to go get it.

"I wouldn't be doing that," said Farmer Parker, but I couldn't hear him. I ran blindly out, behind the manure spreader, jumped up in the air, trying to catch my treasure map, grabbed it with one hand and ...

Splat-split-plat-slap-splat-splat-split-plat-slap-splat-splat-split-plat-slap-splat-splat-split-plat-slap-splat—

Pieces of smelly soggy manure, all sizes, shapes, colorations, hit me all over my head and body, like it was shooting out of a machine gun from a Saturday morning gangster movie.

Every inch of the front of my body, face, arms, and head was riddled with cow dung, and more was coming at me every second I stood there!

I couldn't move. My arms stuck out like I was a frozen scarecrow. I was covered head to toe with manure splotches ... hot, wet, steamy cow manure splotches. Farmer Parker had leaned on his side, looking around at me, shaking his head, like he tried to warn me, but the wagon was still moving. It was almost empty now, and a farmer doesn't stop until a load is empty—or full, depending on the nature of the chore. Wagons were meant for loading or unloading. Nothing on a farm was about play. It was all about work. It was about getting things done and moving on to the next chore, while daylight and the weather held. My foolishness didn't stop the task at hand. I wasn't hurt. The spreader kept rolling.

I wiped what gunk I could off my face with my map, out of my hair with my hands, and the front of my t-shirt. By now the manure wagon was completely empty. Farmer Parker stopped, pushed the lever forward, tied the reins to it, jumped off, and handed me his bandanna kerchief to wipe my face.

"You need a tub," he said. With his glove he brushed big globs off my t-shirt and jeans as best he could.

Without moving my lips or opening my mouth any more than I had to, I thanked him for the ride, walked across the field towards the maple and elm trees, shaking a leg now and then, as a cat with a wet paw does. I was on my way to meet up with Holbrook and Dale. Farmer Parker watched me walk away.

I climbed through the fence and went down the hill into the cemetery.

Holbrook, Dale Barber, and Mary Crane were waiting. I was surprised to see Mary.

"Holbrook didn't have a ride," she said. "Tommy Kellish called and asked me if my dad could drive him so I rode along, too. Is that okay?"

"Sure," I said.

Holbrook's eyes bugged out at the sight of me and he yelled, "What happened to you? Stay away from me! You look like an outhouse!"

He started laughing, doubling over and holding his sides.

"I know exactly what happened to him," said Dale. "He got caught on the working end of a 'honey wagon' and it got the best of him."

I was trying not to talk until I could splash some water on my face.

I had heard people talk about honey wagons—now I knew for sure what it meant.

"I need a hose," I said.

Dale said, "Let's go into Delphi Falls. We'll find a hose and a place to talk there."

Walking into town, Holbrook was careful not to let any of the manure splotches rub off on him. He walked on the other side of the road or several feet in front of us, stepping backwards so we could talk.

"Don't worry, it happened to me once, I learned my lesson," said Dale.

"What was the lesson?" I asked.

"Stay on the wagon until you're sure it's empty."

"Oh … right," I said.

Walking through town we saw Bases, the Mawson kid. Everybody called him "Bases" because you'd never see him without a ball in his hand. He even held a baseball while he ate. Bases leaned back in a porch chair waiting for a ride to a baseball game he was playing in. He had his spikes on, leaning them up over the rail, his chair tilting back, rocking in its balance. He was throwing his ball with noisy slaps into the glove on his other hand, like he was either trying to keep time until his ride came or break the glove in, except the glove was older than he was and everyone knew that time had its own notion of standing still in Delphi Falls.

"Got a hose, Bases?" Dale asked.

Seeing the mess I was in, his next throw flew over the porch railing, bounced in the grass. The chair legs slipped out from under him like they were stilts on ice. Rolling and holding his stomach, gasping for breath, he pointed at the hose by the porch, motioning approval. He finally stopped laughing enough to sit up on the stoop and watch Dale hose me off. I took off my t-shirt, wrung it out, and put it back on. My teeth were chattering. I was shivering, but at least I didn't smell like the working end of a honey wagon any longer. Mary walked over to the sidewalk, picked up the baseball, walked back, and handed it to Bases.

We all sat on the porch steps. I told them about gourmet Mike and the rabbit, and what he was going to do to it. I told them we needed to save the rabbit so Mike wouldn't have to be arrested or go to an insane asylum or anything like that.

They all agreed, we couldn't let that happen.

Then Bases said, "You guys need a plan. What would Dick Tracy or the Phantom or any of the 'Sunday funnies' detective guys do in a case like this?

"The Hardy Boys would hide the rabbit and stall for some time to think," I answered.

Mary looked down at the floor of the porch and said, "A rabbit needs food and water. They just can't be hidden all that easy. They could chew their way through a cardboard box. Where can you hide it?"

I jumped up. "I've got it! Dick just built a tree house, on the side hill, in a big tree no one knows about. No one will ever think of it."

Pointing at me with his baseball, Bases asked, "Where's the tree house?"

I looked up at him, gathered my thoughts, and said, "If someone didn't want to be seen, they should come down the ridge, right on top of Farmer Parker's south pasture hill, follow the path from his corner fence down into our woods. They wouldn't miss it. It's not far from our house, but so steep up the hill no one can see it from there."

Dropping his glove and baseball on the porch he interrupted, "Hold on a minute. I've got an idea. I'll be right back out." He ran into the house, letting the screen door slam.

Holbrook stood up quickly, pinching his t-shirt with his finger and thumb like he was holding a teacup. He pulled the cotton shirt away from his stomach and yelled, "EWWWWW, I got some of it on me! Get it off! Get it off!"

Dale and Mary looked at him, like, *Aren't you the same guy who made fun of Jerry for the past half hour, and wouldn't come close, because he was covered with it?*

Bases burst out of the house, picked up his baseball and glove, letting the screen door slam again just a split second after his mom shouted at him not to slam the door. "Okay," he said, "I've solved it, but you're all on your own. That's my ride coming." He pointed to a car turning onto Main Street.

We all got serious, looked, and listened. We didn't say a word ... we just listened.

Bases leaned in and said, "I just telephoned Paul Shaffer. He is in your brother Dick's grade, Jerry. He lives on your road down by the Butlers."

"Yes," I answered.

"Well, he raises prize rabbits to show at the state fair. I told him how to get to the tree house. He said he would leave a carrying cage in it as soon as we hung up. When your brother Mike comes back, you have to figure a way to get the rabbit from him. Take it to the tree house, put it in the cage, and then call Paul Shaffer to come get it. No one will know where the rabbit went or what happened to it. His telephone is New Woodstock 37. But if you forget it, Myrtie, the operator, will know it."

This was perfect. We felt like we'd accomplished something, maybe saved a rabbit from being murdered. Mary told Holbrook her dad could take them home. She asked if she could use the telephone. We split up. Dale started walking the mile to his house, down Oran Delphi Road. I started walking the mile towards mine, down Delphi Falls Road. Holbrook took his t-shirt off, hosing the spots off the front of it, while waiting for Mary's dad.

There was nothing better than best friends.

CHAPTER FIVE

BUNNY MAGNATE

When Mike came home, I was waiting just inside the barn garage door, out of sight. I could see him drive towards the house and park and pull the emergency brake. My knees began to shake, but I stayed quiet and unseen. He got out of his car and walked into the house. I saw that he had nothing in his hands, so I ran, as fast as I could, over to the car, grabbed the rabbit from the box on the front seat, closed the lid back down, and bolted up into the woods with it. Just as promised, there was a carrying case in Dick's tree house. Paul Shaffer must have found it easy. I left the rabbit in it and closed the door latch. Then I hurried back down the hill to the house, sat on the front porch—trying to catch my breath—waiting for all Hell to break loose when Mike came out of the house looking for his rabbit.

Mike finally came out, pulling the top sprig from a radish he had in his hand. Then he tossed the sprig on the ground, popped the radish in his mouth, and began chewing it with his mouth open in loud crunching sounds. He motioned a "hey" to me and walked over to his car and started opening the passenger door to get the rabbit.

"Want to pet the rabbit one last time? Give it a carrot?"

It was all I could do not to give him a piece of my mind, but I relied on the Hardy Boys' cool and calm in the face of danger.

"Already have," I blurted.

Mike said, "Oh?" and pushed the car door closed again, biting into the rest of his radish. I had to think fast.

I shook at the knees because he was really big, six feet six inches tall, and could pulverize me if he wanted to. I had to keep him from looking in the box.

"Want an omelet?" I stuttered.

In a stroke of brilliance I added, "I gave the rabbit a carrot."

Slowly, as he finished swallowing the last of the radish he'd been chewing on, savoring its rank flavor, he smiled, and said, "There any eggs in the house? Let's go make omelets."

I didn't even know what an omelet was but I went in with him—in part to celebrate my victory and in part because I was hungry. I knew what eggs were, they weren't rabbit or some stinky cheese or frog, so I said okay. You have to watch those gourmet guys ... keep an eye on them real close. I was nervous all the time we ate the omelet, which, except for the green pepper in it, wasn't all that bad. Mike said he had to make a telephone call, so I waited for him to do that and leave. After he was out the door, I picked up the telephone and asked Myrtie for New Woodstock 37 and told Paul Shaffer he could come on and get the rabbit.

I headed out the back door and up the side hill to Dick's tree house. He'd built it up off the ground, without a ladder attached or even climbing sticks nailed into the tree, so you had to jump up a ways and grab onto a board to be able to get into it. He said that would make it harder for enemies to get into it. I think he just ran out of wood or nails, or met a girl, or had some other distraction. That happens to really smart people. The neat part about the tree house was that he'd built it in one of the few trees that leaned out over the side of the hill, about forty feet above the ground below. If you could get in it, you could look down at the house, the barn garage, driveway and everything. I watched Mike back his car around and drive out through the gate down Cardner Road.

I gave the rabbit another carrot and the two pieces of lettuce I had in my pocket, and we waited for Paul Shaffer.

It wasn't long before I heard him coming over the ridge, down the hill and into the woods. He was blowing on his harmonica. He wasn't playing it loud enough to give him away—just loud enough to pass the time, while walking through the woods. Different boys had different superstitions about the woods, ways of walking through it alone. I know—I was almost just getting used to the woods myself. My mom kept telling me there were no dinosaurs up there, but I sure kept finding a lot of fossils near the bottom of the falls. When he got outside the tree house, he put the harmonica in his pocket, jumped up, grabbed onto the crossing board, and pulled himself into it.

"Hey," I said to him.

"Hey," he said.

"Mike left, but he always forgets books or something, so there is no telling if he would just turn around and come back," I said.

"I'll take it back up through the woods, then," said Paul, "instead of on Cardner Road."

"Can I come with you?" I asked.

"C'mon," he said.

Paul climbed down from the tree house. I handed the carrying cage out to him, then climbed down myself. We started up the hill, through the woods, towards Farmer Parker's side hill pasture up to the ridge. When we would get to a barbed-wire fence, I'd hold the cage, put my foot on the lowest wire and hold it down while I pulled up on the next wire above. This left a gap big enough for Paul to crawl through. Paul would climb through it. I'd hand him the cage over the fence, and then he'd hold the wires for me. When you're kids in the country, you learn how to do these things. A simple barbed-wire fence won't slow you down a bit. We helped each other, because we knew a tear or rip in a shirt or pants, caused by a sharp barbed wire, were good for a certain lecture on the cost of clothes and on trespassing.

As we walked, Paul told me how he was getting his doe rabbits ready for the State Fair Livestock Competition in September. He had all spring and summer to get them to the right weight and coat. Easter was just a month or so away.

Paul loved his rabbits and had blue ribbons over the inside wall of his garage.

None of the talk about doe rabbits made any sense to me. I figured he liked making dough—as in money, not bread.

It was no time at all before we were walking along the top ridge, above where all the cows were grazing, and we passed the back of Doc Webb's place. He blew "Oh Susannah" on his

harmonica while we walked. We passed the back of the Butlers'
place, and then to the ridge behind his house.

We climbed down the hill and walked into their back yard
to the garage. Attached to the outside wall of the garage, about
five feet off the ground, were three rabbit hutches with chicken
wire on the sides and screen wire on the floors. One big cage had
four beautiful, floppy-eared gray rabbits which looked alike. He
called them his doe rabbits. Two other cages were smaller. One
had a rabbit in it that looked just like the other four in the big
cage. One cage was empty. When I pointed to the lone rabbit,
Paul said it was his "buck" rabbit.

I wasn't sure what that meant—like was it for sale for a buck?
"Buck" and "doe"—I never knew he liked money so much. You
couldn't tell it by listening to him play his harmonica, and he
sure never told my brother Dick about it. Sometimes you just
can't figure out older guys at all. Who would have ever thought
Mike could think of murdering something or even be a gourmet, and all the while going to college, right under everyone's
eyes, to be a doctor?

I was a guest at his house, and Paul was doing me a big favor,
so I wasn't going to be rude and ask him why the one rabbit,
"buck," was all alone and all the "doe" rabbits were in the other
cage playing together and having all the fun.

"Want to see my picture with my ribbon in the paper from
last year?" Paul asked.

"Sure."

He ran into the house to find it.

Just then, Dad drove up and blew a quick honk on his horn.
He rolled down his window and said, "Hop in, son—I'll give you
a ride home."

I jumped up onto the porch, saw Mrs. Shaffer through the
screen, and said, "Would you tell Paul that my Dad came and I
have to go, Mrs. Shaffer?"

"I will, honey. You run along and say hello to your mom for
me."

"Yes, ma'am," I said and jumped off the porch and hopped
into Dad's car.

Just as I was about to close the car door I yelled, "Wait!"

I remembered we had forgotten to put the rabbit in the cage. It was still in the carrying case, on the ground, where animals might get to it. I ran back over, reached in, and took out the rabbit. I looked at the empty cage next to "Buck," then at the cage where all the doe rabbits were playing. I decided their cage would be more fun for mine. He wasn't in trouble, like Buck, and needed to meet some new friends. He had just lived through enough problems. I opened the cage, put him in with his four new friends, closed the door, and hooked the latch.

I felt good when my rabbit looked up at me, almost like it was thanking me for saving its life.

"Bye, and behave," I said. Then I ran back, jumped into Dad's car, and we drove off.

"How'd you find me?" I asked Dad.

"Myrtie," he said.

"How would a telephone operator know where I was?"

"Simple. I picked up the phone, asked her if she knew where my brood was, and she told me. Mike was probably on his way to see Nancy, his girlfriend, in Syracuse. Dick was probably at the Dubas in Fabius, and you were most likely at Paul Shaffer's house."

"How would Myrtie know all that, Dad?"

"Did Mike come home and make a call from the house?"

"Yes."

"Did you call Paul Shaffer's telephone today?"

"Yes."

"Well, there you go—and Dick probably talked to Duba this morning. Now hop out, and see if there is any mail in the mailbox, will you, son?"

I was totally amazed at how smart my dad was—and now, at how much Myrtie knew about everyone. I remembered how she found a way to get a message to Holbrook's house for me. Myrtie could be a really good help to the Hardy Boys and my detective work, I thought.

I got back in the car, and Dad drove in the driveway around back of the swings, where he always parked, and stopped the car.

Inside the house, Dick, Duba, and their two friends Jimmy Conway and Jimmy Dwyer were playing Pitch. It looked like Duba was winning—he had the most pennies in front of him.

Speaking to me and Dick, Dad asked, "Which of you want to get up really early and help me sample Brewerton before the sun comes up?" He walked down the hall towards his and Mom's bedroom.

Every once in a while, Dad would meet a bakery truck in some small town and hang a loaf of bread on everyone's door so people could see how good the bread was. Sometimes Dick or Mike went with him. I never had yet.

"What's trump?" asked Dick.

"Hearts," said Duba.

"We're going to Suburban Park in Manlius when Mr. Duba picks us up," said Dick. "You go with Dad."

When Dad came back in, I told him I was going with him.

"Great," he said. "We'll stop on the way back and do some fishing at DeRuyter Lake, if you want."

After supper, Dad told me to get right to bed because three in the morning came awfully early …

"Pssssssssst! Pssssssssssssssssst!" said Dad in a low whisper.

"I'm up, Dad, I'm up," I answered.

I had slept in my clothes, so I got up, put my sneakers on fast, and went outside to Dad's car. He was putting some fishing poles and things in the trunk.

"Hop in the backseat and get some sleep. I'll wake you when we get to Brewerton."

Before I could fall asleep, I asked him what we were going to do.

"Every now and then it's a good idea to advertise a product by actually letting families have a free sample of it. That lets them try it free, and see if they like it."

"So, is that what advertising is?" I asked him.

"Sometimes," he said. "Advertising is getting the word out about your product to a lot of people. The more people who know about it, the more product you will sell—even if only a small number of those people buy it. It's in the numbers. Sometimes it's commercials on the radio that let everyone know about it. Sometimes it's ads in the newspaper that let them know. Sometimes it's giving away samples, like we're going to do today. Today we are going to hang a warm loaf of bread on over a hundred doors in Brewerton right before people get up for breakfast, before they open the door to get the morning paper off their porch or lawn. When they do, they will see our bread. Maybe they will try it for breakfast. If only twenty percent like the nice warm bread, that could be forty new bread customers. It's the numbers, son."

"How do we hang the loaf on the door, Dad?"

Dad slowed down, pulled off the road, came to a stop, and got out. Dad loved talking about business to anyone who was interested. He always said that every question deserved a good answer. That's how we learn, he would say. He opened the trunk, pulled something out, and slammed it back down. He got back in, reached over the back of the seat, and handed me a chip-board-like paper Indian headdress, which had colorful printed feathers all around it.

"With these," he said.

He pulled the car back onto the road and started driving again. I crawled over the seat, to the front, holding the Indian headdress. I tried it on. It went around my head, with colorful cut-out feathers sticking up all around it. It looked almost real.

"Kids will love these," I told him.

It had the name of the bakery in the back. It stayed on your head by attaching the two holes in the end of it like a lock.

"How?" I asked.

"How to you, too," said Dad, and we both laughed.

"We put the bread in the middle of the head bonnet and the holes on the ends—the same ones that lock and hold it on your head—will also fit right over a doorknob and hold a loaf of bread. We'll use three headdresses for every house, so it will be stronger, hanging on the door. Besides, if they have more kids, each will get one, that way. It's the numbers, son."

Dad was nice like that.

The bakery truck was waiting for us, and then it followed us all around the town. I would run up to every door and hang the headdresses with the loaf of bread on every doorknob. When

I got back to the car, Dad would hand me another, all ready to hang. If I could see any clue that the home had more than three kids living there, I would leave five or six headdresses around the bread.

When we were done, Dad turned the car around to go back home. Driving through town, near dawn, we could see kids already wearing the Indian headdresses.

"New customers?" I asked Dad, pointing to the kids.

"Happy new customers," said Dad.

My dad was smart. I had just learned how to advertise.

We headed to DeRuyter Lake.

I was still amazed at my dad. While we caught sunfish and perch, I kept asking him more questions about advertising. He would always say the same thing, "It's the numbers." We packed the fishing gear up and headed for home.

As we drove in through the gate, we could see gourmet Mike's Chevy. Mike was sitting on one of the swings. He looked upset. (Mom had called him and made him come home for an emergency family meeting.) Dick was walking out of the house carrying an encyclopedia. Dad drove around behind the swings and parked.

"Now you've done it," said Dick.

"Done what?" I asked.

"I don't know," he said. "Mom is on the phone with Mrs. Shaffer, but I think you've had it."

We all went in the house to the kitchen. My heart was pounding because I probably was going to get stomped for stealing Mike's rabbit. We waited for Mom to get off the phone. Mike sat up on the kitchen counter, grabbed some grapes from a bowl, and waited. Mom came out of the bedroom into the kitchen with her hand to the side of her face, like people do when they have a toothache.

She stopped, caught Mike's eye, reflected, turned around, and looked at me like maybe I should be in jail or reform school.

"Young man, where did you get the rabbit you took over to the Shaffers' house?"

I knew she knew.

"I couldn't let it get murdered."

Mom turned and looked at Mike again. The confession came easier than they both anticipated. Mom and Dad then looked at each other for the punishment phase.

I didn't care, murder was wrong, they both knew—even the president said that.

"Jerry, the rabbit you took from Mike was an Easter present for Mike's professor's daughter. Your brother was watching it for him while he was traveling so she wouldn't find out about it. It was meant to be a surprise."

My jaw dropped.

"It was?"

I stared up at Mom; I looked over at Mike; I looked up at Dad. I looked around at Dick who kept jerking his head towards the back door—motioning for me to take off as fast as I could and maybe run away while I still had the chance.

"Young man," Mom said, "it seems you put a buck rabbit in with the Shaffers' breeder does, and now there is a slight problem ..."

Standing there, with the encyclopedia open in his hand, Dick interrupted like he was Ben Franklin or someone: "Rabbits have a gestation period of four weeks, can have litters of as many as eight to twelve rabbits when they birth," he read proudly and then stared at me, jerking his head again, like if I was ever going to run away from home, he'd cover the door for me, but now would be the perfect time.

"He wasn't a buck rabbit," I declared. "He never got in trouble of any kind."

Dad belched out a short giggle, kind of smirked, but Mom twisted her eyebrows like a horsewhip and gave him a stern look, to be serious.

"Jerry, when a rabbit is a boy, they call it a buck, and when a rabbit is a girl, they call it a doe."

"Uh-uh. Nah ... no way. That's deer," I insisted.

"AND rabbits!" smarted off Dick, pointing to a section in the encyclopedia.

"Jerry," Mom asked, "do you have any idea, at all, of how babies are made?"

Dick raised his hand, started hopping up and down as though he was in school, wanting to be called on. Dad made a fist, and with his middle knuckle gently knocked on the top of Dick's head, a couple of times, as fair warning to shut his mouth, unless spoken to. Mike just stared down at me, feeling sorry.

"Yes," I said confidently. "People get married."

Dick blurted in one long breath, "Well, your bunny just got married four times, and four times eight is thirty-two baby bunnies—or, times twelve, is forty-eight baby bunnies in four weeks."

"Is that true, Mom?" I asked.

"Yes, dear, I'm afraid so. What you need to know is that rabbits are livestock. If you want to save these bunnies from being sold, for meat or fur, you will have to think of some way to place them in homes where they can be pets."

"Want me to look up livestock?" offered Dick. Dad gave him another knuckle knock on top of his head.

"How long did he say?" I asked—looking up at Mom.

"Four weeks!" said Dick, slamming the encyclopedia closed with a pop.

Everyone stood there without saying a word, staring at me. Then Dick added, "Oh yeah, baby rabbits are called kittens."

Dad took the encyclopedia away from him.

Mom leaned over with a stern look in her eye, to drive home her disappointment, and said, "Young man, you owe your brother an apology. Unless you can retrieve it, you owe Mike's professor the cost of the rabbit that was to be a gift to his daughter. You owe Mrs. Shaffer for its care and feeding and you owe a promise that you will take the litters off their hands, when they come, if you don't want them to become livestock. Do you understand me?"

My mind reeled and went blank.

Rabbits-bunnies-kittens! I was a wreck. My whole day flashed through my head. I got up at three in the morning. I put chipboard headdresses and loaves of bread on every door in Brewerton and caught four sunfish all before anyone here in the kitchen ever even woke up this morning. How could I have possibly gotten into so much trouble in that amount of time?

I closed my eyes, slapped the palm of my hand on my fore-head—*splat!* Dick was right, running away was probably the only way out of this mess. I turned around in a daze, not even feeling the slap on my forehead, walked from the kitchen through the laundry room, out the back door, and up the steep side hill into the woods to run away. Maybe Dick was right.

Mike got off the counter and followed me. I could see him out of the corner of my eye as I began climbing the hill.

"Wait up," he shouted.

He probably wanted to beat me up for losing his professor's rabbit, the Easter present for his daughter. I pretended I didn't see or hear him.

"Wait up," he shouted again.

I didn't have any idea where I was going, but somehow know-ing he was following me made me a little braver. I went higher and deeper into the woods, up over the first falls, then the second falls where I had never been before. I came to a clearing where there was a fence for a pasture. I got through the fence, trying to hold the wires from tearing my shirt. Then I turned around, looked Mike in the eye, and held the wires for him, admitting I knew he was with me. He stayed quiet, but crawled through.

We walked through the field towards a tall, fat apple tree in the center. We were both startled to see two very large Belgian workhorses standing under it. We stopped walking, sat down on the ground, and watched the horses. They were twice the size of Farmer Parker's horses, Sarge and Sally. The leaves on the apple tree started to bend in the wind, which was gusting up. We could see the horses' manes blowing in the wind. The clouds started to darken and roll. The sky was clouding, moving, the wind started blowing all the trees.

"This is the Pettacabbage place," Mike said. "The Pettacabbage family came here from Europe, where they lost their farm because of bombs during the War. They're really good farmers. Those are their Belgian workhorses. They're big, but they won't hurt us."

"Wouldn't matter," I moped. "My life is over, anyway. Like a 'stupido' I think I rescued one rabbit from you, and now thirty-two or more might get murdered because I'm such a lame brain."

CRRRRRAAAAAAAACCCCCCCKKKKKKKK!

Like a giant axe, a bolt of lightning shot straight down, through the clouds, ripping the top limb from the apple tree with one swipe. The horses bucked up and galloped off to a covered shed on the far end of the pasture.

Mike pushed me quickly down to the ground and plopped down next to me.

"Stay on the ground!" he shouted. "Lightning strikes the tallest things in an area, and we'll be safe on the ground, until it blows over."

I peered up and saw the big top tree limb, still attached by a thin piece of bark, flapping and bouncing up and down on the ground in the wind. I began to trust Mike knew what to do. It felt just like we were in the movie newsreels of the War, waiting for the bombs to drop out of airplanes on us.

Lowering his head to the ground, Mike said, "When I was your age, I did a lot of things I thought were right but wound up to be dumb and embarrassing. Don't worry about it."

"You did? Like what?"

"I'll have to think. I'm sure I did some really stupid things. You did what you thought was right. You're still my brother, always will be my brother. Don't worry about it. Running away is never an answer."

Sometime just before the rain started, I got so tired from being up so early in the morning and from climbing the hill that, lying next to Mike now, I fell asleep.

When I woke, he was already sitting up. The storm had passed, but it was getting late. The sky was getting dark. The ground was soaking wet. It must have rained a lot while we slept. We both knew that, to get back, we would have to climb back down the hill and past two seventy-foot waterfalls.

"Some storm. Feeling better?" Mike asked.

"Yeah."

"Let's go home, okay?"

"Okay."

We got up and started towards the fence we would have to crawl through, to go home. I held the wires for Mike, and then he held them for me. As we started down into the woods, above the second waterfall, Mike stopped and turned. His face was all serious, like we may be in danger. He warned me to be careful, as the ground was wet, real muddy, and very slippery.

We walked a little way further.

Then he stopped and turned around.

Now I was getting scared!

"Okay, here's the deal," he said. "We have to climb down, right at the edge of both the upper second falls and the lower first falls. They have high dangerous cliffs, tons of water flowing after a storm. I'm going to have to carry you on my back. But before I can do that, you need to know, I will need both my hands free, to grab onto trees and limbs, to keep us steady from falling and sliding down over the cliffs. It will be up to you to hang on, stay on my back without any help from me. Can you do that?"

"Yes," I said.

"Are you sure?"

"I'm sure."

I wasn't as afraid now, because I trusted Mike.

He said, "Okay, then—you get on my back, and don't let go until we're on the ground by the back door of the house, okay?"

"Yes."

Mike bent down on a knee. I piggybacked on him, wrapping my arms around his neck, clenching my hands together. When he stood up, my legs just fit around him. I locked my feet up in front of him. Mike leaned forward to keep his balance and stepped very carefully, like Hawkeye from *The Last of the Mohicans.* He would grab hold of one small tree just ahead of him, securely in his right hand like a ski pole, to keep his footing. Stepping carefully forward, he would reach out and take another small tree in his left hand. I held on with all my might and closed my eyes when we got too near the cliffs. Slowly, deliberately, we moved through the woods. The closer we got to the upper waterfall and its cliffs, the louder the water crashed, like thunder, rumbling the ground around us, the tighter I would hold on. If I opened my eyes, I could see down the cliff. I knew if we slipped, or fell, we could both die. I kept them closed as much as possible. I could sense, with each step, Mike carefully choosing which tree or branch he would grab next, as he stepped forward to the next one he could trust. Just when we got to a point where the noise of the upper waterfall was behind us, I could see down the cliffs of the first falls. Down below it, the noise got louder again. This waterfall was bigger, even more dangerous. Mike very carefully stepped over the top edge, onto land, while he held onto a pine tree he could get his hand around.

I was too scared to cry, but I trusted Mike would do his best to save us. I tightened my grip.

This hill was much steeper. It led straight to the cliff.

In the distance, I could see Dick's tree house, so I knew we were going to be safe. Mike told me to hang on, tight, because, although we were safely away from the falls and the cliffs, we were coming to a very grassy, steep, slippery hill. With no trees to grab now, his feet would slip and slide forward a bit. Then he would turn his body sideways, slide sideways a little, leaning down, grabbing whatever grass and weeds he could from the side of the hill, with his fingers for balance, until we reached the bottom.

"You can get down now," he said.

I slid off his back. We just stared at each other.

Mike looked down at me and said, "Dad taught me something, Jerry, and you should know it, too. Don't ever be afraid to do what you think is right. You did what you thought was right. We all do dumb things. Now you're in a pickle. But you're very smart. Smart enough to figure this thing out, the jam you're in. You just don't think you are. Figure it out. Never be afraid to make mistakes along the way. It's the best way to learn."

He looked me straight in the eye.

"I'm sorry I took your rabbit," I said.

Mike extended his hand for me to shake.

"Well, now you can get it back to me so I can get it to the professor, right? No harm, no foul. Deal?"

"Deal," I said, taking his hand and shaking it.

We both looked back at the churning water pouring over the roaring lower waterfall, turned, and went into the house. I never thought Mike was weird ever again.

In the house no one asked us any questions. They saw we were safe and left us alone. Neither of us ever talked to anyone about what we had just gone through together—*we could never expect to describe it,* and no one would ever believe it, anyhow. We knew we had just experienced something that would bond two brothers together, forever.

Mom came up to Mike and said, "Mike, please take Jerry to Mary Crane's. He'll show you where to go. The Cranes invited him to supper. Jerry? Go put some dry clothes on and get ready to go. I'll pick you up at eight and bring you home."

Mike and I didn't talk all the way to the Cranes' house. We knew things were different between us now. When I got out of the car he said, "Good luck. You can do it."

For the first time I believed I could.

Mary was sitting on her front-porch rocking chair. As I walked up, she turned and puffed away a curl from in front of her eye. "I heard about the rabbits and the mess you're in," she said. "Don't worry, we can sell them for Easter."

"We can't sell thirty-two rabbits," I said. "We don't know thirty-two people who would buy them. If they don't buy them, I'll be stuck with them and still in the same trouble I'm in now."

"What are you going to do?"

"I'm thinking," I said.

Mary's mom leaned in to the screen door and said, "Jerry, your brother Dick is on the telephone asking for you. You can get it in the kitchen."

"Hello?"

"You know that GASCO gas station in Manlius, the one Mom always goes to after church?" Dick asked.

"Yeah."

"Well, it caught fire and burned. It must have been an explosion, too. County sheriff has a reward for information to catch whoever started it."

"How much is the reward?" I asked.

"Fifty dollars," said Dick. "They would never give it to a kid, unless he was over eighteen. But if you can figure a way how, you could use the money to get you out of trouble with the rabbits."

Then Dick added one more sentence before he hung up—a sentence that only a Hardy Boys aficionado would have caught, on his best day—and I caught it myself.

That sentence was: "What I can't figure out is why Sonny's sleeping cot was in the front room of the gas station, not in the back, where he normally sleeps."

Dick hung up, and I went back out on the porch to where Mary was.

"How much would it cost to get thirty-two or forty-eight Easter baskets, like the Easter bunny brings, and fill them with candy? An Easter bunny would do that."

"Probably a lot," Mary said. "What are you thinking?"

"How much is a lot? And do you even know where we can get some baskets, enough candy to fill them, and still have room for a small bunny?"

"Mr. Moore has little baskets, over on Pompey Hollow Road, down by you. He sells apples in them, at his apple farm. I saw him unload a truck full of them. I'll go ask him how much fifty will cost. My dad will drive me. I can handle the candy," Mary added.

"How can you handle the candy for all that?" I asked.

Mary stood up and motioned for me to follow her. In her room, she got on her knees and pulled out the middle drawer of her bureau, like it was the vault at the Tully bank. It was completely filled—to the brim—with candy of every kind. This candy she had collected every Easter and Halloween, for years. Then she opened the bottom one, which was filled with jelly-beans of every color!

"If you can get the money, I can get you Easter baskets," she said as she closed the drawers. "I'll tell you how much money you'll need, after I talk to Mr. Moore, tomorrow."

I was amazed.

Mom picked me up after supper. Mary said she would let me know about the baskets when she found out.

When I got home, I went outside for a walk. I had to think.

I walked out to the front gate, then down Cardner Road to the bridge, just before the alfalfa field. I leaned on the bridge wall, stared at the water still rushing down as a result of the storm.

All of a sudden, I had an idea. It was all clear to me now, and it depended on only one thing. I stepped back, stood straight up, and took a second to rethink the entire idea in my head again, so I wouldn't forget any of it. Then I walked quickly back up Cardner Road. This just had to work.

When I got in the house, I went to Mom and Dad's room. It was empty. I closed both of the doors and picked up the telephone.

"Myrtie? This is Jerry Antil."

"I know," she said. "Some storm, eh, hon?"

I told Myrtie about all the trouble I was in, and what I had to do so that thirty-two to forty-eight bunnies wouldn't become livestock and get murdered. Every once in a while Myrtie would excuse herself to switch someone's call, or connect someone, but she listened to every word I had to say.

I told her about the reward money and what the clues were telling me as a junior detective.

"I think the man who works at the gas station either started the fire by accident, with a cigarette or something, or he set it on purpose. Maybe he had a friend stay there for him, who was careless. I think he put his sleeping cot in the front room, because he knew he would get burned if he stayed in the back."

"Interesting," said Myrtie.

"But I'm too young to collect a reward, Dick says," I said. "I need money to help save these bunnies."

Myrtie told me to let her think about it. She would call me when she had an idea, or if she needed me to do something. I didn't even ask her how she would know where I was, because by now I was convinced she always knew.

I hung up the phone and went to my room. No one said anything to me about anything. When someone was in trouble, everyone knew it was best to just leave him alone to work it out, unless he asked for help.

The next morning Mr. Crane dropped Mary off at the house and drove off. When she knocked on the door, I stepped out on the front steps.

"Say I can get the baskets, say you can get the money," she said. "How are you going to get thirty-two or forty-eight kids to want them first, and then how are we going to deliver them, if and when they do want them?"

"I'm going to advertise. It's all in the numbers, Mary. Let me worry about the advertising," I said. "Then, you're going to drive me around in the '38 Dodge pickup we have out in the alfalfa field. Down next to the bridge. We can deliver them all in that."

"I am!?" she asked. "I'm ten!"

"Can you drive a stick?"

"Yes."

"Can you back it up, drive it forward, whenever you want?"

"Yes."

"So, what are you afraid of? You're driving. But don't say a word to anyone, or we'll get clobbered, or arrested or something."

"What if it's hard for me to see over the steering wheel," Mary offered.

"Then sit on a pillow," I told her.

"Well, we need to go to Mr. Moore's and get the baskets. Dad took me there before we came here. Mr. Moore told me he paid six cents apiece for them and would make us a fair deal. You don't have to pay him until later," she said. "I told him you and I would walk over."

"I wonder if there's any gas in the '38?"

"Why?"

"Let's go."

We walked to the front gate and down past the bridge, and sitting in the alfalfa field was the old '38 pickup someone had left for Dad to use to haul rocks in and hadn't picked it up. I wiped off the windshield best I could, wondering if there was any gas in it, and flipped the key to Mary.

"Huh?" she said, startled.

I removed the cobwebs from the cab and steering wheel and said, "You drive. I have to think. It's only a mile, just down Pompey Hollow Road. You know the way already and there's no traffic—so you drive."

She looked at me like I was crazy, but got in and started it up. To drive it, she had to sit on the very front of the seat, holding tight to the steering wheel to keep her balance and reach the foot pedals. Off we tumbled through mounds of grass in the alfalfa field and onto the road, Mary stretching her neck up to look through the middle of the steering wheel.

When we got near the Moore apple farm, Mary pulled off the road into an entrance of a pasture, stopped, and turned it off. She didn't want to take any chances getting caught driving. She also didn't want to spook Mr. Moore into thinking he was aiding a couple of potential delinquents, regardless of how good our mission was. We had to walk about two hundred and fifty feet to his house.

Mr. Moore saw us crossing his lawn. He opened the door and lifted up a bulky burlap bag filled with something, tied with a string at the top. He pushed the screen door open.

"Here, Jerry and Mary—here are sixty one-quart baskets, just for good measure. They're a gift from me and the missus. You're doing a good thing. God bless."

I took the bag—it wasn't heavy—and thanked him. He went back behind his screen door, and watched us walk away, back up Pompey Hollow Road.

Mary drove us back toward my house while I inspected the baskets.

"Look," I said. "Some have pink dye on the rims, some have blue dye on the rims—they'll be perfect for Easter."

A truck was coming down Pompey Hollow Road towards us from the other direction. Mary mumbled through her teeth, "Please don't see me, please don't see me, please don't see me."

The man in the truck was Mr. Vaas in his milk truck filled with milk cans. He was laughing, slapping the outside of the door of his truck with his hand, pointing at little Mary driving. He whistled and waved as he drove past. Mr. Vaas was out delivering farmer's milk to the dairy.

"He won't tell," I said. "He's Randy's dad, the boy in the desk behind me in school."

Mary drove in our driveway and parked the truck next to the barn garage. She pushed out her lower lip and puffed the hair curl away from her eye.

"You'd better clean this up if we're going to use it. And make sure it has enough gas."

I smiled at her and stepped out.

I took the burlap sack into the garage barn and put it on a table for later. Mary called her dad to come get her.

At supper, Mom, Aunt Kate, Dick, and I were eating spaghetti, meatballs, and sausage. Spaghetti was like a celebration at our table, because everyone liked it. Mom mentioned that Dad would be there anytime, but we weren't to wait. She asked me if I wanted to say grace—I think because she knew I was in the biggest trouble of anyone at the table and needed all the help I could get.

"Bless us, oh Lord, and these thy gifts for which we are about to receive, from thy bounty, through Christ, Our Lord. Amen."

I was starved. This was my favorite supper. Well, maybe the lobster that gourmet Mike brought home one time for Dad's birthday was better, but we only had that once.

We could hear the front door opening and the hall closet open and close. Dad walked from the living room through the dining room with a big smile on his face. He was loosening his tie and taking his business suit coat off, to put in his and Mom's room, next to the dining room. When he came back out, he rolled up his sleeves and sat down at the head of the table, ready to eat. He looked at me.

"Jerry, me boy," he started, "I want to personally congratulate you, and tell you how very proud of you I am."

Everyone stopped eating and stared at him.

I stopped sucking a strand of spaghetti and stared up at him, motionless. I didn't know if he was serious, or joking.

"I am not going to spoil it by revealing your resourcefulness, or any of your plans, or secrets …," he said.

I'm getting clobbered! I thought. I didn't even know what "resourcefulness" meant.

"… but here, son, here is your reward, for helping find the culprit who set fire to the gas station in Manlius. Everyone: Jerry, our junior detective here, came up with the clue the police needed. A man, who moved the cot, was questioned, and he confessed to accidentally dropping a lit cigarette, setting off the fire. Now, I know you have very good plans for this money, so here it is—all of it. I'm not even going to ask how you intend to use it. I want you to know, we all trust that you will do what's right."

With that, Dad pulled some bills from his shirt pocket, counted out ten five-dollar bills, and put them in front of my plate, near the middle of the table. I still had a strand of spaghetti hanging out of my mouth as I was bent over the plate. All eyes at the table followed the money from his hands, to where he counted and stacked it, one bill at a time, and right in front of me. We stared at that pile, more money than Dick or I had ever seen, in one place, at one time, before.

I bit off my spaghetti and looked at Mom, who was smiling at me. I looked around; Aunt Kate and Dad were smiling. I looked at Dick, who had a confused look on his face. I knew he was trying to think of how I thought of the right clue with the information he gave me. I reached in front of my plate and took a five-dollar bill, handed it to Dick.

"Thanks for telling me about the cot. It gave me the exact clue I needed," I said.

Dick smiled big, took the bill, held it up to the light, like he'd seen someone do in the movies, to be sure it wasn't counterfeit. He said, "Thanks, glad I could help." He folded it into his pocket proudly.

Then he gave me a wink, like he would be there for his little brother if I ever needed him, picked up his fork, and stuck it into a meatball.

Tears came to my eyes for a second. It was just that miracles were happening, but better than that, all the family was rooting for me, and the rabbits.

I was happy. That felt good.

I left the rest of the money in front of my plate all through supper. We celebrated my good fortune—without saying it. Everyone knew I might be able to save the rabbits from becoming livestock and getting murdered.

After supper, I walked over to where Dad was sitting and whispered into his ear, "Myrtie?"

"Myrtie!" he answered and smiled as I walked away.

I walked over to Mom and gave her two five-dollar bills.

"Mom, please don't ask me anything, but will you buy me something nice, for Myrtie? Something she will really like, and really needs? Tell her it's from me?"

Mom looked me in the eye and smiled. "Yes, of course, dear."

The next day, around noon, I waited on the road to ask the mailman if there was such a thing as a postcard that already had a stamp on it. He told me there was. They cost three cents each. I had to get rid of maybe forty rabbits. So I knew, according to Dad's advertising numbers, I needed to advertise to two hundred kids. I asked him how much two hundred of them would cost.

"Six dollars," he said.

I counted out six dollars.

"I'll leave them in the mailbox tomorrow," he said. "I have to get them from the post office when I get back from my route."

When they came, Dick and I sat down and wrote my name and address on the front of every one of them. That way, if anyone ever put any of them in the mail, they would come through the mail to me.

Perfect!

Now all I needed to do was tell two hundred kids about the rabbits and baskets before we could get forty to want them.

We needed the numbers!

CHAPTER SIX

IT'S THE NUMBERS

At school recess every day, for a week or more, all of my friends who'd met in Delphi Falls—Mary Crane, Dale Barber, and Holbrook—and even the boy who sat behind me in class, Randy Vaas, volunteered to help me tell all the kids to meet us out by the schoolyard fence for a secret meeting. During the course of the week nearly every kid came.

After the kids circled around, I made the announcement:

"Raise your hand if you think your parents would let you get a free, live Easter bunny for a pet and Easter basket, with candy in it, on Easter Sunday. Think about it before you answer, because if your parents won't let you have a pet bunny, don't raise your hand."

In five days, more than ninety kids raised their hands. We gave each of them a postcard, and told them their parents had to fill out their name and address and mail it back.

Then, after my announcement and the kids' show of hands, Mary would make an announcement:

"Now, here's the secret oath. If you send the card back, do you promise to set your alarm clock for five o'clock on Easter morning, and be by your front door, so the basket and bunny can be dropped off quick?"

"Yes!" everyone shouted.

Dale Barber would always be there, listening to the whole presentation, waiting for someone to ask what would we do if we ran out of bunnies on Easter—but if no one asked, he shouted it, like he was part of the crowd: "What if you don't have enough bunnies?"

"Good question," Mary answered. "The bunnies will go to the first kids who send the postcards. The rest will just get a pretty Easter basket, with candy."

Everybody clapped.

Out of the ninety postcards we handed out, fifty-seven came back to me, each with the name of the kid and their address on it. All of them were either in Delphi Falls, Fabius, Pompey, Apulia Station, or Tully. Mary and I got Barber and Holbrook to get addresses so we would know where the kids lived.

Dale, Holbrook, Mary Crane, and even Randy Vaas said they would all help on Easter morning.

Just after supper one night, Paul Shaffer called and asked me to come over.

When I got there, he showed me four carton boxes in his garage. They were filled with baby bunnies.

"Forty-four," he said. "All healthy."

I never saw so many bunnies in all my life—some white, some white and gray, and some gray.

All I could do was …

"Gulp!"

"Easter is Sunday," Paul said. "They'll all be weaned by Wednesday."

I didn't know what that meant, but I said, "Great, can we come get them at four o'clock Sunday morning?"

"Huh?" said Paul.

"I'll give you a dollar now and a dollar on Sunday, if we can come at four in the morning," I told him. Paul's eyes glazed over in a gleam as he smelled money, kind of like my brother Mike's do when he gets a whiff of some stinky cheese.

"Two dollars now, two more on Sunday," he said.

"Okay."

"Swear?" he said, holding up three fingers like a scout.

"Swear!" I said, holding up three. Neither one of us was a scout, but we figured that was as good as anything.

"Deal," I said. I counted out two dollars, handed them to him. I got Mike's rabbit, put it in a carton box, and started walking back to my house with it.

My alarm clock started clanging so loud at three on Easter morning that I jumped out of bed, knocked my desk lamp over fumbling for it, and stuffed it under my pillow in one motion. Then I found the off button, not wanting to wake the whole house. I got dressed the best I could in the dark and snuck down the hall, hooking my belt. When I got outside, Mary was already there, out by the barn garage. Her dad had dropped her off after her paper route. She was in her blue bloomer gym shorts, a wool sweater, and sneakers. She had the '38 pickup backed into the barn garage already and was loading the baskets, placing them in rows in the bed of the truck. She was spooning jellybeans in the bottom of each with a feed scoop, to weigh them down. Forty-four would be filled with candy and delivered with bunnies; thirteen would have extra candy, and no bunny. She'd already planned for enough candy.

I had my spiral writing pad with everyone's name and address broken out by town. We were ready.

"Are you sure we won't get caught?" asked Mary, rubbing the sleep out of her eyes.

I was a morning person.

"It's Sunday, Mary ... It's Easter, Mary ... It's three-thirty in the morning, Mary."

Mary was all business. "Just stop," she blurted. "You're making me dizzy," she said, in an irritated tone. "You owe me nine dollars and eighty-five cents for candy."

I dug in my pocket, pulled out some crumpled bills, and handed her ten dollars.

"Now get in the truck, let's go," I said.

With the lights off, she started the '38 and drove slowly out of the barn garage and down the drive. I kept checking in the back to make sure none of the baskets were blowing around. We pulled onto Cardner Road, turning left up the hill. As we passed Farmer Parker's house, his kitchen light went on, making Mary jump. She thought we might be seen, or caught, but it was just a coincidence. Farmer Parker was just getting up.

"It's milking time," I said.

Mary seemed to get calmer the farther she drove. We passed down by Doc Webb's, then the Butlers' place. She slowed down and pulled over into Paul Shaffer's driveway. She turned out the lights and shut the truck off.

Paul came out of the garage, walked to my side of the '38, and asked, "You got my money?"

I stepped out of the truck and gave him two dollars.

In the garage, with three flashlights, we were trying to figure whether it would be best to put the bunnies into the baskets here, or keep them all in one carton and put them in the baskets when we delivered them.

Seemingly out of nowhere, the moon flashed a bright silvery reflection off the side of a big, long, midnight-black car driving up with its lights off. It turned slowly into the driveway, grinding the stone pebbles as it crunched to a stop, just behind the '38 pickup.

We all froze.

It looked like the president of the United States was coming to arrest us all. Certain it was we all almost had heart attacks. Mary backed away, stepping behind one of the bunny cages next to the garage to hide, in case she had to make a run for it and dash up the back ridge. Then we all saw it was Dick's friend Duba getting out of his father's car—it was the big, long Lincoln. Duba's and Dick's best friends Conway and Dwyer got out as well. They told us they had come to drive us, for Dick. Dick had asked them to help get us out of the jam. They were all thirteen. No licenses, but thirteen, and figured they could get away with sneaking the Lincoln out, if they were quick about it and had it back before daylight and before Duba's dad woke up.

I was amazed. Knowing we were ten, Dick's thirteen-year-old friends showed up to volunteer to drive us so we wouldn't get in trouble. Dick kept it a secret all this time, even stayed home so no one would get suspicious.

Older guys had come to help!

Just about that time, Barber drove up in his dad's Packard. Was he ever happy to see Duba, Conway, and Dwyer already there to do the driving. He beamed a grin in the headlights.

"It's a danged miracle," Dale whispered.

He knew for certain that if his dad ever found out he'd taken the Packard, he would become mincemeat. Worse than mincemeat if he drove it all over the countryside. Right after Dale came, Randy Vaas's dad drove up in his milk truck, Randy got out, and the truck pulled away, on its way to the dairy. This was getting good. Randy was ten but wanted to be there for us, too. His dad was the one who saw Mary driving the '38.

Randy said, "Where's Holbrook? We would have gotten him."

"I came straight from my paper route, I forgot about him," said Mary.

As soon as Randy and Mary got it out of their mouths, Duba jumped into Mr. Barber's Packard and said, "I'll get Holbrook— I'll only be ten minutes. I'll have to drive through Fabius, so I don't want to get caught driving the Lincoln."

Everyone knew he was right. He backed the Packard around and slowly he went, lights off until he was on down the road a ways. Then the lights came on and the car lurched into speed squealing the tires.

"Oh, geez," said Dale, watching his dad's Packard quickly disappearing down the road, its engine revving.

We knew the towns we had to deliver to only had one or two streets, so we could do it safely. Nobody was out driving this early, anyway. It was about that time my brother Mike drove up. He said he was there to help and he would drive straight back to Syracuse after we were finished. This was too good to be true.

Soon the Packard pulled back in and Holbrook got out with Duba. Holbrook was barefoot, in jeans and a pajama top. Duba had to go into his house in the dark and up the stairs, find him in a room filled with five brothers and no lights, and wake him up without waking up the whole house. Holbrook only had time to grab his jeans and his glasses.

We divided up all the names from the postcards by the towns they were in, and divided the baskets by car. We counted the rabbits and put the right amount in each carton box. Mary carried the boxes out and put them in the right cars.

"You might carry the rabbits and baskets separately or the candy could get peed on," Mary announced.

Mike would drive Randy in his car to Fabius. Duba would take Dale up to Pompey, circling around to Tully in the Lincoln. Dwyer and Holbrook took Apulia Station in the Packard. They would all meet up at Shea's store in Fabius to switch cars and head home. Mary and I would take Delphi Falls in the '38. It was just down the road.

We all had to get home after our deliveries, pretend we never left the house, and go to church. With Mike's and the older guys' help we would be done in no time. We agreed to meet at the Delphi Falls cemetery, at one o'clock, to talk about how it went.

Well, not exactly.

The kids all agreed to meet, but when we asked Duba, Conway, and Dwyer if they wanted to meet with us, they told us not to even think about it. Helping us out was one thing; being seen with us in the daylight was another. Mike had to go right back to Syracuse.

Kids understood these things.

"Mush, you huskies!" I said, just as Sergeant Preston of the Royal Mounties would tell his faithful lead sled dog, King, on the radio. "On, King!" he would shout.

"Wagons-ho!" said Dale, in a raspy loud whisper, as if we were in a John Wayne Saturday morning picture show.

"Be careful, you guys," said Mary.

"Don't get caught," growled Duba as he slammed his car door closed.

We backed the cars and the '38 around and out, headlights off as we rolled away, in both directions, before pulling the lights.

Mary, sweating bullets, but with more confidence knowing nobody had licenses, made it into Delphi Falls. When we stopped at each house, she would slouch down in the seat so she couldn't be seen. One kid asked me who was driving the truck, and I told him the Easter bunny and that no one could see him! That seemed to work.

"Please don't see me … please don't see me … please don't see me."

Mary would keep mumbling this every time a car or truck would come down the road and pass by.

We had everything delivered without a hitch—every kid was right by the door, like they promised, and everyone loved their bunnies.

We all accomplished our missions in no time at all and drove back home while it was still dark, as proud as Superman. Mary's dad was parked out by the front gate, leaning on the window, asleep in the car, as we passed. He knew she was helping out delivering Easter candy and was waiting to give her a ride home. Mary drove in and parked the '38 by the barn, exactly where it was before. She stepped out and started walking out to meet her dad down by the road.

"Hold on, I'll drive you out," I said. "First give me a hand, will ya?"

I went into the back of the barn garage and rolled Dick's popsicle cart to the back of the pickup. Mary grinned and helped me load it in. I drove both her and the cart to the gate and we all lifted it into Mr. Crane's trunk. He tied the lid down with a rope.

"Mr. Crane, if you can fix this, Mary can use it. It should be a good moneymaker for her. It'll hold popsicles and fudgesicles if you put dry ice in it, I think."

Mary smiled and nudged her head down on my shoulder. "Thanks, Jerry."

I got in and drove back to the barn garage, parked, sneaked into the house, and went back to my room.

I felt my whole body collapse on the bed, but couldn't sleep right away, thinking of our great adventure.

Later in the morning, Mom woke us up for Easter Mass.

I opened my eyes and stared over my head, out through my window, thinking about the almost two-month-long nightmare I had just gone through. I thought about Mike showing up out of the blue and helping.

At the church, St. Anne's, in Manlius, I was sitting between Mom and Dad while Father Lynch was getting ready to serve Communion. When the collection basket came around, I pulled out the wad of money I had left and counted how much it was—fifteen dollars. I unfolded and handed Mom ten dollars and asked her if she would buy a savings bond for Mary Crane—and then I dropped the five-dollar bill in the basket.

I looked up at Mom and she smiled.

Dad gave me a wink and held his hand out for me to shake it.

Everyone knew I'd come through for the rabbits for sure, with the help of all my family and the best friends any boy could ever have. What felt best was that they trusted we would do the right thing, and didn't ask any questions.

On the way home from Mass, I leaned over and told Dick thanks. I also let him know I'd given the popsicle cart to Mary's dad to try to fix—and told him I said it would be all right for Mary to use it and try to make some extra money with it.

"She can use the extra money," I said.

"How about Holbrook?" asked Dick.

"He needs like a part-time job or something. He needs more money than from popsicle sales," I said.

"Who showed up?" he asked.

I leaned over and whispered, "Mike came from Syracuse to drive and Duba came and was driving his dad's Lincoln. Dwyer and Conway were with him. They bailed us out big time. Really big time."

Dick beamed a smile out the car window, happy our brother Mike had showed up and that his school friends had come through for me—for him. He had a look on his face as if it felt good knowing he and his friends were able to do something good. He leaned over and whispered in my ear, "You kids see trouble again, SOS me. You know SOS?"

"Yes. Dot, dot, dot—dash, dash, dash—dot, dot, dot?"

Dick wrenched his lips in an agreeing smile, turned his head, and looked out the car window again at the farms going by in great satisfaction, feeling good about himself and his friends.

I was beginning to realize just how smart he was. It dawned on me Dick had figured out how to help us with the rabbits long ago—by maybe getting Mike there, by maybe leading me with hints on how to earn the reward money, by getting the other drivers—without even talking or bragging about it.

Because of Dick's brains and Mike's "buck" rabbit, it was a very happy Easter for everyone, *especially* for a lot of kids in Pompey, Fabius, Apulia Station, Tully, and in good old Delphi Falls.

Later, at the cemetery, Mary's dad dropped Holbrook and Crane off. Holbrook had a clean t-shirt on this time. Mary was in her new Easter dress. Dale and our friend Randy were already there.

Mary said, "We should say thanks to Dick's friends and your brother Mike.

"I already told Dick thanks, after church. He said if we ever get in trouble we can just SOS him."

Hearing SOS gave us chills.

We all knew, from listening to the telegraphed shortwave radio signals all during the War, that SOS was the most important signal you could ever hear in Morse Code. It meant there was big trouble. It meant "Save Our Ship!"

"I'll write Mike a letter at college and thank him," I said.

Everyone looked around at each other. The possibility of more adventures was dawning on us with the thought of the SOS. Each of our minds began to flutter in the afternoon sun, reminiscent of the flickering and sounds of the clacking movie projector in the darkened Saturday morning picture show. Our imaginations let us wonder, in our own ways, just what other adventures we may have in store for us. What else could we solve together, especially with the help of the older guys?

Who would have dreamed one little rabbit could have been such a big adventure?

Just then Bases came walking up the drive into the cemetery. He guessed we were going to be here when he saw Mary's dad drive through Delphi Falls. He wanted to show off a brand new baseball he got for Easter. After passing it around, he stuffed it in the back of his worn-torn baseball glove and asked Mary to kindly latch it to a belt loop on the back of his jeans, to hang for safekeeping.

I thanked everyone for being there for the rabbits. We all felt pretty good about making so many kids happy, especially today.

Dale said God would be very proud of us this Easter.

Randy suggested we consider starting a best friend's club and said he would be proud if we included him.

We stood in a circle, piled our hands together in the middle, and asked, "Pals for life?"

"What do we name it?" asked Holbrook.

"We need an important-sounding club name," Mary answered. We all thought.

Dale felt inspired again, stood up straight, stepped up on a tombstone, raised his arm like a preacher, and announced: "The Pompey Hollow Book Club!"

"Book Club? Book Club!? Will we have to read books?" asked Holbrook.

"Not a word if you don't want to," said Dale, "but carry a book if you leave the house on another mission. There ain't a mom in the county who will stop us from going to a book club meeting, even on a school night."

Dale was eloquent.

"You might stop saying *ain't*, then," suggested Mary.

In full agreement, we spit in our hands and shook on it.

"Can girls be in your club?" Bases asked, his eye catching Mary's new Easter dress.

What next occurred began as a very loud, stone-cold silence.

Holbrook bolted back, thinking of how, if it weren't for Mary, he would have never had a ride. Vaas stepped back, and thought of Mary counting out all the rabbits and always being there for us. Dale said, "Oh, geez," and remembered all the days Mary was there for us, at the playground fence talking to kids. I thought of Mary driving and finding the baskets and helping anyway she could.

Mary's neck raised up slowly, like a well-oiled submarine periscope. She leaned back from the circle of friends and, in a robotic motion, reached around behind Barber, dug her hand deep into the baseball glove hanging on Bases's belt loop, her fist clenching the brand new shiny white baseball stored there for safekeeping and lifting it out. She stuck the ball under her chin, stepped back from the group even further. Turning away, she methodically gathered and lifted both sides of her yellow Easter dress with her hands and stuffed it like drapes into the side waistbands of the blue bloomer gym shorts she had on underneath.

Looking Bases dead straight in the eye, with a bead you could only read about in an Edgar Allen Poe thriller, Mary took the ball from below her chin, rubbed it generously with her thumb. She twirled her arm backwards, in three full windmill-like circles, kicked her left leg up, rolled her eyes back in her head—then heaved Bases's pretty, brand-spanking-new Easter present straight over the tallest cemetery pine tree she could see (it looked like a knuckleball), barely missing a crow's nest. The baseball cleared three trees in the cemetery, in fact, with ease. In time, it hit the road down below with a thwack that sounded like a broken bat, landing farther than most of us, including Bases, could have rolled it down a paved hill. About that time a long black feather from a frightened mother crow gently floated down, in circles, landing in the middle of the friends. Bases stuttered, stammered, searching his brain for the words for an apology, and how he could ever explain to his mom, a girl, why and how he'd lost his new baseball, or to the team counting on him to pitch today's game with it, without getting a considerable thumping. He cleared his throat and carefully crafted his new position: "How about anyone who shows up when you need them can belong?" he suggested, still imagining his new ball bouncing its way down the road towards Delphi Falls. Mary pulled her Easter dress from the sides of her gym shorts waistband, straightened it like the little lady she was, and brushed the loose hair from her face back up over the top of her head, tucking it in. Un-sneering her eyes, she smiled as though nothing had happened, and spit in her palm, again. We all leaned forward and shook again. Not only was the Pompey Hollow Book Club official and forever, it was coeducational.

CHAPTER SEVEN

IDLE SUMMER, HANDS

"Holbrook and I figure if we spent the summer hopping tramp steamers maybe in Casablanca or Pago Pago or somewhere," I said, "we could sail part of the world. He could make money working cargo holes to buy a water heater for his mom and maybe a telephone for his sisters and I could explore the world with him, and become a famous writer."

"That's nice, dear," Mom said. "Pass the potatoes to your brother."

"You'll both need earrings," said Dick. "You should get gold ones, be sure it's pure gold, no gold-plated crap."

"Don't say 'crap,' dear," warned Mom.

"That way if you get throwed in the brig you can get your bail money. You could melt the gold down, maybe with a candle. Aaargh!"

"'Thrown,'" said Mom. "Don't say 'throwed.'"

"Can't they bite on it and tell if it's gold?" I asked. "I saw a pirate or someone bite gold in Hong Kong, or Bali or somewhere, at the picture show. I think it was Bob Hope. I wouldn't have to melt it down, I don't think. "

Dad stepped in: "Jerry, you and Holbrook have been camping out a lot this summer. Have you met with any of your other friends? Don't you kids have a club like other kids?"

"The Pompey Hollow Book Club," I said.

Mom smiled. Dad asked, "Do you have regular meetings? What are you reading?"

Dick gazed across at me. He knew the truth. He wanted to hear what kind of explanation I had for the Pompey Hollow Book Club.

"Well, we met once at Barber's house, but we just helped him stack hay bales. We made Mary president. Mrs. Barber fed us lunch with lemon meringue pie and Mr. Barber gave us each fifty cents. It'll be easier for us to meet after school starts. Summer is busy on farms. Dale has a lot of chores. Besides her paper route, Mary sells popsicles with her cart, sometimes in Delphi Falls, so she's busy."

"Now we're getting to the bottom of it," Dad said. "Sounds to me like you and Holbrook need something extra to do this summer, like Barber and Mary. Idle minds are a devil's workshop, aren't they, Mommy?" Dad grinned down at Mom.

"Huh?" I quizzed. "We're not idle; we're just bored sometimes, so we camp out."

"Camping's fun, son, but you'll both like having a project or a responsibility, too, like Dale or Mary. I know your friend Randy rides with his dad nearly every morning, delivering milk cans to dairies. Dick here washes dishes part-time at the Lincklaen House on weekends. I just had a thought. What do you and Holbrook eat when you camp out?"

"We cook Spam and eggs in an old skillet Mom gave us, sometimes we cook hot dogs or cans of soup or corned beef hash. We tried making toast but it catches fire. If we have ears of corn, we throw them on the fire then shuck 'em after they cool off. Why?"

"I'm impressed—basic cooking, at your ages. What if I could show you a type of cooking but with flour, sugar, butter, eggs, milk, and spices—a world you could both earn money from, right away? You could learn it in a day. It only needs practice after that."

"You mean baking, Dad?" I asked.

"Well, I would have said baking, but thought you may think it's only for girls. You'd learn some of the basics at the bakery—but you could use what you learn to teach yourselves more. You could earn a living anywhere in the world. In fact, if you learned to bake and could help around the kitchen here, say, with family desserts, we might even raise your allowance by a quarter a week—whatcha think, Mommy, think we could?"

Mom smiled approval. She heard the learning word, not the allowance word.

Dad added, "Holbrook could get a job at any bakery. I'm thinking the Tully bakery, close to his house, earn extra money for a water heater or telephone, whatever he needed. I know the owner."

"Okay," I answered.

Dad went on: "Son, if you could bake, you could earn your way around the world on a tramp steamer anytime you were ready to set sail. Every sailor or deck hand needs to eat. Get word to Holbrook that we'll pick him up early in the morning and go to the bakery for a short course on baking. Tell him we'll have breakfast at Bucky's."

"Okay."

Dad then looked over at Dick. "Dick, get the water softener instruction manual from your mother. If you can figure out how to keep it cleaned and running, I'll raise your allowance, too. Quarter a week. But you have to change the filters and add the salt or chlorine regularly, and keep it running."

Dick and I exchanged a look across the table. Mom and Dad were generous but neither of us remembered ever getting a regular allowance.

Dick was saving up to buy a car of his own and had twenty-six dollars from washing dishes. "I can do that, easy," he said to Dad, and then he tried: "Can I get a cash advance?"

Dad didn't answer. "Tell Holbrook, Jerry," he said. "I'll introduce you to a baker who could open a new world for you. Seems you both already have a flair for cooking, somewhat."

The next morning Dad came into my room early, already in his work suit.

"Jerry, me boy, rise and shine. Let's go get your friend, have breakfast, and then go meet a baker."

I got ready and met him outside.

After getting into the car he drove around the swings he parked behind for the summer shade, and we headed first to Holbrook's and then on to Cortland.

At the diner, Dad took a shiny quarter out of his pocket.

"Call it, Bucky!" he shouted, not taking his eyes off the flying quarter on its descent. Holbrook's eyes opened wide as he stared up at the quarter in flight. With a big grin he watched Dad slap the quarter down to the counter when it landed.

"Heads!" yelled Bucky.

Heads it was. Dad slid the quarter over the counter towards him. Bucky tipped his paper cap, and placing both hands on the counter he lifted his legs up sideways almost above the counter and clicked his heels together.

Dad said, "Bucky, the boys are about to become bakers. Jerry so he can handle his new chore of making desserts for the family. His friend Bob Holbrook here, so he can maybe get a part-time job to earn extra money." He explained to Bucky how, since we'd grown up during the War, from about 1940 to 1946, 1947, we didn't have the advantage they did of licking the spoons, learning how to bake just by watching or helping our moms, our grandparents, or others while they baked every Saturday.

Bucky said, "No sugar! War time and the sugar being rationed, there was none left to bake with for most families during the War—only a minimum amount. With the War over, sugar is available again."

Bucky reached over the counter and shook Holbrook's hand hello.

"During the War sugar was needed all over the world to feed the fighting boys and the wounded in the Red Cross hospitals," he said. "Here at home we had to go without desserts most the time. Sugar rationing was important; we had to feed the troops who were fighting for us. But to help you both out, I sure enough got some easy old recipes I dusted off after the War if you both want them."

"Thanks," Holbrook and I said.

After breakfast, Dad took us to the "cake kitchen" part of the bakery in Homer, where they made all the cookies, cakes, and sweets. Everything smelled good, like spices and raisins and sugar. People moving about were dressed in white with long white aprons and paper baking caps. The cake kitchen was across the street from the bread bakery. Dad reached on top of a locker, grabbed two paper baking hats, and put one on Holbrook's head and one on mine.

We all sat on stools at the small employee coffee counter, waiting.

A baker came around from behind the mixing machines, walked over to us, sat down across the counter with a cup of coffee in his hand, and asked Dad, "What can I do ya for, Mike?"

Dad said, "Me boy, Jerry, and his friend Bob would like to learn about baking and making desserts. Maybe earn some extra money. I thought you might be able to give them some simple pointers, some basics."

The baker grabbed my hand and while shaking it he said, "Mighty glad to know ya, son. Jerry, is it?" He then shook Holbrook's hand. "Mighty glad to know ya too, son. Bob? You done both came to the right man. I can out-bake and out-dessert any bake-off at any county fair. I'll be happy to teach them, Mike."

He poured himself another cup of coffee, filled a cup for Dad, and wedged a pencil up under the side of his white paper baking cap.

"How many we baking for, boys?" he asked.

"It should last 'bout a week—four, maybe five at the table each night," Dad answered for me. "For Bob here, there are eleven or so in his house."

The baker man reached over by the phone that was on the counter, took the white pad sitting next to it, tore the top half from the bottom half, and slid half to each of us. He took the pencil from his hat and the ball point pen from Dad's shirt pocket and handed them to us.

"Baking is simple, boys, if you always do it right," he said. "You might want to make notes. Rule one, baking is just like carpentry. If you don't measure exact, it won't hold together. Use the exact measurement always, right temperature always, and perfect time always. Never guess when baking. Follow the recipe. Cooking and baking are different. There may be a dozen different ways to cook a hamburger or make a soup—but there is only one way to bake. Remember that and you can bake anything. Rule two, you have to learn volume. A two-layer cake can go maybe six or eight ways depending on how you cut it, but the same volume in a one-layer sheet cake can serve sixteen or eighteen, so I would go with sheet cake—same amount of cake going twice as far."

He continued: "Just think volume, boys. If you put dough on a cookie sheet with a small teaspoon at home, you'll get more cookies to a batch from your dough than you will if you put it on with a larger tablespoon. If you ever work for a bakery, Bob, they'll tell you exactly how much. Smaller pieces of dough will mean more cookies."

It was all making sense to Holbrook. He was good at math. The important thing was baking wasn't just for girls and it wasn't how much we baked but how we served it: in portions that would last for everyone and last most the week.

I said, "Is it like having one or two scoops of ice cream?"

"Exactly, son. People like two scoops, but they're happy with one, also."

Holbrook piped up: "It's making whatever you have go around so everyone can have some."

"Mike, the boys are smart. It's good to run out, though. You don't want desserts every night of the week. A dessert should be a surprise. If you're in a hurry, always remember egg custard. It's quick, easy, and I'll give you a recipe. You can bake it in the same baking dish you use for a sheet cake. Oh, and if you want to get fancy, add some pieces of raisin bread to your custard mix, and it will become raisin bread pudding by magic. Same time, same temperature."

The baker looked at Holbrook and asked, "How many in your family, son?"

"Eleven kids," said Holbrook.

"I thought I heard Mike right. Hold on, son."

With that, the baker winked at Dad, stood up, and walked back to where the ovens were. I looked up at Dad who was smiling back at me. When the man came back, he handed Holbrook a rectangular glass baking dish, an oily metal baking pan, and a tin for making twelve cupcakes.

"The baking dish will fit in this pan, son. Put water in the pan when you make custard. Bake the custard resting the dish in the water. It won't scorch or burn."

He went back to the ovens again and came back this time and handed Holbrook two big cookie sheets, a measuring cup, and two pie tins.

"For a mixing bowl and rolling pin, you're on your own, but your momma will have them. This will get you started."

Holbrook sat there amazed, looking up at the pile of baking stuff that was now his. He didn't know what to say. He thanked the man and promised he would become a good baker and maybe grow up to have a restaurant of his own someday.

"Boys, I just want to try something you make sometime. Promise me I can?"

We both told him yes. I handed him back his pencil and Holbrook handed Dad his pen.

Dad helped pick up all the baking things the baker had given Holbrook, to take out to the car. He lined newspaper on the backseat and set the trays, pans, and baking dish carefully on top.

"I have a quick meeting at the bakery so I'm dropping you both at the library. Get the book *African Queen*. You want to go around the world on a tramp steamer? You'll like the adventure. It's about Africa, the jungles, and a small steamboat. Either I'll come get you when I'm done or you both just walk over to the bakery. Tell the librarian I'll bring the books back when you're finished reading them."

In the library Holbrook pulled out the encyclopedia and read about baking cakes and bread and pies and looked for cookbooks. I found the title *African Queen* in the card-index drawer. I memorized the Dewey decimal number for it on the index card. That told me what section and aisle the book was in, what shelf it was on. Like a code.

The book's beginning was slow so I cracked halfway into it. It's about two people on a scary river journey during World War I. It talks about a lot of jungle and all sorts of wild animals. This man, Charlie, owned a small cargo boat—the African Queen— and he delivered mail with it somewhere in Africa. The lady, Rose, had pretty eyes. After she told Charlie that Germans in the gun boat on the lake at the end of the river had murdered her brother, who was only a harmless Christian missionary, and that she wanted to go down the river and blow up the German ship,

Rose then kissed Charlie really good. So then he said okay, and from then on he called her Rosie. A kiss can do that. I know. I saw it in the *She Wore a Yellow Ribbon* movie. Together they managed to steer the boat all through the winding, dangerous jungle waters, past deadly crocodiles, hippopotamuses, wild jungle birds, and monkeys, just so they could blow up an enemy gunboat—if only they could get to the lake.

Holbrook and I left the library, me with the book under my arm, him with two baking cookbooks.

On the way back to Holbrook's house, Dad stopped at the Tully bakery. He took Holbrook in and introduced him to the owner. The man invited Holbrook to come back and work part-time, whenever he could. He said he would teach him everything he needed to know.

When Dad and I got home I went to my room and lay down to read the part from the *African Queen* book where Charlie got out into the swampy water to pull the boat through the weeds and leaches crawled all over his body, sucking his blood. It got scary so I put the book down to think about the baking and what I would bake first.

I fell asleep.

CHAPTER EIGHT

UNDER ATTACK

"Ahhhhh! The beasts! The beasts!"

Shouting, tossing, turning, rolling off from my bed, flopping onto the floor—I started slapping my face, neck, and arms as I yelled:

"Pull them off me!"

"Cooooo!"

"Get them off me, Rosie!"

I woke up—startled from a bad dream—sat up, opened my eyes, looking around to see where I was. I wiped the back of my hand across my sweaty forehead, stretched my arms back, and leaned on my hands to catch my breath and fully wake up.

I was dreaming I was on the African Queen, and about Charlie Allnut and Rose Sayer when the river got shallow and Charlie and I had to get out over the side of the boat and down in the dark black water so we could pull the boat through the swampy reeds and leaches attached to our skin with suckers that wouldn't pull off and they hung on sucking our blood.

I shivered thinking about it.

I stood up, went to the kitchen to get the egg basket off the top of the ice box, and started walking to Mr. Pitts's farm to collect the eggs like I do every week. I needed some air.

When I walked back home with the basket full of eggs, I walked over to the front of the barn garage to see where the noises were coming from.

The old '38 pickup was backed into the end bay and both Duba and Dick were on their backs on the floor under it like surgeons—well, more like moonshine runners—trying to connect the brand new, what they called "glass pack," mufflers Dick had bought with some of the money he'd earned from washing dishes up at the Lincklaen House in Cazenovia on weekends when they had weddings.

"Glass pack" mufflers could get a guy a traffic ticket for making car tailpipes noisy in Syracuse. Some kids called them Hollywoods—they made a lot of rumbling sounds when a jalopy (car) revved its engine while taking off or when the driver popped the clutch to gear it down. Neither Dick nor Duba had a license, so it didn't much matter.

Standing there with my basket filled with eggs, I announced my return. Neither Dick nor Duba heard me, or at least paid any attention.

"Small crescent?" asked Dick with his hand sticking out from under the car, looking for a little help.

I picked up the wrench and put it in his hand, stepped over and leaned out of the garage to see Dad driving in and around back of the swings and park.

Most times when he came home he'd just wave and walk into the house, but this time he walked under the swings and over towards us.

I warned Dick he was coming our way—but he wasn't worried. Dick and Duba actually mastered the "cover up" and had a knack for being able to tell the truth in such a way they could wrap it around some smelly cheese-like fib and no one, without proper training in law enforcement, could ever tell. That was unless, of course, the county sheriff caught them both red-handed, dragging or speeding a back road (without licenses), and brought them home to their moms and dads along with the truth from the law's point of view.

"What's going on?' Dad asked.

Dick stuck his head out from under the car. "The muffler and tailpipe are filled with rust holes, so Duba and I are putting new ones on."

"Good," said Dad. "Holes in mufflers and tailpipes can be a noisy nuisance. Good job."

I looked at Dick like he was going straight to hell for lying, but then I thought, He did tell the truth ... he just didn't embellish it with any important details that could get him a ticket in Syracuse.

Dad took the egg basket from my hand, turned away, and started walking to the house. He paused, turned back, scratched his head, stepped into the barn garage closer to the '38 than he was before, and bent forward.

"Dick, I hate to be the bearer of bad news, but the pickup doesn't even belong to us, son. It was loaned to me to haul some rocks. You've spent your money on something we don't own. Mr. Kehoe will be coming by to pick it up anytime now."

"He already came for it, Dad. Duba and I offered him twenty dollars for it and he took it. He bought a '48 already and said he couldn't afford the tires for it and this one, too. The '48 holds more in its bed. He took the twenty dollars and was happy. He gave us an extra key, too."

Dad looked pleased. Dick and Duba could now do something they always wanted to do: stay under the hood of a car.

"Jerry, I have a quick meeting at our other bakery up north in Carthage. You flew to Watertown that time; it was close, but you've never been to Carthage—just east of it. Want to ride with me to pick up a boat motor near there? If I want the motor, I have to pick it up before this weekend."

Seeing the basket of eggs in his hand reminded me of something. I blurted: "I saw six pheasants up by Mr. Pitts's fence—in the cornfield. I left corn behind our fence so they might move into our woods and not stay out in the open where they could get shot by hunters."

"They're safer in the field than in the woods, son," said Dad. "They can run and fly to escape in the field better than in the woods. Want to go?"

"What kind of boat motor?" Dick leaned out and asked.

"Evinrude, half-horse, I think—a small one, made before the War. One of the bakery salesmen said his grandfather gave it to him along with a wooden boat. He already had a bigger motor, and offered if I wanted it for you kids, I could have it and we could maybe get it tuned up and running. He'll keep the boat. I thought we could take it by Brown's Hardware in Cortland for a look. Jerry, you want to go? We'll be back tonight. You and I can take it to the hardware store Saturday."

He looked down at my bare feet.

"Get some shoes on. We'll go fishing. Trout and salmon, I hear."

All I could think was if a salmon ever got on our line we would all have heart attacks. We wouldn't know what to do.

I said, "Sure," and ran into the house to get my sneakers. When I came out of my room, Dad was talking with Mom, who was meeting with Mrs. Cerio about a new idea to get volunteer teachers to start night courses at the school for farmers and their wives who might like them. Some of the farmers and their dads went off to the War at eighteen and didn't have a chance to go to college when they got back to the farm. Mom called me over to check my knapsack.

"I don't see a toothbrush," she said.

"We should be back before supper," said Dad.

I pulled my toothbrush out of my jean pocket and showed her. She took it from my hand and dropped it in the knapsack.

"Get a roll of film out of my purse for your camera," she said.

"Mom, I saw six pheasants up by Mr. Pitts's fence, in the cornfield. I left corn behind our fence so they might stay in our woods and not get out in the open where they could get shot by hunters. Dad thinks they were safer in the field because they can run and fly easier there."

Mom said, "Nature takes care of her own. They may go in and eat your corn, but their instincts will have them return on their own to the cornfield where they may be safer. That's the way nature is, Jerry—so have fun in Carthage with your dad. Take pictures."

Mom was good at knowing these things and putting a mind at ease—even though she was ready to let Mike murder a rabbit just for science the time I thought he was going to murder it.

Then she added: "Wild pheasant is a game bird, just as the fish you catch are game. People hunt and fish game to eat. You mustn't forget that."

Seemed animals could hardly win in the country.

Dad pulled around the swings, all the time looking in the direction of the barn garage at Dick and Duba under the '38.

"I hope they keep the noise down from that muffler in places where it would annoy people."

"You know what they're doing, Dad?" I asked, dumbfounded.

"I can read. The box he had the old muffler laying on said 'glass packs'. I know what glass packs are. They're noise makers."

Then he added, "The mufflers aren't illegal. The noise they make, in some cities, is."

Dad was like that. He would let us make our own decisions—as long as we were ready to accept the consequences.

We headed down Cardner Road.

"Where's the boat motor?"

"It's at a camp up on the Black River just beyond Watertown, closer to Canada," said Dad, turning in Delphi Falls to head north.

All I could think of was the name of the river—Black River—and the African Queen. I'd never ridden with anyone in a boat with a motor before, so this would be an adventure.

"I thought we would get a little fishing in," Dad said. "Then you can go ahead and take the boat and drive it up the river to the Carthage reservoir where I'll be to meet you, and we'll put the motor in the trunk. He wants the boat in Carthage so he can haul it filled with supplies back to his camp."

"Huh?"

Dad looked over at me and smiled but didn't say anything.

"What do you mean, *me*, Dad?"

"I want you to drive the boat into Carthage. You can do it. Just follow the river. The river will do most of the work."

"Me? Drive a boat with a motor?"

Dad grinned. "Jerry, me boy, pretend you're captain of your very own cargo tramp steamer headed off to Casablanca, or maybe even to Pago Pago."

Leaches crossed my mind.

Driving north, we stopped at a bait house I'd never seen before and got worms—our favorite bait—a new bobber, and some sinkers for Dad's fishing box. He bought a flashlight with a lantern handle on it in case I needed it. Then he picked up two tuna fish sandwiches wrapped in wax paper and asked if I wanted them in the boat, in case.

In case of what? I thought. Why would I need a flashlight with a lantern handle on it or extra food?

"What if the motor conks out," Dad said, "and you have to wait for help to come and it gets dark?" He offered all that without my asking any questions. I felt better.

"What if it does?" I asked.

"The Black River flows north," he said. "Just let the boat float on its own or set the oars and row it to Carthage and park it by the steel bridge just before you get to the reservoir. There will be a can of gas in the boat, but the motor should make it."

Eventually Dad slowed down to turn off the highway onto a narrow dirt farm road that went straight through a large fifty-acre hayfield. Land this far up in northern New York didn't have the huge hills that looked like mountains like where we lived at Delphi Falls, or even like the hills around Cortland. On the entire back side of the field we were driving through were crowded woods with tall trees, many with green velvety moss up high on their trunks, and sprawling thick bushes everywhere. Once through the hayfield, we entered the woods. The dirt road began to wind like a snake around the trees in short, sharp curves, back and forth as though we were in a real jungle.

In Delphi Falls, I was used to the woods being up high on the sides or the tops of steep hills and tall cliffs by the creek. This was a ground-level woods just like in a Tarzan jungle. This was just like Africa.

We eventually drove up to a wood-planked cabin painted a light shade of green just on this side of the wide river. Two squirrels were running around on the moss-covered wood shake roof. Dad parked in front of it and told me to check out the boat while he went into the cabin to find a broom. I looked through the car window at the river. All of a sudden my brain registered with reality and kicked in:

"Oh, my God!"

The river water was wide and as black as coal. I got out of the car and had my first close look at it and how black it was. I felt my heart sink and could almost see the crocodiles and hippos attacking my boat from the deep dark river, just like in Africa.

This can't be good, I thought.

Dad brought an old broom from the cabin, which wasn't locked, and handed it to me to sweep leaves out of the boat to get it ready. As I swept, I noticed the boat bottom was dry, which was good. I asked Dad why the river was so black.

"It has something to do with the minerals in the soil, but it isn't black everywhere—only around Watertown and Carthage, and maybe Camp Drum, I think. There are a lot of twists and turns in it between here and Carthage," he said. "You'll see it all."

I could hear birds, especially crows making noises. Every sound seemed louder and more alive here on level ground than it did in the hills back at home near my camp. Maybe the river made it all echo so much. Maybe the thundering noise of the two waterfalls at home covered those animal sounds up. I watched an eagle high in the sky, circling.

I didn't dare ask Dad how deep the river was because I was afraid he'd tell me and give me a heart attack.

He handed me a dollar bill to keep in my pocket, and we packed the boat with my supplies, the lantern flashlight, and an extra can of gas. Then we both walked out on the wooden dock with our poles and cast our fishing lines for a while, but we had no luck … not even nibbles. I wondered how fish could even live in such black, dark water, or what they looked like if they could.

"Jump in the boat and see if you can start it, Jerry me boy. Pull the choke out until she revs up, and then push it back in. The throttle is on the handle. You turn the handle one way to go faster, the other way to go slower—you'll get the hang of it. Just remember to turn it slowly. Watch out for floating logs and go around them."

I made certain to listen and hear every word.

The motor started on the third pull of the cord. Dad threw the rope line into the boat and shoved me away from the dock.

"Go out to the middle of the river and back a few times to get the hang of it. If it conks, just row it."

It was easier than I thought—and it was fun turning the boat around in the water and watching it push a wake of water in front of it.

I felt like a sea captain.

From the shore, Dad pointed towards Carthage, indicating which way to go. He stood tall and saluted me, a sharp salute, like I was now a captain, turned and walked toward his car to put fishing gear in the trunk.

He got in behind the wheel, door still open and his foot still out on the ground, watching me putter slowly on up the deep black river for a few minutes.

I think he missed being a kid and having adventures like the one I was about to go on.

He smiled and waved good-bye, lifted his leg in, backed around, and drove off, leaving me on my own.

I was alone on a strange river.

Other than my imagination scaring me at every turn, the ride down the river was an adventure.

There was not a doubt in my mind—this was one of the best adventures of my entire life. It felt exactly like being deep in the jungles of Africa every second I was there. I watched the eagle drop from the tallest branch of a towering tree and try to swoop up a squirrel too long at rest. The eagle missed, but the squirrel rolled over two times scurrying on the ground to safety from the wind gust caused by the eagle's wings.

I ate both my sandwiches with one hand, steering with the other, without a worry in the world.

Coooooooooooooo!

The river ride eventually took me into the northern city I'd never been in before. Boating into Carthage was a new experience for me. It was my tramp steamer ride. Soon I could see cars moving about high up above the river bank. I wondered if they could see me and if they knew I'd just navigated downstream several miles, alone, fearless.

On the right, up ahead, I could see the big old steel bridge and Dad's car parked on it. He was waving at me from the railing.

I thought of my airplane ride when he was there to meet me when I landed. I was distracted by the loud noise which sounded a lot like our waterfall behind our house in Delphi Falls. The sound confused me at first.

Then I saw it. I realized what it was.

I could see a calm thin flat water line stretch across the whole river. No ripples in it like the rest of the river. I grabbed an oar. Just beyond it I could see tree tops in the distant background peeking up behind it. The calm line was where the river flow stopped and it began to pool, about two hundred feet ahead. This was obviously the top of the reservoir-spill dam Dad told me about—and for sure the boat could go over it in heavy waters, straight down, me and all, if I didn't get to the bridge quickly and tie up.

This really can't be good! I thought.

Dad and his friend were now down by the mooring under the bridge waving to get my attention and yelling, "Cut the engine. Cut the engine!"

They threw me a rope to catch. Reaching for it I kicked the flashlight over the side into the dark black river. It sank like an anchor, disappearing out of view. I grabbed the rope.

"Hang on tight while we pull you in."

My heart was pumping like the steam engine on the African Queen. Dad pulled the boat in and began to tie it securely to the dock.

Dad's friend shook my hand and helped me out of the boat.

"Congratulations, young fella," he said. "You just traveled a few miles through wilderness and brought her in safe and sound."

He then began detaching the small motor from the boat while Dad finished tying the boat up under the bridge wall and out of the path of possible overnight rain. The man was going to come tomorrow with his bigger boat and pull this one, filled with supplies, back to his camp. I stood there staring down the deep black river, playing it all back in my mind.

I thanked the man for the ride and for trusting me with his boat. Dad set the boat motor in the trunk of the car and drove a few blocks to the bakery.

I'd never been inside the Carthage bakery, only the Homer bakery. It was just as noisy and as brightly lit. The bread oven seemed as big as the building. They were baking bread on the oven's turning wire conveyer racks and making doughnuts in another area. Everything smelled good. People were everywhere working and waving hi to me as we walked by, even though they didn't know me. One man stepped from behind a stainless steel table and handed me two hot doughnuts and told me there was water for tea or hot chocolate in the break room.

Dad pointed and said, "Take the doughnuts to the meeting room over there, son, so you won't bother the busy bakers. I'll come get you when we're ready to go."

The meeting room ceiling lights were already on. I had never seen a meeting room before, except maybe in a movie at the Saturday picture show. It looked important. There were big maps on two of the walls that looked like blow-ups of the New York State map in my geography book at school.

A long shiny wooden conference table in the middle of the room had a piece of glass on the top and eight leather chairs around it. I put my hot chocolate and one of the doughnuts down on a piece of newspaper and walked over to the wall to look closer up at all the maps. The closer I examined them, the better I could see all the lines and circles carefully drawn on them. They looked like drawings of Tinker Toys. Lines and circles were everywhere. There was one circle around Binghamton, which was a city down below Cortland; a circle around Cortland; a circle around Utica, east of Syracuse; a circle around Syracuse; and a circle around Watertown and Carthage. Then there were smaller circles around all the smaller towns with lines connecting them to the bigger circles. Lots of lines and circles.

I bit into my second doughnut, thinking, just as Dad came in and said we could head home.

"What are the maps for, Dad? Is this a secret room?"

"Well, secret from our competition. They show all the bread routes for both our bakeries—Homer and Carthage. The circles are the cities or towns where all the grocery stores are that a route salesman delivers loaves of bread to in their bread trucks. The lines are the bigger bread trucks that deliver cartons of bread to all the delivery trucks in the circles. Remember the truck that delivered bread to us in Brewerton so we could hang loaves on doors in the Indian head bonnets?"

"Yes," I said.

He pointed to one of the lines that went from a circle around Cortland to a circle around Brewerton and said, "That truck is this line, number thirty-one." Dad loved teaching things to people who listened. He even got a desk lamp and held it up near each of the maps so I could take pictures in its light with my Baby Brownie camera. I learned something new today. Besides learning how to drive a boat, I saw how bread got from the bakeries in Carthage and Homer to all the stores all over a lot of the state. I knew someday I was going to try it out—see how far I could go just by hopping bread trucks from town to town, connecting from truck to truck. I had a feeling someday this knowledge could help my detective work.

CHAPTER NINE

SHERIFF JOHN

Dad took a quarter out of his pocket.

"Call it, Bucky!" he shouted, not taking his eyes off the flying quarter on its descent. Dad slapped the quarter down to the counter when it landed.

"Tails!" yelled Bucky.

It was heads. Dad slid the quarter over the counter towards him and said, "Just throw in a hot chocolate for Jerry me boy with my coffee, if you will, my good friend."

Bucky tipped his paper cap kindly. "It will be my pleasure, kind sir," and placing both palms on the counter, he lifted his legs up sideways almost above the counter and kicked his heels together.

Just as he landed his feet down and was about to speak, something caught his eye through the front window of the diner. "What's going on over there at the hardware store?" he asked.

As Dad and I turned and looked, we could see a county sheriff's and a deputy's cars parked in front of Brown's Hardware store across the street. People were standing around talking at the front door.

Dad looked up at the clock on the diner wall and said, "It's too early, they aren't even open yet. Let's walk over and see why the sheriff is there. Bucky, we'll be right back."

I ran to the car and grabbed my Baby Brownie camera out of my knapsack on the backseat and both rolls of 127 film. Walking across the street, I loaded the camera. Dad told me not to take any pictures unless someone said it was okay.

"Hi Mike," said the sheriff to my dad, "Which one is this?"

"Sheriff, meet Jerry, me boy," said Dad.

I put my hand out like Dad and Mom taught us.

"Hi, young man," he said, shaking my hand. "I'm Sheriff John A. Price, and it's always nice to meet any son of Big Mike."

"Can I take pictures?" I asked him.

"Sure, go ahead. Just be careful and don't touch anything."

"What happened?" I asked.

"Burglary," he answered.

"Is that like robbery, Sheriff John?"

"Jerry, a robbery is when someone says, 'This is a stick up!' A burglary is when they sneak around like weasels in the night and break into places when no one is around."

My heart jumped into my throat. I was standing at the scene of a real crime. What would the Hardy Boys do? I asked myself. They would watch and listen, I told myself.

I listened to everyone talking.

Someone had broken the lock on the door with a crowbar, but it wasn't anywhere to be found. It looked like maybe all they took were shotgun shells, but the owner wasn't sure.

I stood by the door and got chills just looking at the same door where desperate crooks were standing in the dark middle of the night breaking into this place. It was like I was in a mystery movie. My Baby Brownie didn't have a flash so I had to be smart and be sure there was some light on everything I took a picture of. I had to remember to stay calm so I wouldn't overlook a single clue.

I snapped a picture of a messy pile of 12-gauge shotgun shell boxes.

On the floor was a folded, bent-up book of matches with the name Kelly's truck rest—Groton, New York, on it. I didn't touch it but I took a picture close enough so I could read the name in the lens.

I couldn't help noticing how neat everything was throughout the store except for where the burglars had apparently stolen things.

On a hunch, something I learned from reading Hardy Boys mysteries, I walked around the entire store, step by step, remembering I was walking in the same footsteps as the desperate criminals. If I saw something that looked like it was messed up or out of place, I snapped a picture of it with my Baby Brownie.

The hunting licenses pad was one of those things, because it was hanging two inches over the side of the countertop. I took a picture of it and of the ballpoint pen on the floor below it.

I took a picture of the shotgun rack because there was a small .410-gauge shotgun lying on the counter in front of it. I saw a Daisy BB gun outside of its box on the floor. I took a picture of both.

I could hear the sheriff talking about maybe dusting the place for fingerprints, but he suspected the burglars wore gloves, and that so far, from the looks of it, the only thing missing seemed to be shotgun shells. Someone else said the cash register didn't appear to be touched—money was still in it and in the cigar box under the counter. Maybe the burglars thought the cash register might set off an alarm and just didn't see the cigar box.

The sheriff said, "Some people are just getting their feet back on the ground after the War; could be they just needed shotgun shells to hunt for food with."

"Go over to the diner, son," Dad said. "I'll be there shortly. Order something and eat."

I said thanks to Sheriff John, went outside, looked both ways, and ran across the road to Bucky's.

I had important detective work to do.

The second I was inside the diner, I said hi to Bucky again, and asked him if he could change a dollar bill for me. I stuck my fingers in my secret pocket and pulled out one I kept for emergencies. I unfolded it and pressed it on the counter. Under his palm he slid three quarters, two dimes, and a nickel to me.

"Whatcha gonna eat, young man?" asked Bucky.

"Is the phone a nickel or a dime?" I asked him.

"Nickel," said Bucky. "Is there trouble over there? You want a hot chocolate?"

"They had burglars. Can I get an egg sandwich with mayonnaise and bacon and a hot chocolate, please?"

"Coming right up!"

I lifted the receiver, put it to my ear, reached up to the coin slot, and dropped a nickel in—*ding*—then dialed the "O" and listened for the operator.

"Opporatorrrre, how may I assist you, paleeze," said a sharp, loud voice on the phone.

"Operator, can you get me New Woodstock 62 in Delphi Falls, please?"

"One moment, paleeze."

Her accent made me feel like I was in a movie. I hoped I had enough change for a long distance call all the way to Dale's house.

In the reflection off the two tall shiny coffee urns behind the counter, I could see Dad starting to leave Brown's Hardware and saying good-bye to Sheriff John. I heard static on the phone and then I heard Mrs. Barber answer: "Hello?"

"Hold for aalooong disteeeance," said the operator. "Paleeze deposit twenteeee cents, sir."

I dropped in two dimes—*ding-ding, ding-ding*.

Dad walked into the diner and looked at me on his way to the counter. I could see he was curious why I would be making a telephone call, but he had a pleased look in his eye knowing I'd figured out how to use a coin operated telephone. Bucky poured him a fresh cup of coffee.

"Hello, Mrs. Barber, is Dale there?"

"Why Jerry, this is a long distance telephone call, I could hear the coins drop. Where on earth are you, lad? Let me hurry and get Dale for ya, dear."

"Hello?" Dale said.

"I'm in Cortland," I said.

"Are you actually calling me long distance?"

"Yes."

"Oh, geez! That's what Mom said. My first long distance coin operated pay phone telephone call in history."

"We need a Pompey Hollow Book Club meeting right away. Something's up and we need to meet today, if we can, so I can tell everybody what I know. Can you call everybody?"

"Today? What time?"

I looked around at the diner clock on the wall and calculated how long Dad normally stayed in his office reading his mail on Saturdays and then the thirty-five-minute drive home from then if we didn't stop to fish.

"Say two hours from now. I'll get my dad to drop me off at the cemetery on the way home and I'll just wait if I'm early."

"Okay," said Barber.

I hung up so the call wouldn't cost me any more money. I only had quarters left.

As always on Saturday, Dad went into the bakery office. This time he told me Mom wanted me to go try shoes on at the General Store for school. I first walked down a block to the drugstore and gave the lady my two rolls of film for developing. She told me it would be Wednesday before they could be picked up. I wrote "Wednesday" on my jean pant leg so I wouldn't forget to ask Dad to pick them up for me. I walked back towards his car. I saw Mr. Stillwell in the general store and waved hi to him through the window. I went into the store and tried on Buster Brown shoes. I told him about the burglary at Brown's Hardware. I told him they weren't sure if anything was missing and the money was still in the cash register. Mr. Stillwell said his lock was broken just a month ago, and when he saw money still in the cash register, he didn't say anything—

"Did they mess anything up?" I interrupted.

He walked over to a corner in his store where he had hunting boots.

"There were open boxes of boots everywhere, all small sizes, but none missing," he said.

I tried on some shoes, took the pair Mr. Stillwell said fitted me best, and walked over to the bakery. Dad was standing outside talking with someone. He looked over at me.

"Let's go home," he said. "I'll go pay Mr. Stillwell for the shoes. Want to stop and do some fishing?"

I waited for Dad to be in the car before I asked, "Dad, instead of fishing today, can you just take me to the Delphi Falls cemetery and drop me off? The Pompey Hollow Book Club is having an important meeting."

Dad gave me a look, kind of like, "What books could be so important to interrupt some Saturday morning fishing?" but he didn't ask any questions.

"We're on our way, Jerry me boy, we're on our way. Next stop will be the Delphi Falls cemetery."

All the way up Route 11, I looked at the big red and some white barns and farms going by along the way. I remembered how, during the War, men in white coveralls with a POW sewn on their backs worked the farms. They were the enemy *prisoners of war* our soldiers had captured in Germany who hated Hitler and could be trusted and put to work on local farms that needed helpers. Many of the American farm boys were drafted into the army and were over in Germany fighting or on ships or in submarines or in bomber planes and fighter planes around the world fighting Hitler and Mussolini and Japan. I remembered the POW prisoners never smiled or waved back when we drove by them during the War. I don't think they were allowed to. The big barns reminded me of the hardware store. I couldn't help wondering if there was a formula—some numbers—like there was in advertising or even baking, something that might fit it all together somehow, to help us catch the crooks.

"We're going to catch the crooks," I said. I couldn't hold it in any longer. "Dad, the Pompey Hollow Book Club guys are going to try to catch the crooks. We all read books, sure, but we all like trying to do good stuff like that better. Just like you always said kids should do during the War, Dad—help out, without having to be asked, if we ever saw someone being hurt."

Dad smiled over at me like he knew something was up, bigger than books, but also like he was proud of our very nature and our spirit of adventure for wanting to catch the burglars. He drove me proudly to the cemetery and pulled into the entrance to let me out.

"Just don't worry your mother," he said as I opened the door and got out of the car. "Son, remember Dick and Duba helped you with the rabbits? Think maybe they can help you again?"

I smiled but didn't answer him and started walking up into the cemetery as he drove off. The Pompey Hollow Book Club felt a little more important to me now, somehow, with Dad knowing the truth about us.

Mary, Dale, and Holbrook were already there. Mary had been in the middle of selling popsicles in Delphi Falls, so she'd just parked her cart behind Bases's place and Dale and she had walked to the cemetery together. Holbrook had gotten a ride from Mr. Crane, but he would need a ride home unless he wanted to wait until Mary was finished selling popsicles.

I started telling them all about the hardware store burglary and the pictures I took and to see what they thought, and I asked them if the Pompey Hollow Book Club should send an SOS to Dick and Duba for help.

"Brown's Hardware was busted into last night by burglars and something about it doesn't look right. I took pictures of everything I could but there are a lot of clues around so I know I missed some."

"What do you mean something doesn't look right about it?" asked Mary.

"I'm not sure. The sheriff thinks some poor guys did it, down and out from the War. From the clues, I think kids did it, but I'm not even sure about that. It doesn't look like anything was taken. Why would someone break in somewhere and not take anything? It's a mystery."

Barber stammered in awe. "HOLY COBAKO! You actually met a real live sheriff?"

Mary interjected: "Who wants to vote on our trying to solve the crime?"

We all spat.

"We'll need the older guys, Dick and Duba, for sure," said Barber. "They're smart and can drive."

"Who wants to get the older guys to help?" asked Mary.

We all spat.

"Jerry, was Dick telling you the truth on Easter Sunday when he said we could just SOS him and the older guys if we ever needed their help again?"

"Yes. He meant what he said. He liked their helping us with the rabbits. He told me so. He also liked you having the popsicle cart to make extra money. He said all that. I promise."

"Who votes on Jerry going ahead and giving Dick an SOS signal to see if they'll help us out with this?" asked Mary.

We all spat.

The vote was cast and agreed to.

Mary said, "How about from now on, we have regular meetings at school? We can meet every Wednesday at lunch? First meeting bring a book you've read and we'll trade them off to read so we don't look stupid if somebody gets suspicious or asks too many questions about our club. Barber can still call emergency or weekend meetings here in the cemetery."

Everyone agreed.

The meeting was over.

We all walked into Delphi Falls to stroll with Mary and watch her sell popsicles door to door from her cart. She treated each of us to one, half-price, before Holbrook and I walked back to my house and Dale headed to his.

When we got home, Dick was in the barn garage with Duba, both under the hood of the '38 pickup.

Holbrook and I stood at the doorway. Stepping in closer I cleared my throat and declared in a loud enough voice for them both to hear: "Dick! Dot, dot, dot; dash, dash, dash; dot, dot, dot."

Dick raised his head out from under the hood and looked around at me and then over at Holbrook. He saw we were serious.

"What's up?" he asked.

"Brown's Hardware was broken into during the night and there are a lot of crazy clues. The crooks got away," I reported.

Dick looked at Duba, looked back at me, and asked, "Is that the hardware store in the big red barn right at the bridge in Cortland?"

"Yes," I said, "it's on the left side of Route 11 going into Cortland, across from Bucky's."

"Okay, me and Duba will take a look."

I asked Dick, "Is this an official SOS you guys are taking, then? You'll help us?"

"No, not yet—not until we know something. We have to check it all out, ask around. We'll let you know if and when it's a good SOS. You'll know when it is. I'll tell you."

CHAPTER TEN

BACK TO SCHOOL

I looked at the crayoned "X" on the Tuesday square on the calendar on the kitchen wall. Today was Saturday, Labor Day weekend. School started on Tuesday.

I was halfway through a peanut butter and jelly sandwich when the phone rang. I set my sandwich down, ran and grabbed it.

"Hello?"

"Jerry?" asked Dick.

"Yeah?"

Dick blurted into the telephone, "We're taking your SOS official. Have your club at Mike Shea's store on Tuesday—lunch hour!"

Then he hung up.

I didn't even ask him what he was thinking about or what he and Duba came up with. All I knew was it might be another adventure for us. I had to get word to the Pompey Hollow Book Club to be in front of Shea's store just down the street from the school in Fabius at lunch hour on Tuesday. That was good enough for me.

As soon as I hung up, I picked up again and got the operator. "Myrtie, this is Jerry. I need Dale Barber."

"An early Saturday morning call so soon after you talked with Dick. Sounds important," said Myrtie with a giggle.

"It is for sure," I said.

"One minute, honey, I'll get the Barbers'. Let me know if you ever need my help again."

"I will, thanks, Myrtie."

"Hello?"

"Mrs. Barber, this is Jerry, is Dale there?"

Barber got on the phone.

"Can you call Mary?" I asked. "Dick and Duba took our SOS for sure—we have to be at Shea's store at noon on Tuesday. All I know is Dick and Duba took our SOS, I don't know anything else; I'll call Kellish and have him tell Holbrook. Can you call Mary?"

Barber rallied like a trooper: "ROGER WILKO! OVER AND OUT!" and then he hung up.

It gave me chills knowing everybody in the Pompey Hollow Book Club was about to learn about a secret meeting set for the first day back at school in front of Shea's store.

Tuesday morning was antsy because we weren't sure what Dick and Duba had in mind or why we were meeting—but we knew our first SOS call to the older guys was like no other call any of us had ever made.

Besides the Pompey Hollow Book Club, both Dick and Duba and some older kids they knew showed up in front of Shea's store. The agriculture and mechanic teacher, Mr. Ossant, who happened to be walking by, paused on the sidewalk and leaned on the maple tree, biting into an apple, to see what the commotion was all about. Student passersby gathered, kids on lunch break, pausing to see what was going on. Crowd gatherings in 1949 could be entertainment and just social, or they could be serious gatherings. It was natural for kids to flock to a crowd just to see. Most kids growing up through the War only knew about the War through movie newsreels, as brave young soldiers were being sent all over the world to fight enemies and maybe die so we kids could be safe and free. None of us could do anything about that War except pray. But there wasn't a man, jack, kid among us who didn't have romance and bravery running through his veins. We were ready to volunteer; if we heard someone may need help, we drew to it like bees to honey. With party lines in those days tying up telephone lines, kids relied on gossip; no telling how many kids would show up. About a dozen or so today, but we could count on many more next time when word got out.

Dick and Duba were waiting on the top step in front of Shea's store. They had already asked Mike Shea, the owner, if he would join us outside because maybe he could help us. Dick's thinking was that Mike was a store owner and maybe he could give us some ideas.

Looking out at the dozen or so gathering around, Mike Shea said, "Well, since nobody can get into the store, I might just as well be out here getting some sun."

"Listen up," yelled Duba.

We quieted down.

"There was a burglary in Cortland—at Brown's Hardware," Dick began. "It's that hardware store in the red barn on the left just before the bridge, and it looks fishy."

"Real fishy," said Duba, and with only giving that little tidbit of information, and without a pause or a hesitation, he asked, "Who's in?"

No one had a clue what being "in" meant, but just the same, every Minuteman in the bunch raised his hand, accepting the challenge. Mr. Ossant, the agriculture teacher, raised his hand only because he always thought he was one of the kids. His shop was out behind the school and he saw kids more than he ever saw any teachers.

The general feeling in the air was that any adventure to kick off the school year was welcomed.

Dick started: "When Duba and I went to investigate the burglary, no one who worked in the hardware store thought anything was stolen. Now why would someone go and bust a door open and ransack a store in the middle of the night and not take anything?"

"Real fishy," said Duba. "We need to investigate more and look at all the evidence."

I raised my hand and said, "I took two rolls of film with clues to the drugstore in Homer to be developed. They're ready tomorrow. I have another roll at the Tully drugstore—stuff I shot in Carthage." I interrupted my thought with: "Oh! I saw Mr. Stillwell at the general store in Homer. He told me his place was broken into about a month ago, and he didn't see anything the crooks took either."

"Fishy," said Duba.

This was getting good. I got goose bumps.

"We need an investigator," said Dick. He looked out among the kids and caught the eye of Marty Bays, a red-headed boy in a grade ahead of me and the other club members.

"Marty, don't you have a driving permit for hauling milk to Apulia Station?"

"You betcha I do … and I'm an official reporter for the school newspaper, too. I'm trained to investigate, get the answers, and keep my eye on the prize."

"Can you get away to Cortland?" asked Dick.

This mission required more than just talent, it required means—Marty could drive and he had his dad's truck every morning.

"Sure enough can," said Marty. "My early morning milk run to Apulia Station just may run a little longer than usual if I mosey on down to Cortland."

Everyone laughed, knowing Marty didn't have a license but that farm kids could get special driving permits. His permit let him drive the milk cans to Apulia Station—which was just before Tully and on the way to Cortland a county over, so maybe there wouldn't be any state prisons involved in case he lost his way and got caught, was our thinking. He'd probably only be taken home after a deputy sheriff bought him an ice cream sundae at the Tully drugstore and soda fountain and told him not to do it again.

"Good," said Dick, "you check out the hardware store people, the general store people, and find out everything you can. Tell 'em you're writing a story."

Duba spoke up: "Sounds like there might be more than one burglary—what if there's more?"

Dick wanted to stay concentrated on the task at hand. "When can you go, Marty?" he asked.

"What say I do it on Thursday? That-away I can pick up the pictures Jerry took from the drugstore while I'm there, if that's okay—but I'll need some money to pay for them."

Knowing Thursday was a school day and Marty would be gone the better part of the morning, a couple of kids volunteered to go with him. Duba and Dick decided to keep truancy at a minimum and told Marty to go alone and take a tablet for a lot of notes.

"Yo!" said Marty.

Then Dick reminded the ag teacher, Mr. Ossant, and the store owner, Mike Shea, that they didn't hear any of that. They said, "Hear what?"

"Who can meet here Friday to hear Marty's report?" Dick asked. Everyone raised their arms.

"Good luck, Marty," said Duba, "and don't get caught."

With that we broke up the first meeting. Most of us went into the store and got our candy or gum or whatever caught our eye from behind the glass that we had enough pennies or dimes for. Dale borrowed fifteen cents from someone and I borrowed a nickel from Dale, forgetting I still had a dollar eighty left in my secret pocket from the Black River ride and my long distance telephone call.

Mr. Ossant walked back to the school, alone, so as not to be seen with our group.

A passel—more than a dozen this time—showed up at Shea's for the second meeting, plus Mr. Shea and Mr. Ossant again.

Duba stepped up on the store steps next to Dick and turned to the kids. "Listen up."

Dick lifted his t-shirt and pulled out a spiral notebook he had tucked under his belt and a pencil from his back jean pocket. Not to spoil his reputation for never opening a notebook, he handed it down to Mary Crane, Holbrook, Barber, and me, hoping one of us would take notes if we needed to. Then he said, "Marty—whatcha got?"

We didn't recognize Marty standing in amongst us, dressed the way he was. His red hair was all wet and slicked back, parted, and combed like he was going to church. He even had his Sunday go-to-meeting coat and bright red tie on, trying to look like he was a hotshot reporter in a city press conference and ready just in case there might be newspaper photographers lurking about Fabius on a school day. He had a clipboard in his hand this time, and a pencil over his ear. Marty stepped confidently to the top step of Shea's store, turned to us, straightened his tie, and barked liked he was running for president and there were a crowd of thousands there.

"I want to thank everybody for covering my back Thursday and special thanks to whoever managed to get me the 86 on the Social Studies pop quiz I wasn't there to take."

Not wanting our meeting to wake up the whole county, Dick blurted, "Keep your voice down, Marty. We can hear you plain. Just talk. Let's hear what you got to say."

Marty loosened his tie and lifted his clipboard to read his report. Someone had written on the backside of it in crayon, "The Fabius Flame—only news that's fit to be tied!"

He began: "Number one: sometime in the night between Friday evening and Saturday morning a week ago, the Brown Hardware store in Cortland was broken into.

"Number two: although it was first believed that the perpetrators purloined several boxes of 12-gauge shotgun shells, this reporter has discovered that no shotgun shells were, in fact, taken.

"Number three: this reporter interviewed the proprietor of the General Store establishment in Homer, one Mr. Stillwell, and discovered a similar break-in less than a month ago. The first thought, in this break-in also, was that nothing was taken— however the proprietor soon discovered a cash shortage of $207 from his cash register."

Dick interrupted, "What about the hardware store?"

Mary murmured approval of Dick's interruption; keeping Marty focused was a good thing, as she didn't quite know where he was taking us with his report.

"Number four: with the new information, this reporter returned back to the hardware store crime scene to further investigate … further. I discovered, upon my return, there was $565 missing from their cash drawer, only found out at closing on Monday, them staying closed on Saturday because of the burglary and on Sunday for church like everyone else."

Dick interrupted, "They told us no money was taken."

"Correctomundo," Marty snickered back. "So did the General Store people at first—only to discover they were short $207 from their till."

Dick stood back and let him continue.

"Number five: before I deducted any conclusions, I went to the drugstore in Homer and picked up the photographs taken at the scene of the crime by one Jerry Antil, to see if they could provide any further clues."

Mary leaned into Dale and whispered, "I wonder if we grab Marty and took his tie and coat off and messed up his hair, would he talk faster and get to the point."

Duba barked, "Listen up."

Our very own Sherlock Holmes, boy reporter, pressed on: "It is clear to me that photos one, four, six, and seven clearly indicate a kid was involved in the crime."

"How?" asked Dick.

Mary had an intuition and interrupted before Marty could answer. "Old crooks aren't interested in BB guns and .410 shotguns and size-nine hunting boots."

Marty added, "The pictures also prove the kids involved were not burglars or robbers, or why else didn't they take these things and not just look at them like a window shopper would and put them back down? Photos two, five, eight, and eleven clearly indicate an adult was involved and most likely perpetrated the hardware store crime with a kid or kids. The picture of matches leads me to believe the adult is a smoker; the picture of the hunting licenses tells us all of them could be over eighteen; the ransacked size-twelve hunting boots and the messed up boxes of 12-gauge shells tells us it was an adult; the missing money tells me they have done this before and will probably do it again. If it was a kid alone, he would have looked at .410 shells after looking at the .410 shotgun, and no one did, and most kids have no use for money other than helping out their folks. It was probably an adult and kid team."

Half clapped at Marty's deductions. The other half clapped, too, thinking he was starting to look better in his coat and tie.

He continued, "Country kids don't have a lot of places to spend money, farms being so self-sufficient. The thought of money to a country kid or the need for it rarely comes up, except for comic books or bubble gum."

Barber spoke up, "He's right. Country kids just don't steal. It's not in our nature."

Dick jumped up on the steps with Duba and Marty, grabbed the pictures from Marty's hand, and started thinking of questions, as if he was inspired. He thumbed through each of the pictures and started looking closely at the picture of the opened cash drawer in the hardware store.

"Watch this," I told Holbrook and Barber. "Dick's brain is clicking. I've seen that look before."

Dick asked, "Who's good at math?"

He was a genius at it, but this was no time to show off.

Two kids raised their hands.

"What are 243 minus thirty-six and 651 minus eighty-six?"

Someone shouted out almost immediately, "Two hundred seven and five hundred sixty-five."

Dick made a mental note of who had shouted out in case he needed to skip a math test and could bribe this person to take his for him; then he nudged Duba like he was ready to come up with a plan.

"Watch this," I said to Dale and Mary. "Dick and Duba know exactly what to do now."

Dick took a deep breath, looked around, and waited for Duba's "Listen up."

He started to talk, then had a thought, paused, and wrote something on a piece of paper resting on his bent-up knee. He handed the paper to Mike Shea while asking him if he wouldn't mind going into the store and making a telephone call for him. Mike read the note, nodded approval, and went into the store.

Dick began, "Marty did good with his investigating! Jerry did good with his pictures!"

Holbrook punched my arm.

"But we aren't done yet. We're going to need volunteers, so listen up."

"Listen up," echoed Duba.

"First, if you leave a twenty-dollar bill, a ten-dollar bill, a five-dollar bill, and a one-dollar bill in a cash drawer, in their slots, it looks like there is money in all the slots of the drawer if you were to look fast and you would think no money was taken until after the cash count at closing the next day when you came up short. That is how the General Store was missing $207, which took them a whole day to miss. There was a bill in every slot."

Cheers went up, and Dick continued: "And if you leave a fifty and a twenty and a ten and a five and a one—that's how Brown's Hardware didn't know they were missing $565 for two whole days. It is very clear these burglaries were only for one thing— the cash drawer—and because of the mess they made, and with the single bill in each slot of the cash drawer covering it up, cash was the last thing the owners thought was missing until long after all the clues got cold and the crooks left town."

Duba was whacking Marty on the back so hard congratulating him, he fell off the top step.

Mike Shea came outside and whispered something in Dick's ear. Dick looked down in the direction of Holbrook, Crane, Barber, me, and Bases. Above the noise he asked, "What's your club called, again?"

"The Pompey Hollow Book Club," said Dale.

Dick winced at our name, but faced the older kids. "We've solved how the crooks took the money, we think. Who here wants to be volunteers in the Pompey Hollow Book Club and actually catch the crooks?"

"Do we have to read anything?" someone guffawed.

"Only the Sunday comics," laughed Duba.

Every hand went up and then came down clapping approval. Everyone gathered was amazed at what we'd learned so fast and how the older guys had deduced the clues. Seeing hands in the air wanting to be in the club, Barber leaned into Mary and whispered, "Mrs. President, there's money here if the Pompey Hollow Book Club could draw a bigger crowd and charge dues."

Dick announced, "Mr. Shea just telephoned the hardware store about picture number five—the picture with the hunting license pad leaning off the counter. Just as I suspected, the pad of hunting licenses and carbon sheets behind them were each individually numbered, and the license and carbon sheet with number 134 on it is missing from the book. We find hunting license number 134, and we find our crook."

The kids roared—it sounded like someone hit a home run.

Dick shouted, "The problem now is that Mr. Brown, at the hardware store, knows too and is calling the sheriff to tell him about the hunting license clue we discovered—so we'll have to work fast if we want to get to the crooks before the sheriff does. Still in?" he shouted out.

Heads nodded yes.

Dick took his glasses off and rubbed them on his shirt and put them back on and asked what time it was.

Duba knew Dick's brain was loaded for bear and ready and told Dick so the crowd could hear, "We've got twelve minutes before the bell rings. Listen up, everyone."

Dick looked around, impressed at some girls who had showed up, wondering which of them he maybe wanted to kiss sometime or take to the amusement park in Manlius with him and Duba on a Sunday. We could see his mind thinking as he was stalling until something came to him. Then he campaigned with arm up in the air:

"Do we just find 'em or catch 'em?"

"Catch 'em," Mary shouted.

Mr. Ossant stepped up on the first step weakly waving an arm in the air and said, "Boys and girls, I'm with you all the way—you know that for sure, boy and howdy—but do ya think maybe we should think this through? Burglary is a purty serious crime and it could be desperate criminals we are dealing with. What say we give it some thought before we make a decision and come back another day?"

"Fair enough," said Dick. He knew the deck was stacked in his favor. He asked for a vote. "Who wants to think about it?"

Both Mr. Ossant and Mr. Shea raised their hands but lowered them when they saw no other arms were raised.

Dick asked, "Who here can find the farm-to-dairy hauler routing for all of Cortland County?"

Barber spoke up: "You mean home delivery or farm-to-dairy delivery?"

"Farm-to-dairy."

"I can, if Randy can help me."

Randy's dad drove a milk-can hauler truck every morning. He sat behind me in school. He'd helped us with the rabbits at Easter.

Then Dick said, "Okay, you guys meet up, get that information, and we'll see you here Monday. Same time, same radio station. Get names, addresses, telephone numbers, and everything, guys. Go."

Barber and Randy stepped up the steps into the store.

Dick went on, "Who here wants to try to see how many burglaries there have been in Cortland County?"

I raised my hand. "Holbrook, Crane, Barber, and I can do that. You know—the guys in our club. We can do it."

Holbrook slugged my arm. "What are you saying!? There's no way we can find all that out by Monday. What are you thinking?"

"Relax," I told him, "I got an idea. You, Mary, and Barber, maybe even Randy, Bases, and the Mayor get to the cemetery for a meeting at midnight tonight. Can you see to that? Barber can help get them there."

My thinking was numbers. My theory was the more kids we had involved in what I wanted to do tonight, the less the punishment handed down if we all got caught.

Dick interrupted us, not wanting anyone to over-promise. "Just calling the sheriff won't get you good information," he warned. "County clerks and sheriffs don't make a lot of things public until they're solved. Are you sure you can handle this?"

I blurted, "We got it handled. We'll find out how many. Who can drive us somewhere at three in the morning, if we need a ride?"

Although near everyone was willing, Mr. Ossant and Mike Shea were the only ones of the crowd who had real driving licenses, not just permits. They declined.

"Marty?" I said.

"Yo!" he answered.

I nudged Holbrook to go see if Marty could be at the cemetery at midnight to meet with us, and if he could bring his truck. I reminded him to ask Barber to try to set up tonight's meeting.

Dick looked down at me, remembered the bunny episode, and shrugged his shoulders like we just may be able to do it. "Duba and I'll check out the Kelly truck rest diner on the matchbook this weekend, without being seen," he said. "No talking about any of this and we'll meet here Monday for your reports and a plan—noon."

Dick told Mr. Shea and Mr. Ossant that it was important for them to make it on Monday, too. He said he didn't know why, but he just thought there may be a use for them. Mr. Ossant smiled, turned, and walked back towards the school.

With the few minutes before the school bell, everyone jammed into the store and grabbed whatever they could for a snack and threw money on the counter and hurried back to school before it rang.

Rule one in an SOS with the older guys, we were learning, was that everyone stayed out of trouble at least until the mission was finished. Everyone felt this was something very big, but Mr. Ossant's warning made us realize the seriousness of what we might be getting ourselves in for.

It made it even bigger and better.

Just before midnight, I headed off in the dark through Farmer Parker's driveway, out behind the barn, up the hill, and into the back pasture on my way to the meeting at the cemetery. I could see my way using the stars and three-quarter moon. Being in a tree-filled cemetery in the dark of night could be enough to unsettle a boy. While climbing down off the hill from the hayfield into it, I could see the weak headlights of Marty driving his dad's pickup and bouncing up the cemetery drive. Holbrook, Barber, Crane, Randy, and the Mayor were all riding with him. One was in the cab with Marty and four were in the back end.

I had a lot on my mind, and was busting to tell what I'd learned in Carthage with my dad, which was only just starting to make sense to me. As soon as they all jumped out and gathered around in the dark, I said, "I saw secret maps at my dad's bakery in Carthage that may help us, but I'm not sure how, yet. I can show you pictures of the maps in the daylight. My dad held a desk lamp up near them so I could take pictures with my camera without a flash. What I remember was the circle and lines drawn on the map look to me like all the bakery trucks are connected somehow—all the way from Carthage down to Binghamton. My dad showed me. He told me if I studied the routing chart map, I could figure out how to hop a bread truck from town to town. If I had a couple of days to meet all the schedules, I could go to any other circle on the map, riding on bread trucks just by knowing their numbers and what their store routes were. Dad explained it all."

"It sounds like treasure maps with secret codes," said Holbrook.

"Yes. They're in a secret room, too, I think. The maps show that the bakery in Homer and the one in Carthage are connected like Tinker Toys—lines and circles—to every town in the counties of Cortland, Onondaga, Thompson, Madison, and some others, which means that a bakery truck driver goes to every grocery store in every one of them every day."

Dale spoke up: "Oh geez! Holy cow! In one day the truck drivers could maybe ask all the grocery stores who was robbed and then tell us who was broken into and who lost money."

"Just what I was thinking," I said.

"What about stores that don't sell bread?" asked Holbrook.

Mary interrupted. "Store people in small towns all belong to a thing they call a fraternity, like the Rotary or something like that, and they all talk to each other. The grocers will know everything that's going on."

Marty grinned. "I got a feeling I know where this is going," he said. "Good thing I filled 'er up and told my ol' man I was staying over at Antil's all night, because it sure sounds about like we're all heading down to Homer to talk to some bakery truck drivers."

"I told my mom I was staying at your place, Marty," said the Mayor.

"So did I," said Holbrook.

"So did I," said Bases.

"I didn't," said Mary. "No one knows I'm gone. I'll climb the tree to get in my room when I get home."

Everyone laughed at the tangled web we were weaving just so we could catch some criminals before some adult caught them first or put a stop to our trying.

"Good," I said. "You can all stay at my place and go home in the morning. We'll drop Mary off on our way back."

"When do we head to the bakery?" asked Marty.

"We can't go until two-thirty in the morning; no one is there until then—no drivers, anyway," I said.

We all decided to just sit around and tell jokes to kill the time.

Marty was the only one with a wrist watch with hands that glowed in the dark. The Mayor fell asleep first.

Turns out we all fell asleep.

"Time to head out," said Mary, poking at each of us. "Get up and let's head to Homer. We'll be there just about three, as we planned."

"Anyone got any money?" Holbrook asked, rubbing his eyes. "I'm hungry."

Everyone dug in their pockets, pulled out what they had, and opened both their palms in the middle of the group so a match could shine on the loot. We had two jack knives, two rubber bands, an empty rabbit's foot key chain, a burned-out radio tube, the beginnings of a marble-sized ball of tin foil from gum wrappers, plus seventy-nine cents and two Indian Head pennies that were for saving and couldn't be spent.

Remembering I had some of my dollar and the dollar left in my secret pocket that Dad gave me on the Black River, I took it out and handed it to Holbrook. Holbrook took it into account with his inventory and said, "Good, we can eat."

"We'll go to Bucky's Diner after the bakery," I said.

Marty was a good driver and was used to driving in the dark, delivering milk cans to the dairy pickup at Apulia Station every morning before school. It wasn't long before we were turning left in Tully and heading south to Homer and the bakery.

Too far to turn back now, I thought.

When we walked in the door where all the trucks were backed in and being loaded with cartons of warm bread, the gang followed me up the stairs into the driver's room, where a lot of men were having coffee. I saw a man, Lindsey Pryor, I knew from a time we picnicked at his house when his wife had a baby. I walked up to him.

"Aren't you Mike's boy?" Mr. Pryor asked. I told him I was and these were my friends. I asked him how his new baby was, the one we all came up to Cincinnatus to see one morning when his wife cooked us breakfast. He smiled and finally remembered. "Baby's fine. What are you boys all doing up at this hour? Are you in any kind of trouble?"

I reached into my back pocket and showed him pictures of the maps I'd taken in Carthage and asked him if the drivers in the circles on the map around Cortland could help us. We told him what we were trying to do, and that if we wanted to catch the crooks, we needed to see how many places in those circles had been broken into and what was missing. A lot of the bread truck drivers gathered around to listen.

"Jerry, here is exactly what we are going to do for you and your friends. Our boys will find out all they can. Won't we, fellas?"

All the men agreed.

"I'll put the results in an envelope, seal it, and ask your dad to give it to you when he comes home at the end of the day, that is, if I see him today. It'll be Monday if I don't see him today. Will that be soon enough?"

We were amazed that we might be able to pull it off and deliver good answers to Dick and Duba by Monday, just as we promised.

"Now you all run along home, before you get me in trouble," Mr. Pryor laughed. "Your daddy would skin me. Go on, now, git."

We were making so much progress; we decided to raid the ice box at home and save our money for a Saturday morning picture show sometime. On the way we forgot to drop Mary home. When we got back to my house, we walked in quietly, and everyone sat around the table in the dark, resting and waiting for my signal before we each took turns raiding the icebox. We could hear Dad in the bathroom, shaving and getting ready for work. When he came out of the bathroom and walked through the dark towards the kitchen for some juice, I surprised him with a quiet, "Hey, Dad."

And knowing how much my dad liked adventures, I proceeded to tell him what we had all been up to this morning and about meeting with Lindsey Pryor at the bakery.

Dad turned and walked back, in the dark, pulled his and Mom's bedroom door closed so we wouldn't wake her, flipped the dining room light switch on, and sat down at the head of the table.

"Well, I'll be," he said, beaming a smile at all of us. "Is this the famous Pompey Hollow Book Club? Read any interesting books lately, gang?" Dad chuckled, implying he knew about our club and supported us.

"Uh huh," I said. "Me and Holbrook read *African Queen*."

"You read the maps, too, Jerry, me boy. You read the maps. Did the Pompey Hollow Book Club figure this all out just by looking at those maps in Carthage?"

"We're smart, Dad. Kids growing up in a War have to be smart, or the enemies can win, remember? We made Mary president. She's smart and we all voted for her. If any of us see something where we think we can do good, like the hardware store burglary, our club just does what we think is right."

Mary spoke up: "Kids from the War can sometimes see things grownups don't have time to see, Mr. Antil. We only want to help do good like we were taught. Doing something is better than doing nothing. The War taught us that. Dale is in charge of calling meetings. Jerry is in charge of getting the older guys to help us, if we need them. Holbrook is in charge of getting other kids to help us, like Marty here. Marty drove us tonight."

Dad looked around the table, recognizing Mary and each of the boys with me. He smiled with pride and said, "You're all smart—there's no getting around that one, young lady. Well, I do admire your spirit, kids, so I'm going to do you one better. Everybody get in my car, sleep the best you can between here and our drive back to Homer, and we'll have a nice breakfast at Bucky's. Then I'll set you up with a table in the break room and as the salesmen come in from their routes, you can hear what they have for you."

"The drivers?" I asked.

"We call them salesmen, son," said Dad. "They are bread sales-men. And Mary, I'm going to call your mom and dad at sunup, and tell them you're okay and not to worry."

Each of the guys witnessed the very same dad I bragged about all the time, actually in action—and just as I always described him, he came through, again. Dad went back into the bathroom to tie his tie. We got up from the table and walked toward the door.

"Shotgun," said Holbrook. We went outside, climbed in the car and waited for Dad to come drive us to Homer. We were all asleep before the car turned onto Cardner Road heading back again to Homer. We collected all of the information we needed by breakfast time. Then we headed back. Driving back we pulled up to Holbrook's and let Bob out. Then we stopped at the Crane's and let Mary out. Mr. Crane was sitting on the porch step read-ing the newspaper. He had already delivered her papers because of Dad's call to him. He waved at Dad. We dropped Randy off at his house, Bases in Delphi, and Barber at his house. When we got home, Marty woke up and woke the Mayor beside him. He said he would drop him on his way home. Marty honked and waved as he drove off. He knew the Mayor lived on a back road and he had a good chance of not being seen driving.

CHAPTER ELEVEN

THE PLAN

Dick and Duba had played poker with friends at Conway's house on Saturday night, so they pretty much knew what was found out about the milk runs and routes. They came to the Monday meeting already with some plans. Dick and Duba had skipped out of a study hall so they could get to Shea's before the meeting and go over details.

A car drove up, pulled around the corner, and parked on the other side of the street, not too close to Shea's. Mr. Ossant got out of it and walked around to the front of the store and took his place next to the maple tree, letting it shield him from cars passing by. Some of the kids walking to Shea's during lunch break gathered around the Pompey Hollow Book Club along with some of the older guys.

Duba and Dick got up on the top step, and Duba started the meeting: "Listen up."

Dick said, "Let's hear reports."

Barber spoke up first. "There are twenty-three milk pickup routes within a thirty-mile circle of Cortland. If we need to contact every single farmer in most of the county, a couple of us can go to three dairies and tape a message on every milk can the trucks pick up and return to the farmers so the farmers won't miss seeing it."

"Very nice," said Duba.

"But wait, there's more," said Holbrook. "We know the crook stole the hunting license number 134. Why don't we send every farmer that number this way so when anyone wants to hunt pheasant or deer on their posted land, they can look at the hunter's license? If it's 134, they could call Shea's store to tell them the name and address the crook wrote on the license. This could be one way we catch them."

Everyone cheered at the brilliance of the "milk can route" discovery. Dick and Duba looked totally impressed.

"Somebody write the note, let's get it attached to the milk cans," Dick said. "Okay with you, Mike?"

"Fine by me," said Mike Shea.

"Next report," barked Duba.

Mary, Holbrook, Barber, and Randy each rolled out a portion of a big map Dad got us from the bakery. Mary and Holbrook got on the top step and Barber and Randy on the lower step. They held all the pieces of map together to make one large display. There was a big black circle drawn around the center of the map. Dick and Duba stepped out into the crowd and turned around to watch. I took a look at my notes, lifted a ruler I brought as a pointer, and made our report, pointing at the map.

"In the past ten months there have been break-in burglaries here in Freeville, here in Dryden, over here in Munsons' Corners, up here in Summerhill, here in Moravia, and over here in McGraw, and the two we know about, here in Homer and here in Cortland. All in all, there was more than $1,297 stolen and every store was messed up, just like the hardware store was. All little-kid stuff. But here's what we want you to pay attention to."

I pointed at the big circle on the map.

"If we draw a circle connecting all the towns where someplace was broken into, dead in the center of the circle ..."

I pointed the ruler to Groton.

Duba and Dick shouted it together: "GROTON! Right where the truck rest diner is from the matchbook you took a picture of!"

They both jumped on the top step again, clapping their hands, applauding our efforts. We all stepped down, smiling.

Mike Shea and Mr. Ossant were amazed.

Dick asked, "Any objections, Mike, if we arrange the burglary of your old empty store across the street for this coming Saturday night?"

Mike Shea gave a big belly laugh at just the idea of it. "You get me some volunteers," he said, "and we can have that old place spiffed up sparkling and stocked with useless inventory from the storage in the back and looking prosperous by Thursday—cash register and all."

"Any volunteers?" yelled Duba.

All the Pompey Hollow Book Club kids raised our hands.

"Meet me every day, lunch hour, and we'll get it done. I'll see you all get enough to eat," said Mike.

The rest of the hands in the group went up with the mention of food. The promise of food also guaranteed the attendance would likely double by tomorrow at noon.

Dick started to organize his thoughts and attack plan. "Jimmy Conway, what do you call that new monster tractor I see at your farm that won't fit in your barn, and how big is it?"

"It's a Minneapolis Moline, four times the size of a regular tractor. Dad got it to drag four plows at once."

"Ooooooooooooooooooh!" murmured through the gathering, still accustomed to seeing workhorses doing most of the hauling and plow-pulling.

"Three times taller than a car," said Dick. "Does it have a fork lift in front?"

"Sure does. And it can lift twice its weight."

"Good. Duba, Dwyer, and I will come by your place later to come up with a plan," Dick told Jimmy.

Then he turned to Mr. Ossant and Mr. Shea.

"Saturday morning, just about lunchtime, the Pompey Hollow Book Club, plus Duba, Conway, Dwyer, and me, will need a ride in our old '38 pickup to the truck rest in Groton. We need to lure out the crooks with bait. Can either of you drive us and wait in the truck once we get there?"

We needed a driver with a real driver's license. We didn't want to get caught breaking the law while trying to catch some criminals. It may be a conflict of interest.

"As much as we want to, kids, there is no way we can be directly involved with something like this," said Mr. Ossant. "You know we would if we could."

"My dad will drive us," said Mary. "Everybody who's going, meet up at the Delphi Falls cemetery at ten, Saturday morning."

Dick understood the hesitance of Mr. Ossant and Mike Shea to contribute to our potential delinquency, so he made a plea in another direction. "Can we at least get you both to get a poker game going in the fire hall on Saturday night after dark and get Sheriff John A. Price and maybe a deputy or two to play with you?"

"We can do that, can't we?" asked Mike Shea, looking at Mr. Ossant.

"Boy and howdy! We sure can!" said Mr. Ossant.

"I'll make a few calls," said Mike.

"Mike Shea, can you put $350 in the register across the street in the dummy store?" asked Dick.

"Sure can. Make dang sure you catch them, though." He grinned.

"In very light pencil, can you write 'Stolen from Shea's store' on every bill somewhere?" asked Dick.

"You bet I can!"

Duba broke up the meeting, and Dick asked the Pompey Hollow Book Club to wait a second.

"I want you all looking like ragamuffins Saturday. Poor as church mice," he said.

"That won't be hard," said Holbrook.

We all told him we would. We each had an idea of what they were about to be up to. They'd never let us down in the past. We headed back to school before the bell rang.

CHAPTER TWELVE

IN THE SOUP

Saturday morning, cars crept into the Delphi Falls cemetery, one behind the other. It looked like a funeral. Finally, Mr.
Crane drove in with Mary and Holbrook. Dick and Duba asked
the Pompey Hollow Book Club members to line up on the dirt
road into the cemetery. They walked around inspecting us. They
were generally impressed with our disheveled appearance. Our
clothes were torn and wrinkled. Dick spaced us along the dirt
drive about five feet apart.

"Everyone get down and roll in the road dirt."

We complied and were getting the understanding of the
purpose. We willingly rubbed our faces with road dust. Then we
stood up.

"Perfect!" said Dick. "Let's go."

"Hold on!" said Mary. "Now you, Duba, Conway, and Dwyer
do it. Get down, roll around. You have to look the same as us."

Our club wasn't all that old and established, but we could tell
this was one of the Pompey Hollow Book Club president's fin-
est hours. The Delphi Falls cemetery was our turf. Mary actually
made the older guys dance to our tune. She was a natural-born
General Eisenhower. We were proud.

They did it. They even offered a compliment.

"Good thinking!" said Conway.

The rest was easy.

Dick and Duba jumped in the front cab with Mr. Crane. The rest of us climbed in the back of the '38 pickup proudly.

As we headed to Groton, most of us in the back were getting dustier. We passed by the pretend store in Fabius. It appeared to be open and fully staffed. Kids were painting a sign and milling about. Some were taping up "sales special" signs in the windows. A few of them waved as we drove by. When we were near the end of town, by the fire hall, we could see several people carrying in a poker table and placing it in the center of the station for the big game tonight. The shiny red fire engine was parked on the side of the building. We turned left in Tully and drove down through Homer and Cortland and over to Groton. We slowed to a crawl and pulled into the Kelly's Rest Stop parking area—the same one from the matchbook. From all appearances outside, it was a greasy spoon. The front window was filthy. Inside, there was a ceiling fan in the middle of the room, over a counter, with a long, curling stream of flypaper hanging down from the center of the fan. From a distance it appeared to be dotted with dead flies caught in its glue.

"Okay, team, this is it," said Duba. "Pretend it's the best restaurant in town. Listen good and follow our lead."

We all piled out of the '38 and walked in. Mr. Crane stayed outside, lifting the hood and sticking his head under it like we were too poor to get it fixed. Inside there was a kid about my brother Mike's age with a push broom trying to look busy, but he wasn't very good at it. We all lined up and sat down on the stools at the counter—older guys on the left and the Pompey Hollow Book Club four on the right.

"Mind your manners, kiddos," goaded Dick as we each settled on a counter stool.

A man with a two-day bristly beard, dirty apron, and a cigarette hanging from his mouth walked up blinking his right eye like a wiper blade trying to keep the rising smoke from hitting his eyeball. There was a pack of Lucky Strike cigarettes rolled up on the outside of his undershirt sleeve. He grabbed the percolator pot of coffee on his way, picked up four coffee cups through their handles with his thumb and first finger, and walked them to the counter, settling them all down at once. He slid one to each of the older guys while he looked us over pretty good.

"How can I help ya?"

"We want four coffees and four cups of hot water," said Dick. "I'll be figuring on what next after we get that." With his thick glasses, he looked the oldest.

The cook lined up the cups and started to pour the coffees but gave double takes to all our crew, one at a time sizing us up, and it seemed a bit reluctant when he turned to get a pad to write down our order.

Mary looked at the newspaper lying on the counter in front of her and was inspired: "Did you see all that money, Daddy? Why I never seen so much money in all my life. Did you see it, Uncle Harry?"

Most of us choked on our saliva. Dale's face turned a dark shade of beet red. Dick and Duba were mighty proud of the girl's gumption and initiative, but not one of the older guys had any idea who was supposed to play "Daddy" and who was to play "Uncle Harry." They sat there trying to sort it out with stares, elbows, glances, and eyebrow movements. They decided it'd probably be best to wait and see if Mary's blurt opened any other conversations of opportunity. It was now a waiting game.

It was the *Cortland Standard* newspaper on the counter with a picture of President Harry Truman, which inspired Mary. We Pompey Hollow Book Club members saw it and it was right then and there we knew we were proud she was our president. No question about it. This was her day.

Hearing about the mention of money, the sweeper man with the push broom moved closer, getting a little more particular about the floor near Mary's stool, it seemed.

The cook put spoons on the counter by the cups of coffee in front of Dick, Duba, Dwyer, and Conway.

Duba broke the silence and reminded the cook, "The young'ns each get a hot water," waving an arm toward us.

The cook stepped over and set our cups of hot water down in front of each of us and turned to get the tea bags he thought we would want.

Dick and Duba went into action. Dick's decoy was first, as though he was at the Ritz in the downtown of a big city: "Sir, us gentlemen will have us two bacon and egg sandwiches with mayo, but split up, half on each of four plates, if you'll be so kindly."

The cook paused a moment to visualize the math. He squinted his left eye a blink or two from the cigarette smoke rolling up that side of his nose and rolled the other eye up in the direction of his brain for a second of thought. "What about the kids?" he asked.

That was Duba's cue. He could hold a straight face best. He rose to the occasion and went into action: "Sir, is there a charge for the use of your ketchup?"

"No."

"Then the children here will all have soup."

That being said, Duba grabbed the ketchup bottle from the counter, took the cap off and handed it to Barber to hold for him, turned the bottle upside down, and began pounding the bottom of it with the palm of his hand, like a jack hammer, plunging ketchup splotches and spurts into every cup of hot water, one at a time, repeating to each kid in turn, "Stir it, honey. Stir your soup good."

The water in each cup slowly turned several lumpy shades of a murky red with each splash from the ketchup bottle.

"They love their tomato soup," he added, looking up at the cook.

"Mmmm-mmm, good," said Holbrook, under his breath, just like he heard on the radio commercial for soup.

Dick's Minneapolis Moline tractor friend, Jimmy Conway, who never hardly ever said anything, was so inspired by Duba's performance, he leaned in and offered, "Stir it up good, kiddies. Blow on it, case it's hot."

"We will, Uncle Harry," said Mary, with a smile.

At least now we knew who Uncle Harry was—it was Conway. We still weren't sure which of the older guys was Daddy.

Duba jumped in: "Sir, can we trouble you for some soup crackers for each of the little ones? Crackers sort of top off a soup meal, don't ya think?"

"Oh good, I'm starved," Barber announced, handing the ketchup bottle cap back to Duba.

The cook was beside himself with all this dusty pomposity. He didn't know what to say, but he was certain he read about poor folk like us somewhere. He also didn't know what a soup cracker was. Ashes fell from his cigarette to the counter. He swept them off with one tidy swipe of his hand just as he slid a soup bowl filled with oyster crackers over to the middle of the four kids. This was about the same time the sweeper man edged his broom over closer towards Mary.

"What money you talking about, little girl? A bank? A store?"

"Pardon me, son," whispered Conway, well, Uncle Harry. His confidence in speaking up was building now that he had the privilege of being named Uncle Harry. He considered the appointment a responsibility. He leaned toward the sweeper man, looking up and gaining his attention with eyeball contact.

"Pardon me, son, but Betsy Lou here or none of the boys for that matter ain't allowed to be talkin' to no strangers. The way the world is now. Why you could be a German Nazi spy or a communist or something."

"Why I ain't no such thing," said the sweeper.

He almost stood at attention with the broom. He was offended at the mere suggestion of it all. His hand flipped some hair back from his face almost resembling a salute.

"You got any identification, young man, showing you're American?" asked Uncle Harry.

The sweeper was bewildered. He was beside himself. He was trying to gather whatever thoughts he had laying around.

All of us club members at the counter were so impressed. We picked up our spoons and actually started eating the watery soup concoction while listening to pros in action.

Duba stepped in with added authority. "You got any proof, son?" he ordered. "Driver's license? Social Security card? Hunting license? Most anything official will do. No offense meant, son."

"None took, sir."

The sweeper man fumbled for thought and blindly stabbed through pockets with his hands looking for answers, until it finally dawned on him.

"I sure enough got me a hunting license," said the man.

He reached deep in his overall pocket, pulled out a Roy Roger's imitation leather wallet, ran the zipper around three edges of it, opening it, and picked out and handed to Dwyer New York State hunting license number 134.

Duba saw the number on the hunting license, handed it back to the sweeper, and outdid himself. "It sure is genuine," he said. "Number 134."

Hearing the number, Barber spilled his "tomato" soup in Holbrook's lap.

"Sorry about the inconvenience, son, but we have to be careful these days so close after the War. Loose lips sunk ships, you know."

"You're a good American," said the sweeper.

He gazed proudly down at his license and the new sense of power it gave him. He tucked it back into his wallet, zipped it up, and slid it into his pocket.

Dick took a turn on his counter stool, slowly spinning around to face the sweeper, and took the stage: "Betsy Lou's talking about the Fabius trading post on Route 80 up there in Fabius. You may have heard of it—go right in Tully. They have some wonderful bargains. They're only open on Fridays and Saturdays and always have a lot of money in their cash register, it seems, until they get to bank it on Monday. Her aunt's cousin worked there, and was just showing off all braggadocios last week to Betsy Lou here, while we were picking apples at the Moore farm near the Cherry Valley. You know how people do? Let's go, kids. Drink up your soup, grab some oyster crackers to balance your meal—we need to go find some picking work while the sun's still out."

Mary cringed at the Betsy Lou moniker handed her, got off her stool, and pushed the front door open and walked out.

The rest of the Pompey Hollow Book Club downed their tomato soups for the cause. The older guys got up and walked out, munching the last of their half-sandwiches. The check came to forty-seven cents. Dick laid down a half-dollar, swallowed so as not to be rude and talk with his mouth full, and said, "Keep the change, my good man. We'll be recommending this establishment to our friends."

On the drive back to the cemetery, we stopped in Fabius to check out the make-believe store. It looked almost real. The cash register was an antique and piled with money. Each bill was faintly marked in pencil, "Stolen from Shea's store."

Dick and Duba asked Mike Shea if everyone could hide on the second floor of his store across the street and watch for the crooks. Mike Shea said he already thought of that and would have sandwiches and soda pop up there. "What's the plan?" he asked.

Dick said, "Conway's Minneapolis Moline will be around that side of the phony store with a canvas tarp over its front so its size won't scare them." Dick pointed to the right of the store. "When the crooks get here and break in, Duba will crawl around on the ground, get under their car, and pull the engine spark wires out so it won't start. Then he'll crawl back, climb up a wooden ladder resting on the tractor, pull off the tarp, push the ladder away, and ride on the front of it, like it was a giant bucking bronco whooping and hollering. When the crooks come out and try to start the car, Conway will crank her up, do a full U-turn with his forklift front, and go right in under their car from behind them and lift them, car and all, about eight feet up off the ground. Then he'll just back it around with the crooks, head on down Main Street full-speed, Duba still hooting and hollering and keeping them distracted, and they'll deliver them to the fire hall and Sheriff John A. Price and his deputies."

It started off as planned.

The crooks sure enough showed up. Two of them. They parked in front, got out of their car, crowbarred the door open, and broke in. It wasn't long before they came out with the loot and Jimmy had them and their car aloft, heading down Main Street, Duba hollering and shouting. The crooks tried to open the car doors to jump out. It was a good thing Minneapolis Moline Jimmy loved milkshakes and studied just how they were made at the fountain in Manlius. Each time Duba saw the car doors crack open, he would signal Conway to double clutch the Moline giant a few times and shake their innards proper. The tractor made backfiring blasts of fiery sparks like shotguns—so loud that the best the crooks could do in their dizziness was grab for things in the car they thought were door handles, rarely coming close. The backfiring belches woke up most of Fabius.

With all the ruckus the monster Minneapolis Moline made, and kids popping out of nowhere, from behind every house, all following behind the tractor going up Main Street, the fire hall door burst open wide just to see what on earth was causing all the commotion. Every light in town was on now. The tractor turned into the firehouse drive like a giant dragon and came to a stop, and Duba jumped off. The whole poker table now stood there and looked up at the giant tractor's head beams, with the car balanced up high in its craw staring down at them. Minneapolis Moline Conway, as he would come to be known, pulled a lever and lowered the catch like an elevator.

"Put your hands out the windows and stick 'em up!" warned Dick on one side and Duba on the other.

The crooks complied. The sweeper had a white handkerchief in his hand as a flag of truce.

Sheriff John and his deputies stepped to the sides of the vehicle, mouths open. They handcuffed both the men, the sweeper and the cook. They took the box of evidence and told Mike Shea he would have the money back Monday morning.

"That money don't prove nothin'!" snapped the cook.

"Sheriff John?" I said. "Look in that one's wallet. Take a look at his hunting license."

"Why, hello, Jerry," he said, recognizing me from the morning after the hardware store burglary. He took the sweeper's wallet and pulled the hunting license from it.

"Number 134. Well, what do you think of that?"

"There is a reward," said Sheriff John. "Who gets it?"

Dick and Duba looked at the kids.

"How about giving it to the fire department?" a voice in the back offered.

"Yeah, the fire department," more rumbled.

"Anybody thinks they got some reward money coming?" asked Dick.

'Shoot, no," came a voice. "We had more fun, sandwiches, and soda pop than money can buy."

The crowd seemed in favor.

"All in favor of the reward money going to the fire department, raise your hand," yelled Duba.

"Hold on," shouted Bases.

He had popped out from behind the church with some of the crowd.

"How about half the money going to the Fabius Fire Department and the other half going down to the Delphi Falls Fire Department."

Kids cheered. It was settled.

We all left the fire hall feeling good. Most went home. The club and the older guys, except Minneapolis Moline Conway, went to the cemetery, got into our rides, and went our way, savoring another adventure.

The last we saw of Conway that night was his monster tractor heading down Route 80 towards his farm. Cars would pull off the road as it approached them, its high headlamps looking like fire from a dragon. When we passed by Conway in the '38, we all waved and shouted up at him, "Hi, Uncle Harry!"

CHAPTER THIRTEEN

THE THANKSGIVING CHICKEN COUP!

Mom spooned some creamed corn onto her plate and passed the bowl.

"We got a nice letter from your brother Mike today," she said. "He's enjoying college and says hello to everyone and is looking forward to Thanksgiving. Also in the mail, Jerry, was this very nice invitation from your piano teacher, Mrs. Cowling, about the winter school piano recital. I'm so proud and happy to see she wants my boy among the talented participants. Look, everyone, Jerry's name is printed on the invitation, right here, see?"

As she held up the invitation, I lowered my face into my empty plate, for effect.

"Do I have to do it, Mom?" I pleaded.

"Yes, of course. Don't be childish. You'll do fine. Start the sweet peas and pass the bowl to your father."

It was my second year of piano with Mrs. Cowling. I played so badly that the only thing I remembered by heart were two stanzas of "Country Gardens," which happened to be identical to each other. Both last fall's and this past spring's piano recitals were humiliating. I played the same thing. Holbrook said the only similarity between me and Mozart was that we both had an "r" in our names.

Dad threw me a life saver. "We all remember Jerry's recital." He tried to keep a straight face. "Why don't we let the boy find some other instrument he might enjoy more?"

Mom threw a perplexed glare across the table at Dad.

Dick offered: "He really stinks, Mom. Put him out of his misery."

Mom looked at Dick and at the same time raised her arm and pointed to the kitchen. It was a straight, arm-long point-ing of her finger. Eating in the kitchen at home was like being sent to the principal's office in school. You may or may not get a lecture—but at home you sure would be the dishwasher that night.

"Go. Now! March! Jerry has tried his best. Eat in the kitchen. I'll hear no more disparagement."

Mom wasn't whipped; she was weakening, but not without the final say.

"I'll call Mrs. Cowling Monday," she said, "and tell her you won't be taking lessons this year. I'll also call Mr. Spinner, the band director, and see what can be done. My children will expe-rience music and the arts."

I knew enough to go look up "disparagement" in the diction-ary after supper to see if there were any strings attached to her surrender.

"Dick and Jerry, you'll both do the dishes tonight, tomorrow night, and Sunday. Not another word."

There was a cost to my victory.

"And Jerry, if Mrs. Cowling insists you play in this recital, you will play," Mom added.

Dad changed the subject. "Mr. Rowe at the bicycle repair shop in Cortland just happened to have an old reconditioned bike he asked me to look at."

I stopped eating and paid attention to Dad's every word. I'd been hoping for a bike. One I could ride in the Memorial Day Parade in Fabius with my friends.

"He gave me an excellent price for the bike if I would agree to take two guinea hens he'd won at the county fair off his hands. He said they needed the country. He has no place in Cortland for them."

"What's a guinea hen, Dad," Dick asked, "and will you put them at Mr. Pitts's farm with the chickens and geese?"

"No, son, these are real prize show birds, not farm animals. Sort of like peacocks. I'll bring them home tomorrow. I've decided that since you are always reading veterinary books and saving up to buy a car, they should be your chore. I'll open a savings account in your name and make a weekly deposit for you towards new tires for your car, when you get it."

Although Dick and Duba had the '38, he still had his mind set on Lindsey Pryor's old Nash convertible he'd promised to sell Dick for sixty-five dollars. Dick beamed at the thought of new tires.

"The bike will be for Jerry. Someday we'll get a horse or two. I'll drop it here in the morning, between my visit to the bakery and some groceries in New Woodstock and Cazenovia."

"My own bike? It's not even Christmas, Dad."

Dad grinned and said, "Well, you need a ride to the Delphi Falls cemetery from time to time, don't you, son? Can't ride it in the snow; it'll be an early Christmas present—from Santa. I'll stop at Brown's Hardware and get you a small can of paint so you can paint your bike, if you want."

I said, "Yellow."

Mom and Dad looked at each other.

If anyone had asked me why I liked yellow, I wouldn't have told them—it was the color of the ribbon the girl wore in the John Wayne movie I saw four times in Cazenovia. I liked the song, too. "She Wore a Yellow Ribbon."

That night I dreamed about whether or not there was a Santa. What with Dad saying the bike was a present from Santa, and knowing he paid for it. But I didn't pay it much thought.

In the morning I woke up hearing the noise of the chirps. A bird was tapping its beak on my bedroom window. No bird could distract me this particular morning. I was in love.

Well, not girl love.

There was only one girl I was ever going to marry: Olivia Dandridge from *She Wore a Yellow Ribbon*, and I didn't care how many lieutenants of the cavalry I would have to stand down to do it. I knew the other kind of love there was, too, like the love Captain Nathan Cutting Brittles had for God, his country, and the cavalry. He and I had a lot in common like that. When the time was right for me to ask for Miss Dandridge's hand, I would get someone like Captain Brittle's advice—maybe my dad's.

I was about to be in love with my new bike.

I got out of my pajamas, got dressed, and went to the kitchen. Sure enough, there was a little can of paint and a small paint-brush on the counter. Dad left a note that started: "The only yellow they had was house paint. It will dry faster, son. Look in the barn garage."

It was beautiful—simply beautiful! It was sleek, with big round tires, curved handlebars, and a shiny bell with a convenient thumb button.

Tring ... tring ... tring ...

It was all so perfect. I loved my new bike!

First, I was going to paint it. After that, I would ride my brand-spanking, newly painted bike down to the Maxwell place on the corner, where I knew Mary Crane was spending the day with pretty Linda Oats, and show it off to them both. Linda was three grades ahead of me and Mary, old enough to be our aunt or something—but I'd been smitten with her freckly smile ever since the first day I saw her on the school bus when we first moved to Delphi Falls. She and Mary had known each other in Manlius or Syracuse or somewhere before they moved here.

I didn't know why they called it the Maxwell place. I think it was because somebody famous, named Maxwell, used to live there during the Revolutionary War and had his name carved in a big stone on the corner when he built the cider mill.

Next to the house was the big old apple cider mill barn, rotting and falling apart inside. Cider mills were big barns, built right next to a creek or river. They had a tall paddle wheel, almost as tall as the barn, which went down deep into the creek. The movement of the water would turn the paddle wheel, the wheel would turn some gears on the second floor, and those gears would turn a big stone wheel that would smash the apples. Apple juice ran down a drain pipe into a big, open wooden vat, about as tall as my chest, on the first floor. Most of the paddle wheel was rotted now; the barn was still standing there, barely.

The bike didn't take long to paint. I even painted it twice to make sure I did a good job. I moved the brush as smoothly as I could across the fenders, so the brush strokes hardly showed. It was a work of art.

When I was finished, I asked Mom to come over to the window and look at my bike.

"My goodness," she said. "It certainly is yellow!"

I beamed as she continued:

"Don't forget you have a dentist appointment today at Dr. Webb's. Jerry, where are your shoes? I wish you would wear the watch you got for your birthday. I don't know what I'm going to do with you. At least go put your sneakers on and be home before ten. Keep asking people for the time."

I went in the house and put on my sneakers while the paint dried. When it was finally dry to the touch, I walked around it a few times, just admiring it, still not believing I actually had a bike of my own. It was like a dream.

Down the drive I carefully peddled around puddles, so I wouldn't splash and mess my new paint. On Cardner Road it was smooth sailing. I hardly had to pedal at all. I glided down the road like the wind was pushing me.

Farmer Parker's cows were in his north pasture that day, by Cardner Road. Most often, when I walked by them, they'd keep their heads down and noses on the ground as they grazed. For some reason this time they all lifted and turned their heads in unison and stared at me riding by. Maybe they hadn't seen a canary yellow bike before. I started to sing, "Round her neck she wore a yellow ribbon … she wore a yellow ribbon all through the month of May …"

Life was good.

Long before I got to the corner, I tried to think how best to show off my bike to Linda and Mary. Should I casually ride by Linda's house, let her and Mary see me, then turn back? Should I slow down, just boldly turn into the driveway, and ride right up to the door? Should I stop, before I got to the house, get off, and push the bike onto Linda's front lawn, so she and Mary could admire its lines from the living room window?

It was too late. I'd already arrived, so I slowed down, turned into her driveway, and came to a stop near the side door. I got off like I was getting off a horse, and rested the bike on the kickstand.

What speed, what grace, I thought.

I walked backwards up to the side door while admiring my bike, and knocked on the screen door behind me. Mrs. Oats came to the door.

"Hello, Jerry," she said. "If you're looking for Linda, she and Mary are in the mill barn. Be very careful out there, and please DON'T GO TO THE SECOND FLOOR, because it isn't safe. Everything is rotted."

I asked proudly, "Do you like my bike, Mrs. Oats?"

"Oh my," she said. "It certainly is yellow, isn't it?"

I had just finished reading a Hardy Boys mystery book, *The Secret of the Old Mill*, for the third time, where they found and caught the desperate money counterfeiters, but nearly got massacred while doing it. I thought about the two desperate burglars who had busted into all those stores, sneaking around at night, hiding in the dark, stealing all that money before we caught them. I really didn't want to go into the dark and dusty, damp old mill barn, so I didn't need a warning that it was dangerous. I had every intention of being extra careful, just in case there were crooks hiding or something.

The mill barn door was open, just a little, rotted on its hinges; the bottom of it scraped the ground when I pushed on it.

"Linda? Mary?" I yelled. "You in here?"

"We're up here, on the second floor."

I could hear Linda's voice from the very place her mom, not more than two minutes ago, had warned me not to go.

There were stairs going up one wall to the second floor.

I looked over towards the center of the barn, next to a huge wooden vat nearly as tall as I was and longer than a tub. It looked like it was filled with goopy, disgusting, black, swamp-like water. From a distance, it looked as if something was moving around in it.

There was a ladder leaning next to the vat, reaching up to a small square opening in the ceiling to the second floor. I decided to go up the stairs by the wall.

"Don't use the stairs by the wall," shouted Mary. "They're all rotted."

I changed my mind and decided to go up the ladder instead.

When I got next to the vat, it smelled dank and awful. It reminded me of rutabagas—which made me gag every time I had to eat them. The dark, grungy, stinky water in this huge vat smelled worse than a barrel of rotten rutabagas, and I had to hold my breath, or gag. While I climbed the ladder, I kept looking down at the vat, and could swear it had something alive in it. Looking up I could see parts of the sky through the leaky barn roof riddled with cracks and holes.

When I finally climbed through the square opening, I gasped a deep breath of fresh air, and looked around. It was a nice old barn in a way, like a barn with a story to tell, and kind of shaky at the same time, the way it was rotting.

"Be careful where you walk, it's not safe," said Mary.

Linda said, "Mary was telling me about the Pompey Hollow Book Club and the stuff you do. You're all such heroes. Is Mary your girlfriend?"

"No."

First off, I thought, I didn't even know any guys in the Pompey Hollow Book Club who had girlfriends, and second, I didn't know if my mom would even let me have a girlfriend.

"But you like her, don't you? She likes you. *Na, na-na, na-naaaaa, na!*"

Mary's face turned a blushed, beet red.

Now boys, I could figure. We talked the same. We liked the same things. We even knew what each other's thoughts were, at times—even Mary Crane's, at club meetings. I looked over at Mary for a second to wonder if she ever thought about liking me or was Linda Oats just talking. This sort of girl talk distracted me—it was new and very strange to me. I had never heard a girl talk like this before, except maybe to Cary Grant in a movie at the Cazenovia picture show.

"You can kiss me, if you want," said Linda.

I honest to God rode my bike down here to show it off to Linda Oats and Mary. I came into this spooky mill barn, against my better judgment, just to get them to come outside and look at my new yellow bike. All of a sudden, I was on the second floor, where her mom had said not to go, and I was being tempted to kiss the very girl I'd been staring at on the bus since we moved here.

"I dare you," Linda added.

Mary folded her arms in front of her, puffed a curl from her eye with a pout, and stood there tapping a toe, staring at me, confident I wouldn't do it. Her expression then looked down in doubt but then back up at me as if she was hoping I wouldn't do it.

Linda wasn't embarrassed at all—she was smiling.

"Chicken?" she said.

"I'm not chicken," came out of me as easy as it would for any kid at the sound of that word, even though my knees began to wobble.

A boy my age could never let a dare like this go unchallenged, or he'd be branded for life. Even I knew that.

Mary's lips buckled a frown in disappointment.

Linda leaned forward, with a silly smile—her eyes closed, her lips puckered. She leaned forward a little more, and kind of held her cheek out. I considered whether to kiss her on the cheek, on the lips, or just climb down the ladder and go home. I bent over, my knees really wiggling now, and pressed my lips toward her face. Glancing over I could see Mary's lips turned to almost a warning. As it turned out, none of any of this really mattered much, because just as my lips touched what I thought was Linda's face, somewhere, both floor boards I was standing on started to make squishing sounds, wobbling, just like my knees. Then they bent and creaked, and I began to lose my balance.

This can't be good, I thought ...

... And the floorboards creaked again.

I looked down at my P.F. Flyer sneakers sinking into the rain-soaked floorboards; they turned to mush like sponges, under my feet, and then—

CA-RASH!

CA-RUNCH!

Down I crashed, through the hole my weight had made in the floor. I caught my fingertips on a wood beam, which stopped my fall, for about the three seconds I was hanging there, eight feet above the open wooden vat below, still full of the dark, slimy-looking sludge water. My fingers couldn't hang on any longer, my eyes made a silent plea up into Mary's stone-cold eyes, which pretty much looked as though I had it coming, and down into the cider vat I went!

"AAAAAAAAAAAAAHHHHHHHHH!" I wailed.

KAAAA-SPA-LOOSH!

It was like falling out of a top bunk bed into a tub of mud, like when I fell out of bed in Cortland onto Dick sleeping on the floor, before we moved to Delphi Falls—only colder, smellier, and wetter and deeper.

My whole body went underwater, like I was in a deep tub. I sat up to push my head above water for air.

"Are you okay?" yelled Mary, sounding almost as if she cared.

I was not about to open my mouth.

I could see both girls' heads, peeking down through the hole I'd made in the ceiling.

"I think he's dead," said Linda.

"He's not dead, Linda, or he wouldn't be standing up, spitting out leaves," answered Mary.

"Are you okay?" whined Mary again, but in a tone as if it served me right.

I spit out another elm leaf and pulled one off my cheek and two from the top of my head. I looked out through the broken windows on the back side of the mill, where the elm tree was. Two pigeons were sitting on a broken window frame, waiting for me to move so they could take their morning bath. All that ran through my mind was, How did a boy answer that question?

I didn't.

I crawled out of the vat, my clothes covered with rust and mud and goop, stumbled outside, trying to wring the front of my t-shirt out. I pushed my bike home so I wouldn't get the new canary yellow paint dirty. My sneakers made a sloshing sound all the way.

Mom could see me coming up the driveway pushing my bike. She came out on the porch to see why I wasn't riding. When I was close enough for her to see the mess all over me, she quickly ran inside and came out again, with clean underwear, jeans, t-shirt, and a bath towel.

"Not in the house!"

She handed me the items.

"But, Mom," I started to plead.

"To the falls!" was her final word. "Clean up and then get ready to go to the dentist."

I put the towel around my neck, the clothes under my arm, and pushed the bike around back, to the falls, and put it on its kickstand.

I spent time at the falls, swimming around in the icy cold water, staring at my bike standing there, waiting for me like a trusted steed. My mind wandered a little, and I wondered if my lips actually touched Linda on the lips or just her cheek, right before I fell through the floor. It might have been my first kiss, and this was important information to have about a first kiss. I finally decided: definitely her lips.

CHAPTER FOURTEEN

RUNNING AMUCK!

Dick shook my shoulder. "Jerry. Wake up."

I didn't budge.

"Jerry. Get up."

I rolled over, barely opening the crack of one eye, and reached out, fumbling for my clock to see the time. Way too early! I squinted a grumble up at Dick. "What!?"

"The guinea hens are over at Farmer Parker's place again. They're eating Mrs. Parker's garden seeds."

"So!? What day is it?"

This was the best I could do before I had some breakfast.

Nobody liked the guinea hens ever since the minute they hopped out of Dad's trunk and scooted off. The feeling was mutual. They had no use for people and were always roaming off the property, scratching up other people's vegetable gardens and eating the seeds just after they were planted. Our dog, Ginger, didn't even like the birds, and she liked everything.

Dick considered thumping me, but stayed calm. "So!? So Mom wants me to go over and run them off. To get them back over here. It's Saturday, get up."

"Good. Go run 'em off."

I rolled back over, tucking my alarm clock under my pillow. In the "chore" world, we pretty much stayed neutral when it came to someone else's chore problems. I was getting woken up because of the two stupid guinea hens Dad had taken for a special good price on my bike. Everyone knew my chore was walking to Mr. Pitts's farm and getting the eggs every week. Taking care of the guinea hens was Dick's responsibility. Everyone knew that, too. Watching out for them was his chore in return for new tires if he ever got the car he wanted to buy from Lindsey Pryor.

He shook my shoulder again. "Jere, I got a job all day today and tomorrow, if I want it, washing dishes, scrubbing pots and pans up at the Lincklaen House for two weddings. The pay's good. I need the money. I got to be there in half an hour. You go chase the guinea hens home; I'll give you a dollar."

"No."

"Two dollars."

"Nope."

Dick grimaced, shook his head about loosely, as if it was a snow globe hoping for a fluttering of ideas, and blurted, "I'll give you the Daisy air rifle Conway gave me. The stock was broken off but I fixed it like new in wood shop. You can have it."

I rallied. It wasn't often one could get the advantage with Dick.

"The BB gun and two dollars so me and some guys can go to the picture show in Cazenovia."

"Don't call it a BB gun. Call it an air rifle. Mom hates guns. You can even use it on the guinea hens to scare them home. It won't hurt them. Let me see how much I got."

"You sure it won't hurt them? Two dollars," I added.

"Aim at their butts. It won't hurt them. It will only scare them and chase them home."

"And the BB gun is mine to keep?"

"Air rifle. Yes."

Dick jumped out of the room, went to his, came back with the BB gun, laid it on my bed next to me, and put three cartridges of pellets on my desk. I picked the gun up and looked at the newly varnished stock. It had two leather straps hanging from a ring on its side.

"This is nice," I said.

"Get up and get over there," said Dick.

"Where's the two dollars?"

Dick jumped out of the room again and back in as quick. "I only have ten bits," he said, meaning five quarters. "Buck and a quarter and this miniature deck of playing cards. It comes in its own case."

He held a small deck out near my face. It was a deck of playing cards half the size of a regular deck.

"Okay," I said, taking the cards from his hand.

Dick then offered his fine print: "The ten of clubs is missing. No one will know."

He flipped the five quarters onto my bed, looked in my eye for confirmation. When he saw me sit up he lit out of the room and out of the house.

I pulled my jeans on, dropped the quarters into my left jean pocket, and picked up and shook the air rifle to see if the pellet chamber was full. It was. I rested it between my side and bent forearm, as John Wayne did in *Fort Apache*, and headed to the kitchen.

Mom was at the table reading the front page of the newspaper, digging a spoon into half a grapefruit.

"I'm going to Farmer Parker's to chase the guinea hens home for Dick, Mom."

"Good. Hurry, dear."

"I'm going to get some cereal first."

"No cereal. Go get the birds, eat when you get back. Mrs. Parker is beside herself. I don't know whatever possessed your father to bring those creatures home in the first place. They're not domesticated. They are such a bother. Go! Now!"

She had a look in her eye, probably from Myrtie's call telling her that Mrs. Parker was mentioning to folks about our guinea hens spoiling her garden.

Mom lifted her eyes from the newspaper, peered over her glasses, and said, "What are you doing with a gun? You know I don't like guns."

"It's not a gun, Mom. It's a Daisy air rifle. Farmers use them to scare pigeons and birds out of barns. Minneapolis Moline Conway gave this one to Dick. Everybody has one."

"I don't like them. Don't point it at anything."

"Can I go to the picture show with some kids?"

"Young man—move! You accepted a responsibility. Go do your job. We can talk and you can eat breakfast when you get back. Off with you! Go!"

Neighbors in the country liked to be good neighbors so they could mean their smiles and waves at each other when they passed on the road. Mom was not having a good morning. I left the house and told Ginger to stay.

Stepping on the yard at Farmer Parker's, their Border collie ran over to meet me. Buddy and I were old friends. We'd brought the cows down off the hill together a bunch of times. I bounced up on the porch and knocked on the door. I couldn't see Farmer Parker or the horses anywhere. The door opened and Mrs. Parker looked at me through the screen door. She was trying to remember which one I was.

"Hi, Mrs. Parker, I'm Jerry. I'm here to chase the hens home.

"Oh, hello, Jerry. You gave me a start. I had to think. There are so many of you and your friends—forgive me."

"Sorry about the guinea hens, Mrs. Parker. Dick is supposed to take care of them. I'll get them out of here, don't worry."

"It's just when I do my late summer and fall planting. They get at my seeds and bulbs before they can root. Most ungraceful birds, in an odd sort of way, such big bodies for those little legs. They can be such a nuisance at planting time."

I could smell bacon and syrup drifting through the screen door. It must have showed on my face.

"I'll get them out of here," I said.

"Thank you, Jerry. Would you like some breakfast? I have plenty."

"You bet I would. Thanks, Mrs. Parker. Let me get them across the road and I'll be back."

"I'll make some hot chocolate," she said.

I turned, jumped off the porch, and walked around the house to her garden patch on the north side. Sure enough, the guinea hens were pecking away. They tried to look like peacocks, blue-silvery-gray with black heads, white face masks, and pintail crowns. They didn't try very hard. I was embarrassed just looking at them. They couldn't fan their tails like a peacock, didn't lay eggs like chickens, and were pretty much nothing but selfish troublemakers. They belonged in a zoo, not on a farm. I cocked the air rifle and walked out in the open for the showdown. I stood square between the garden in front of me and the distant barn at my back, so I could block their path. I planted my feet.

I shouted best I could before my breakfast: "Shoo!"

Both birds lifted their heads, looked at me as if they were telling me to go find my own garden, and went right back to pecking.

I looked around quickly to be certain no one witnessed that embarrassing moment.

This time I flapped my arms: "Git! Go on, dumb birds, get out of here!"

They couldn't have cared less.

I was about to wish I hadn't taken the job when I remembered: BBs.

I lifted the air rifle, lodged it on my chest by my shoulder, remembering what I had learned from the shooting gallery at the Suburban Park amusement park in Manlius. I took careful aim at one of the hen's butts and squeezed the trigger.

Bop!

The hen jumped straight up about four inches off the ground almost into flight, telling me in no uncertain terms: "Girgle, girgle, girgle, girgle …"

It stood there frozen, staring at me.

I lurched forward, cocking my air rifle for another shot. The hen backed up two steps, turned around, and took off running, the other hen right on its tail. I ran tippy-toed across the edge of the garden, balancing so as not to tumble into the row of beets, went down through the dew-covered, sloping yard, chasing them with war whoops across the road and through our gate. Once on our property they high-tailed it the full distance up the driveway to the green barn. They both ran like they had loaded diapers. I picked up pebbles and flung a handful to help them remember to stay near the barn where they belonged and to quit waking me up on Saturdays.

I walked back up to the Parker's, rested my air rifle in the kitchen corner, ate breakfast, and learned about Mrs. Parker's widowed sister who was coming for Thanksgiving all the way from Erie, Pennsylvania. Mrs. Parker had an old wood stove with cream and lime-green enamel sides and chrome handles, a black top, and tin chimney. It went up the wall and bent into the top of the wall just under the ceiling. Next to the wood stove was an electric oven she was cooking on. She handed me a plate with three pancakes and four strips of bacon.

"Do you ever use the old wood stove?" I asked.

"If the electricity goes out a spell, we do. Or if it gets intolerably cold in the winter, Fay will put a fire in it to warm the place," she said.

"Is that what Farmer Parker's name is, Fay?" I asked.

"Yes. It was his father's name."

Mrs. Parker took a small pot off the burner and poured some hot chocolate into my cup.

"He likes when you come around, Jerry. He was so proud of all your friends for solving that burglary in Cortland. He said it made him wish he were young again. He enjoys watching you learn about the country and farming. You call him Farmer Parker. He's told me he feels that's so respectful. He likes that. You boys and every one of your friends are reared well. Parenting and schooling today must be wonderful," she added with a smile.

"Reared?" I asked.

Mrs. Parker sat up like a school teacher and said, "We can raise our corn and vegetables, but we have to rear our children."

Mrs. Parker sipped her tea, smiling out the window at the dew, probably remembering the days she would walk into Delphi Falls and teach in the two-room schoolhouse.

"Can I use your telephone, Mrs. Parker?"

"Of course. It's an old one. Do you know how?"

It wasn't like ours, where we just had to pick up the receiver and wait for Myrtie to come on. I lifted the ear piece off the hook, put it to my ear, turned the crank around two full turns, and waited to see if Myrtie came on.

She did.

"Hello, Myrtie, this is Jerry, I'm at Farmer Parker's. Can you get me Randy Vaas, please?" I turned and looked at Mrs. Parker. "Myrtie told me to say hello to you for her, Mrs. Parker."

Mrs. Parker smiled.

"Hello?"

"Randy?"

"Yes."

"Barber told me he was staying over at your house last night to ride the milk truck this morning with your dad. They back? You guys want to go see *Annie Get Your Gun* at the picture show? It started last night in Cazenovia."

"Sure."

"See who else can go. I got a buck and a quarter from Dick."

"Hold on a sec," said Randy.

I said to Mrs. Parker, "I like helping Farmer Parker. He teaches me a lot."

Randy came back on the phone. "Dad has to pick up feed and lime in Cazenovia. He said he'd take all the kids that could fit in the cab of the truck. I'll call around and call you back. Is that the movie about Annie Oakley, the sharpshooter?"

"I think so."

"Barber and I'll call around and call you back."

We both hung up.

I thanked Mrs. Parker for the breakfast and apologized for the hens and told her I would see what I could do about keeping them where they belonged, better.

"Jerry, come any time. I always have enough."

I picked up my Daisy air rifle, went outside, scratched Buddy under the collar, and walked back home.

I got to our barn garage and went in looking for a couple of nails and a hammer. I was going to find a place in my room to hang the rifle. When I picked the spot, I pounded both nails in the wall by my bed. After carefully resting the gun on them, the room took on a certain air. I stood back, by the door, and stared at my rifle on the wall next to my bed. The room seemed more grown up for some reason.

Little did I realize that this air rifle on my wall would be the beginning of some problems.

"Come eat breakfast, Jerry. What was that pounding noise?" shouted Mom.

I decided not to test Mom's bad start to her day by telling her I'd already eaten across the road and had just pounded two nails into my bedroom wall. I went to the kitchen, pretended I was hungry.

"Mr. Vaas is driving us to Cazenovia to see the *Annie Get Your Gun* movie; can you pick us up later?"

"Yes, dear, eat your grapefruit."

"You should go see Mrs. Parker sometime, Mom. She's a nice lady."

"I'm certain she is. But wasn't it Robert Frost who said good fences make good neighbors? Perhaps I'll invite her for tea one day."

"If we had good fences, she wouldn't have our guinea hens in her garden," I offered.

Mom never answered me when she knew I had her stumped.

"Mrs. Parker said we had good rears, Mom."

Mom lifted her eyes from the article about Eleanor Roosevelt and peered over her glasses.

By now Mom had learned not to overreact to what she called "Jerry-speak." She waited for a translation to come out. Her neck perked, she crinkled her nose. "Excuse me?"

"Mrs. Parker said me and all my friends were raised *good*."

Mom's eyes smiled. "Raised *well*," she said. "Mrs. Parker said me and all my friends were ..."

I interrupted: "Well, she did."

"That's nice, dear."

The phone rang.

I jumped up from my grapefruit, went into Mom and Dad's room, and picked it up.

Randy said, "Barber and I will be at your house in fifteen minutes or so with Holbrook, Crane, and the Mayor. We'll pick up you, and then we'll go into Delphi and get Bases if he can go. Can you get us all a ride home?"

"Already have," I said.

I figured it best to tell Mom there were five to take home, spread out over half the county, *after* she came to pick us up rather than now, what with her morning disposition being so frail because of two guinea hens.

Mom completely forgot about the *pounding* question and was reaching for her purse.

"I have enough money from Dick, Mom; you can come get us anytime this afternoon."

The good thing about a Saturday morning picture show was that it cost fifteen cents to get in. It started in the morning, sometimes with a Superman serial or cartoon. Then, after the newsreel, around noon, they'd show the feature movie and repeat it all day. You could sit in the movie house the whole time for the fifteen cents. They even let people go in for free to find their kids to take home. Anytime Mom came for us would be fine.

I felt the five quarters in my left jean pocket, slid the case of miniature playing cards in my right pocket, took one last look at my Daisy air rifle on my wall, and headed towards the gate to wait for Mr. Vaas's truck to roll down over the hill next to Farmer Parker's.

Nobody had a truck like Mr. Vaas's truck. I had ridden in it before, with Randy, when he did his early morning dairy run. A 1942 Dodge with a stake bed for carrying milk cans or feed sacks. It was originally made for the War as an army truck. The steering wheel could be unlatched and moved from the left side over to the right side. The truck had pedals and steered from either side. Mr. Vaas thought they did that because different countries, where the War was, had different driving laws for which side of the road you could drive on. Someone else told me it was in case the driver on the left got tired or shot and killed; the soldier on the right could take over without stopping.

Mr. Vaas squeaked the truck to a stop and dropped us off in front of the movie house, right next to the Lincklaen House, and drove away. We had a whole fourteen minutes to wait before it opened, so we gathered up and sat by the curb.

People were really good about driving around us.

I told everyone about the guinea hens and how I got the air rifle. Each of them, except Mary and Holbrook, already had one. I pulled the miniature deck of playing cards out of my pocket.

"He gave me this, too." I held it up for everyone to see.

Holbrook reached deep into his pocket and pulled out a soft piece of fur about the size of his hand.

"Want to trade?" he asked.

"What's that?"

"A chipmunk."

I jumped up and blurted, "Did you murder a chipmunk?"

"No way. My dad backed over it. On Berry Road, with the DeSoto, going to work in the dark. I found it squished when I was walking over to Tommy Kellish's."

Every nose on the curb wrinkled a stomach churning *ewww*.

Holbrook continued: "Mom wouldn't let me use her pancake spatula so I picked it up with a pair of Dad's pliers, hosed the guts off it best I could, and begged Mom to skin it for the pelt. Wanna trade it for the cards? You can use it to polish your air rifle. I promised to hang the wash on the clothesline three Saturdays in a row, if she skinned the chipmunk."

Barber spoke up. "With eleven kids, six girls, this could be a humiliating experience for a boy—people driving by, watching him with a mouth full of clothespins hanging brassieres and panties."

Randy grinned. "To a good trader, you're the one who got skinned, Holbrook."

"Trade?" Holbrook repeated, holding the fur up to my face.

The image of my air rifle on my wall flashed in my brain.

"Trade," I accepted.

The trade was done; the movie house opened. We all quickly emptied our pockets and handed our money over to Mary. She divided it equally, handed it back out—and had fifteen cents to spare. We went to the popcorn stand after paying for our tickets. The fifteen cents we had left over we put in the "iron lung bank" on the candy counter for the March of Dimes, for polio kids.

We loved the movie. All three times we sat through it.

Annie was the best sharpshooter in the whole world. She hit every clay bird and glass ball they threw up in the air. She was better than the man, but they got married anyway and sang songs together. The music was fun. Mary asked me if she could borrow my Daisy air rifle to practice. I said sure. I asked everyone to keep their eyes open in the woods or fields for some turkey feathers I could hang from my gun on the leather strings.

CHAPTER FIFTEEN

IMAGE PROBLEMS

No one knew my secret—about the only other time I took aim at a bird with the BB gun, and shot and killed it.

It was a sparrow. It didn't jump like the guinea hen. I watched its eyes turn blank. Both its feet grasped the twig it was resting on, and its body fell over, swinging dead in the breeze. I climbed the tree, crawled out on the branch, reached to the twig, and lifted the sparrow gently in my hand. Feeling the warmth of the lifeless body did something to me. I begged its forgiveness, buried it with a full-blown funeral—whistled taps and my mourning dove coos—while scratching the words "Poor Sparrow" with my knife on its tombstone.

Ever since that funeral, my BB gun had never been pointed, by me, at anything other than empty tin cans or bottles. Not even at guinea hens.

But because of my chipmunk fur (now tacked on the wall) and my Daisy air rifle looming over it, I was branded a seasoned woodsman, like a Davey Crockett or a Daniel Boone, by most anyone who walked by my room and peered in. The Hardy Boys book I had leaning up against my window to block the porch light from shining through at night, with a *Moby Dick* book jacket to disguise it, didn't help.

I wanted to show a broader literary interest than the Hardy Boys, so I took the *Moby Dick* book jacket from a book in Dick's room. With both the gun and fur on the wall, *Moby Dick* only made me a whale hunter.

The Pompey Hollow Book Club kids were Saturday morning picture show junkies when we weren't fighting crime. We simply knew life as it should be, from growing up half our lives seeing the world in a way it shouldn't be. To us life was about right over wrong, good over evil, and about just trying to remember to make our beds in the morning.

Thanksgiving was a few weeks away. Relatives would be coming home, sometimes staying a week. There could be twenty or thirty family members, friends, and kids around tables celebrating Thanksgiving, having fun and eating a lot of food. There would be tons of leftovers all week.

"Big families have big responsibilities," Dad would always tell us when he handed out our special Thanksgiving chores. Last year I had to help set the table.

But with this Thanksgiving holiday coming, Dad had a different look in his eye, a look like maybe I had matured somehow over the summer and maybe I was ready for a whole new challenge and responsibility in the development of my life experiences. Maybe (it appeared to be on his mind) I could help the family get ready for Thanksgiving in a different way this year—at the helm of a chore befitting my new image.

Holding a cup of coffee, Dad stopped me on my way through the house to my room to oil my BB gun.

"Jerry," he said, "Mike's getting a load of pumpkins, apples, and cranberries for pies and sauces and seasoned bread from the bakery for the stuffing when he drives in from Lemoyne. Since he's the gourmet in the family, he'll be helping out in the kitchen. Dick's going to rake the leaves and pick up the front and the back yards. Your mother is going to drive to Cortland Thanksgiving week and buy a fresh tom from the Rotary fundraiser, but we'll need more than one turkey to feed everyone through to New Years. Son, think you and Holbrook can go up and help Mr. Pitts prepare four geese and ten chickens for cooking and gifting? Okay, son?"

He added: "Your mother and I want to give two of the geese and five of the chickens to the Holbrooks's table for their holidays; they have a large family, too. Eleven, isn't it? You two can help Mr. Pitts anyway he needs help: chop wood to get a fire going for water, whatever else he needs help with. Mr. Pitts will tell you. Walk over this week and work it out with him, son."

With that said, Dad matter-of-factly picked up an axe resting on the kitchen counter, an axe which hung in the barn for chopping wood, and handed it to the one person he now thought was Daniel Boone. Me.

It was even worse than I imagined! I was smart enough to know that preparing the chickens and geese didn't exactly mean giving them a bath and brushing their combs.

I stared up at him with my mouth open, speechless.

"Close your mouth, son; you'll catch flies in it," he said.

I never once caught a fly in my mouth.

Mr. Pitts was a nice old man. He was a friend of mine who watched over our chickens and geese at his little farm, I guess in trade for his being able to eat chickens and sell eggs we didn't use. I walked over and picked up the eggs every week. Dad would drop off bags of feed and stack them on a shelf in his barn, high enough so animals couldn't get to them.

Dad was expecting me, his only son with the daring to nail a chipmunk pelt and Daisy rifle on his wall, and Holbrook, my best friend, to go help Mr. Pitts flat-out murder ten chickens and four geese for the Thanksgiving and Christmas holidays.

I kept my mouth shut and thought.

People who lived on farms raised things to eat. I knew that. That didn't bother me. Hot dogs, hamburgers, and bacon were meat. Still, it was one thing to go to a grocery with Mom and put these things in her shopping basket, but it was a whole different kettle of fish to be standing there with an axe in my hand thinking about the rooster at Mr. Pitts's farm with its *cock-a-doodle-doo*, knowing my job was to get it and nine of the others ready to be cooked.

I killed the sparrow and didn't sleep for days.

I kept thinking.

There was no way I was going to murder ten chickens and four geese. What harm did the chickens or geese do to me, anyway? The chickens cackled around, pecking at the ground, minding their own business, and they gave us eggs every day. The geese chased me, sure, which could be very annoying, but they

also chased away any fox that tried to get a chicken. My brother
Dick chased me around the house, but there was no way I'd chop
his head off.

Dad clicked his fingers three times in front of my face trying
to get my attention. "You okay, son?"

I snapped out of it. "Sure, Dad."

It was final, I thought to myself—our animals living at Mr.
Pitts's house were family, not livestock.

I wasn't going to do it, and was pretty sure Holbrook wouldn't
either. He talked about being a woodsman and about deer track-
ing, but he'd rather be combing his hair and looking at girls. He
couldn't even skin the squashed chipmunk.

I wouldn't dare say any of this out loud for Dad to hear. I knew
if I ever told him I didn't want to do it, he wouldn't make me. It
would remind him of the Easter rabbit fiasco, and he'd just get
an older brother to do it. I couldn't let that happen either.

I turned around, dragged the axe to my room, and slid it
under my mattress.

I had to get a meeting with the Pompey Hollow Book Club
and tell them what my dad wanted us to do.

I went to Mom and Dad's room and picked up the phone.
"Myrtie, can you please get me Tommy Kellish?"

"Are you getting ready for Santa, young man? It won't be
long now."

"Yes ma'am."

"I love the bed comforter you gave me at Easter. I use it
every day. It's so cozy in the chill air. Here you go, hon, you're
connected."

"Hello?"

"Tommy, could you see if Holbrook is working at the Tully bakery today or if he can meet at the cemetery? It's real important."

"Life or death important?" he asked.

"Yeah, this time it's my dad. He wants us to murder a ton of
chickens and geese."

"Uh-oh, that is serious."

"If I know he's not working, I'll call Barber to set up a
meeting."

"If he's home, want me just to go ahead and call Barber right off?" asked Tommy. He knew the cemetery was the Pompey Hollow Book Club's favorite meeting place.

"Perfect idea. Thanks, Tommy."

About forty minutes later the phone rang. It was Barber. "Early morning tomorrow. Sunup. We'll see ya there."

"Okay."

We both hung up.

The next morning I got up and dressed in the dark and walked over through Farmer Parker's place. I went down into his barn and said hello to him while he was milking; then I stepped through the sliding doors and said good morning to Sarge and Sally. I cut through the farm down back of his barn, over the creek, and up the steep hillside wagon road to the top. I crossed the hayfield, feeling the breaking sun on my shoulder, and climbed down on the other side between the maple and the elm into the cemetery.

Climbing down the hill, I made mourning dove coos with my hands, for some noise. Barber and Bases were already there, playing barehanded catch, waiting. We sat on the ground and talked about the *Annie Get Your Gun* movie. It wasn't too long before we could hear the car door of a new Ford open and close. Kids could tell the kind of car it was from the door slam.

The car drove off.

We could hear leaves rustling up the hill into the cemetery, between the tall pine and maple trees. With a morning fog, Holbrook and Crane were kicking the dried leaves around tombstones, deliberately stepping on dead branches and twigs, snapping them with their feet. Normally Holbrook and I could sneak through the woods, like Indians, and not make a sound, but every kid knew, especially in a cemetery so soon after Halloween—not that we believed in ghosts or spirits or anything like that—we just never thought there *couldn't* be ghosts, either.

Mom read me the story once about Ichabod Crane and the Headless Horseman, so I knew what I was talking about. The book was written about Sleepy Hollow and that couldn't be all that far from Pompey Hollow, we figured. We suspected it was all true, so we made noise—lots of noise—walking in the cemetery.

Mary and Holbrook became clearer walking up the hill between the trees. Holbrook had one candy bar in his hand. Mary had three.

I figured her dad had stopped at Hastings' store in Delphi Falls and bought candy bars for each of us.

Mary handed one to Barber and one to Bases, kept one for herself. My guess was Holbrook ate his on the way up the hill through the cemetery and was carrying mine.

Holbrook took the wrapper off the candy bar, broke it in two, and held up both pieces. One was longer than the other, so he took a bite off the longer piece to even them up and held them up again to be sure they were even.

Good friends didn't look at something like this as cheating a friend—we'd just think it was funny.

Everyone savored their chocolate, like grownups do with their morning coffee. Holbrook and Mary were still catching their breath, happy to be safe at our meeting place.

Holbrook asked, "What's wrong?"

He always wanted to get right down to business. He knew my call to Tommy Kellish was a life or death call. What no one knew was it was life or death for some chickens and geese. Everyone stood around in a circle to listen.

"My dad gave me an axe and said for Holbrook and me to go up to Mr. Pitts's place and help him butcher ten chickens and four geese for Thanksgiving and Christmas, and two of the geese and five of the chickens are for Holbrook's mom and dad to have for Thanksgiving and Christmas."

Holbrook looked at me. "So what's the problem?"

"Holbrook. You crazy!? There is no way we're going to murder any chickens or geese!"

Mary offered, "You may have to dip them in boiling water right afterwards to be able to get the feathers off."

Holbrook could smell the gravy. He shrugged. "I don't see a problem."

It was then when Barber added a more educated, one might say more clinical, point of view: "And then one of you will have to stick your hand in their *hiney*-holes and pull out all their guts and clean them."

Holbrook spun around in a complete, dizzying circle. His repartee sank to a low I could only attribute to our talking about chicken guts just as he swallowed his second half of the chocolate candy bar. He muffled a stutter. "Now that could be a problem. What do you have in mind? What's the plan?"

He tried to sound in control but his mind was failing him.

Our president scrunched her nose up, her imagination smelling the air a few times (for warm chicken guts), and flipped what was left of her candy bar up over her head, loping it behind her.

I tried to gather my thoughts.

They were nowhere to be found.

Mary said, "How about the plan is that Jerry goes and tells Mr. Pitts what we're supposed to be up to—murder—but that we want to just go play in his barn all day instead, pretending, while we think of something to tell his dad why we didn't? Jerry tells him we aren't going to murder anything, and that's final."

Bases and Barber said in unison: "Perfect!"

It sounded like a perfect stall.

I rallied. "Holbrook and I will walk to Hastings' store and buy some chickens and geese that are ready to cook. No one will ever know," I said.

"You're all geniuses," said Holbrook, wadding up the candy bar wrapper and tossing it over his shoulder.

I knew the integrity of this adventure was a little cloudy, so I asked, "Who's in?"

Everyone spat.

"But where do you get the money to buy them?" asked Barber.

"We'll walk to the store now. I'll tell Mr. Hastings my dad wants to surprise Mr. and Mrs. Holbrook and their eleven kids, wants to order enough chickens and geese for the holidays, and that Holbrook and I can pick them up in two weeks. We'll ask him if he'll put them on Dad's store charge account."

"But that won't be telling the truth," said Mary.

That minor detail had never deterred us from executing a brilliant idea in the past. "I know," I said, "but this is a life or death situation, and it calls for a really big fib. 'Sides, Mom will understand and be on our side. She hates violence of any kind."

"Bull tacky! If your mom finds out you lied, we will all get our butts whupped but good," said Barber.

"Oh, she'll kill us," I admitted, "but at least she'll understand. Besides, who here wants to be pulling the guts out of a lot of dead chickens and geese?"

Not a hand went up. No one spat.

Bases leaned down, picked up the remnants of Mary's candy bar, flicked a stone chip and a dead pine needle off it, and popped it in his mouth.

"Good thinking, this is some really good thinking," Holbrook murmured, still holding his stomach. "Let's get going."

We all started the quarter-mile walk towards Delphi Falls, taking turns kicking a pebble down the road. This sort of thing helped concentration if a person had a lot on their mind, and right then, we had a lot on our minds.

We were about to have an adventure which was going to be bootstrapped by a fib. That alone could very well have landed us all in very big trouble. Every time one of us mentioned that we should maybe think some more about this before we did it, someone would say something like, "I wonder what chicken guts feel like when you pull them out?" Or someone else would add, "I wonder how hot guts smell?" and we would kick the pebble a little farther than the last time so we could get there faster and get this over with. We were in a situation where we had convinced ourselves we were on the right side of a thin line between right and wrong.

The bell on the store's paint-chipped wooden door jingled. Mr. Hastings, without looking up to see who was walking in, said, "Be right with you after I carry this bag out to the car for a customer.

When he came back in and closed the door, Holbrook and I explained to him what we needed for the holidays, as a surprise for my dad. Mr. Hastings scratched the two-day whisker growth on his cheek and said, "Yes, I can have ten chickens and four geese ready for you in two weeks. Want me to call your mom or dad to tell them when they are ready?"

Like a solemn High Mass church choir, everyone shouted together, "Oh, no!"

Holbrook added, "And if they come in, please don't say anything!"

Knowing just about everyone believed a girl, our president took control. "Jerry and Holbrook will come and get them in two Tuesdays."

"We want to surprise my dad and mom, show them how responsible we can be," I added.

Mr. Hastings smiled over at his wife, who was stacking acorn squash on a table, sizing us all up out of the corner of her eye. Mr. Hastings mentioned to her that—wasn't it nice?—our helping two families celebrate a joyous holiday season was such a wonderful gesture. He told us how proud he was of how grown up we were acting as he unwittingly became a conspirator to our scheme. He told us all to help ourselves to a free crème sickle.

Mr. Hastings was now a part of our deception, unbeknown to him.

Mrs. Hastings just stared at us all as if she had an inkling we were up to something. She'd heard stories about Easter rabbits and free candy. She'd seen Mary pedaling her popsicle cart around Delphi Falls.

There was a simple rule that the more people we involved in our mischief, the more likely we'd get off with a talking if the law caught us—but for certain a whupping if we ever got caught by any of our parents. We knew this from experience, but we couldn't be distracted. The Pompey Hollow Book Club had chickens and geese to save.

That night something new was in the brisk air outside. It turned colder than a big block of ice in a washtub filled with Kool-Aid. I didn't like the shrill windy sounds that came with it. When it got pitch dark with hardly a moon, the winds kicked up into a new mean personality. The trees up the steep hill were moaning and howling, drowning out the noise from the crashing waterfalls. It was enough to curdle your blood. I looked around the living room for something to crawl under in case I had to hide quickly. Even Ginger, our outdoor dog, had somehow snuck in and cowered next to Mom's footstool. Mom just sat under a lamp reading her book, just as if nothing was happening.

This all started after dark, about the same time I turned the living room radio on to listen to a murder mystery. While the radio was warming up, a low branch of a big tree on the side hill up by Dick's tree house started clawing down on the roof of the house over the laundry room like it was raking leaves off the roof.

Dad was somewhere on bakery business. Tomorrow was only a half-day at school, so Dick was staying in Fabius at Duba's.

Mom was sitting in her easy chair, smiling, reading a book about the Von Trappe family and how they sang together.

I was lying on the living room floor, nearly scared to death from the noises outside and from the radio show. I was listening to a chilling murder mystery program with shrieks and creaks of iron doors, shootings, stabbings, and black bats in the belfry looking for blood. Every time I heard a scream through the radio speaker, I would look around to see if anyone was in the room, sneaking up from behind. The wind outside, howling through the trees, didn't help. Every scream would give me a new layer of chills. I'd spin my head back around, look at the glowing radio dial, and convince myself it was only my imagination.

One thing was certain, as soon as "Death at the Haunted Mansion" was over, I was going to bed. It was about to give me a heart attack. There is only so much a boy can take, surrounded by screams, high winds, and cold dark woods at night.

Then it happened:

Zzzzzzap … pop!

The whole inside of the house went black.

All the lights went out; the radio went off; everything electric that made noise, like the icebox, stopped. The house was pitch black, and as quiet as the city morgue in the radio program.

This can't be good! I thought.

My heart skipped a beat as I gulped, "Mom!?"

"Looks like a fuse is blown," said Mom very calmly.

I had no idea where she was now, because I couldn't see her anymore. It was easy enough for her to stay calm. She was a mother and wasn't listening to "Death at the Haunted Mansion" on the radio.

"Can people come out of a radio, Mom?" I asked in the dark.

It was one of those questions you asked and, almost before you got it all out of your mouth, you realized how dumb it was. But I wasn't thinking clearly in the dark. I thought there had to be some coincidence in my just listening to someone's bone-chilling scream through the radio—from a haunted mansion—and suddenly all our electricity going out, leaving the house dark, right in the middle of the scream.

"Don't talk nonsense, dear. I'll see if we have some candles. We'll change the fuse, if I can find the fuse box, that is. I knew where it was in Cortland, but I'm not so sure about this house."

I was on my hands and knees, feeling my way along the living room wall towards the hall to the bathroom, when Mom dropped the bomb on me: "Jerry, we're going to have company all weekend with Mike's friends coming from college, so we'll need eggs. Walk to Mr. Pitts's and get a basket of eggs, dear."

"Okay, I'll put the basket by my bed and do it when I get up in the morning."

"Tonight, Jerry, you have school in the morning."

"What? When!? I always walk and get eggs on Saturday, Mom."

"Right now, dear, while it's on my mind. Stay where you are. I'll bring you the basket."

"Are you serious?"

"Of course, I'm serious. Why would you ask such a question?"

"This is crazy!"

"Don't be impudent."

"Mom, I can't even see you, much less the basket. It's even darker outside. How am I going to find Mr. Pitts's house?"

I could hear the wind picking up, through the dark and trees outside, inviting me outside to the sacrifice.

"The stars will light the road," Mom said. "I'll wait up for you to get home. Off you go."

She nearly stumbled over me while I was trying to stand up in the dark. I grabbed the basket she was holding, just to keep from falling over again. I knew if I tried to talk my way out of this, Mom would give me the "You're the oldest boy here, so you're the man of the house tonight—the eggs are your responsibility" talk.

This talk could sometimes go on for days, so I took the basket, which wasn't my egg basket—it was my Aunt Kate's sewing basket with a broken handle and a big hole in its upper left side scratched through by Mittens, the cat, sharpening her claws. Mom emptied it every time she needed more eggs than usual, because it held more than my egg basket.

I had fun going to see Mr. Pitts, playing in his barn—in the daylight. It was a small barn. He didn't have electricity. It had a stable for his horse, Nellie, and one for his one cow, Bessie. It always reminded me of Christmas. A kerosene lantern hung flickering on a post between the stables, and another hung on the post by the side door that led out to the chicken coop. The barn always had a glow, with the golden straw on the floor, the hay hanging over the loft above, and the bright golden yellow and orange "harvest" corn in the wooden manger bin with the chicken wire sides, set in the middle of the barn. Mr. Pitts called it his "cow corn" because it was stacked and tied standing in the field at harvest time for the sun and air to dry it on the stalk. Then the ears got chopped into two- and three-inch cobs by hand. Bessie ate the cobs all through the winter when there was snow covering the thick green pasture. Against the wall there was a horse-drawn carriage. It had a leather bridle and harness neatly lying in the back of it, behind the seat. He would hitch Nellie up to pull him in it to Hastings' store in Delphi Falls, or other places he needed to go. The chicken coop was next to the barn.

One time I asked Mr. Pitts why he didn't have electricity or a car.

"Well, long as I got matches, a good tooth to strike 'em on, a lantern will do me fine," he'd say. "Ol' Nellie has some good years left in her, too. More than me, prolly. Why would I want to learn to drive one of them jalopy cars for, anyhow? I seen 'em in the big un"—he meant World War I—"and had no use for 'em then, neither. Well, it weren't a big war like the War we just had.

You and your pals saw a bigger one, that's for sure. Well anyway, give me a horse."

Then he would spit his "tabackee" with a *patooooie* sound, wiping his chin with the back of his hand.

Everything Mr. Pitts ever said to me made perfectly good sense—especially on this particular evening. I felt my way along the front hallway wall in the dark to our front door and my possible demise. I mumbled, "If we at least had a kerosene lantern like Mr. Pitts, I could see; if we had a horse and buggy like his, I would be safer getting there. Horses can see in the dark."

"Don't dally, young man. No stalling. Here, put this sweater on."

Without so much as a spark of light to guide her throw, Mom hurled a wool sweater at the very last sound she heard—my voice. It sailed through the darkness like a warning storm cloud and landed squarely in my face.

"Say hello to Mr. Pitts. Don't keep him up late talking. Mr. Pitts has been sick, and your dad's been taking him to a hospital for checkups in Rochester. But don't mention it. Go to bed as soon as you get home. Tomorrow's a school day for you and he's not been well lately."

With an aim like that, who would argue with her?

It wasn't a full moon like it was in "Death at the Haunted Mansion," it was a quarter moon, so I could see the parts of the road and driveway that would reflect its light. The trees next to the house and the woods all down the road were pitch black and daring me; their branches creaked and moaned, the leaves making all sorts of noises, like something wild was running through them. I didn't know these woods.

This can't be good.

I walked almost as fast as I could down the driveway without tripping in puddle holes. I could have walked faster, but I wasn't totally convinced I wouldn't turn on a dime between strides and head back to the house. I made it to the end of the driveway and to Cardner Road. This part wasn't too bad because, way down at the corner, there was a house on the left (where pretty Linda Oats lived) and one on the right where the Burlingame sisters lived. Both houses had lights on. All I had to do all the way to the corner was stare at the lights and keep telling myself I was almost there.

Reaching the corner, I could hear the wind howling through the broken windows of the old cider mill barn next to Linda's house. A shutter clacked back and forth, slapping the outside wall like an angry iron skillet. I had to turn right to go up the hill. Looking up the hill, I suddenly remembered how steep it was, even only halfway up it, to where Mr. Pitts lived. Somehow it looked steeper in the dark. I stood still, near freezing, staring up the hill, wondering if Mom would ever believe me if I told her there were no eggs, if I just turned around and went back home. Not only were there dark, noisy trees on both sides of this hill, all the way up, they were so big they blocked out any chance of moonlight for the entire hill. It was like a black cave that went up. It was getting very serious.

I started up.

I somehow managed to get up to Mr. Pitts's dirt drive. Against my better judgment, I stepped on it and walked in very slowly, approaching his front door. There were no lantern lights in the barn or in the house. I could hear the geese honking in the barn, warning me to leave, to go back where I came from, and I wouldn't get hurt. I hoped he was home, because I hated the thought of going into the chicken coop in the dark alone to find the eggs, especially with no light, from under chickens who didn't want people taking their eggs in the middle of the night, and with a rooster and geese who wanted to protect all the chickens.

None of this was looking good.

I stepped up onto the wooden porch of the small unpainted two-and-a-half-room house and knocked on the window of the front door.

Nothing.

I pressed my face up to the glass, trying to see through what appeared to be a doily lace curtain behind it.

It was dark inside.

I knocked again.

Nothing.

Then I saw a match-spark ablaze, and a small glow of light got bigger and started to move a shadow on the wall inside. I knew Mr. Pitts had lit a match, and then a lantern. There was a warm golden look in the room. My heart started beating again. I could see his face coming closer to the door. He held the lantern high ahead of him, making his shadow bouncing on the floor and wall behind him look like a monster. He was wearing a long flannel nightshirt and a sleeping cap flopped over his ear, like the father wore in the storybook about the *night before Christmas and all through the house.* His shadow moved from wall to wall as he walked to the door. It was like a haunted house filled with ghosts. I knew they were his shadows, though, so that was fine.

He pulled the lacy door curtain aside delicately with stubby callused fingers and peered out through the glass at me—then opened the door and said, "I wondered if Mrs. Antil would be wantin' eggs for the weekend—I been 'specting ya, son."

He handed me his lantern, stepped back inside, and lit another for himself. He pulled his boots on, came out, and led me to the chicken coop.

"Yes, sir," I answered. "It's just that there's no car at home for a ride, so I had to walk, and company coming."

"Walking is good fer ya. Ya oughta get a horse," he chuckled.

He opened the coop door and walked through first. The coop was about half the size of my bedroom. One wall was stacked with thirty square wooden apple crates on their side, floor to ceiling, with straw in each for a nest. There was a chicken nesting in every one of them, murmuring cantankerous morning cackles under their breaths, wondering why the early wakeup.

He put his hand under every chicken, one at a time, and never stopped talking to me, like we were sitting in a barbershop.

"If you *coop* the chickens, son, this is how you collect your eggs. You're the boss, just reach under them quick-like. If you *free range* them, you have to learn where they scatter the eggs, but they will lay the same place every time. You have to beat critters to the eggs free range or they'll eat them. Early morning is the best time."

He took one, sometimes two eggs from the nests of sleepy chickens that never moved and handed them around his back to me to put in the basket.

One egg he handed around was as heavy as a rock. He turned around to catch my eyes, giggled as I looked at the make-believe egg, and took it back. He held it up to his lantern for me to get a good look at it.

"This here one is made from *alabastard*. A new chick thinks it's a real egg, and while trying to hatch it, it puts her in a way and she starts laying her own." He put it back under the chicken.

"If you free range, always remember they sleep high at night and lay low at day. Fences, trees, rooftops, on about anything high enough up to sleep safe."

"What's free range?" I asked.

"S'when you let them free all day and all night, spread the seed for them to peck and scratch at. No feeder. It's more natural for them. I don't have the space—too close to the road."

"Do you like to eat chicken, Mr. Pitts?"

"I eat ham, bacon, and chops. I eat butter, eggs, and cheese. I eat apples and vegetables. I don't ask nuthin' more from a chicken than their eggs. I swallow more tabackee than I care to."

"Mr. Pitts, my dad wants me and my friend Holbrook to come help you murder chickens and geese, but we don't want to hurt any of them. Can all my friends come here and mess around in the barn and just pretend we did? We can get some from the store instead. Can we, Mr. Pitts? Please?"

Mr. Pitts paused, turned around slowly, lifted the lantern. He could tell my eyes looked serious and I wasn't just trying to get out of a chore.

"I'll have to think on that one, son. Mr. Antil is 'specting me to do it. I'll have to think on that one, son. Give me a day. Lemme think on it."

He turned away from me again.

I didn't know why, but I had a feeling Mr. Pitts knew Dad had asked me to help him butcher the chickens and geese. I had a feeling he was telling me all about chickens because he knew the chickens, geese, and ducks would maybe come to our house someday, and he wanted me to know how to watch after them. He may have been getting too sick to watch them. I wasn't sure.

"You like the woods yet, son? Your daddy tells me you like it more than when you first come."

"I like the woods a lot. Not like tonight, though. Best if I can get up there in the daylight and build a fire before it gets dark. Me and Holbrook sleep out. I do alone sometimes. Don't like the big cold winds, though. It's scary with the cold winds."

"Nights like this is for critters," he said.

I didn't need to hear that.

In no time at all the basket was full and we backed out of the coop. He saw to it the door and the gate were closed and latched tight.

"That ought to do ya through the weekend," he said. "On that other thing, come see me after school tomorrow, son."

He took the lantern from me and turned away.

Then he added, "We've had a fox or two lately. Sneaky critters they are. Show 'em who's boss."

I knew foxes liked to get at chickens—and knowing there were maybe foxes somewhere around was not something I wanted to hear, especially tonight ... I still had to walk all the way home.

"Thanks, Mr. Pitts. Good night."

Just as I put my foot on the dark road in front of his house, I heard his door close. I looked around and saw he had blown out the lanterns, and had probably gone back to bed already.

The basket was bulky, so I swung it at my side by its wobbly handle to keep balance as I walked. I started on my way back down the very steep hill.

Something was different. I noticed the wind had stopped, and there were no strange or spooky noises in the woods ... on either side of the road.

It got still.

It got way too still all of a sudden.

Then, from behind me—

Ka-chop!

I froze in my tracks. My heart pumped like a Model A. Something was following me. Was it a fox's paws jumping into the middle of the road? Was it a wild-eyed screaming owl stretching open its claws for a new kill and dropping a snake from its beak on the road in favor of the eggs it saw in my basket?

I started to walk faster.

Ka-chop!

My walk became the fast walk people do in a manner they think disguises fear. Its general purpose is to get away without appearing like it is. Down one of the darkest and steepest hills in the area I went, at a speed which was not smart.

Ka-chop! Ka-chop!

That was enough for me … no time to be smart now … every boy for himself!

I began running so fast down the hill I nearly stumbled at the bottom just trying to slow down. Trying to turn myself left, at full speed, in order to go back up Cardner Road, I could feel my feet sliding inside my P.F. Flyers like they were three sizes too big.

Ka-chop! Ka-chop! Ka-chop!

Louder and closer!

God—I promise to clean my room every week—God, I promise to do anything my mom says—Oh, God—please don't let it catch me.

Running faster than even Superman could without leaving the ground didn't seem fast enough. I could hear my loud heavy breathing and feel my heart pounding all the way through my ears. The thought occurred to me to drop the basket, but for some reason I held it tighter, swinging it even more quickly. My sneakers slapped echoes on the pavement.

Ka-chop! Ka-chop! Ka-chop!

Then it stopped.

There were no more noises.

It happened that fast.

Nothing was chasing me anymore.

But I didn't dare slow down.

"Thank you, God," I panted.

Still running full-out, I figured I was either safe from it now or it was ahead of me, waiting to ambush me, and nothing much else mattered.

I leaped up the front steps and ran inside and dropped the basket on the dining room table, which had a candle glowing on it. I could hear Mom on the telephone talking to Dad, asking him where the fuse box was.

I personally had had more than any one boy could stand in one night; I went to my room, took my sneaks off, got under the blanket with my clothes and socks on, and covered my head. I figured even living through the night would be a miracle. Whatever it was out there chasing me now knew where I lived.

What else could possibly happen?

Mom woke me up in the morning; I got ready for school quickly. I decided to keep all of last night to myself. By not telling anyone about it, it might go away like a bad dream. I didn't know what had been chasing me. All I knew, it was fast, and must have been huge.

The school bus stopped. When I got on, Mr. Skelton looked me over as if he knew something wasn't just right about me but he couldn't put his finger on it, like I was a little green.

If he only knew what I had been through, he would have understood.

I sat down in the very first seat, right behind the door of the bus because it was empty. I grabbed the rail in front of me with both hands, to steady my nerves. The bus started down Cardner Road.

"What on earth? Wonder what that is?" said Mr. Skelton.

He hardly ever talked while he drove.

I looked out the front window to see what he was looking at.

"Looks like broken chicken eggs," he said. "Why, they're everywhere. My goodness! Did you ever? Well I never."

I rubbed my eyes and looked again. Broken eggs— a row of them, in a straight line right straight up the middle of the road.

It was my eggs, I thought to myself. It was the eggs that were making the noise, and nothing was chasing me last night.

I laid my head down forward on the rail in front of my seat, and buried my forehead on the backs of my hands. How could I be in school and so lame-brained at the same time? I couldn't believe I could be such a dunce.

"I wonder how they got there?" I said back to Mr. Skelton, using a Hardy Boy diversionary technique.

I hoped he'd just drop the subject and wouldn't open up a whole conversation about it. Sometimes conversations led to the truth, and I wasn't ready for that.

Later that day, when the school bus dropped me and Dick off, Dick walked in the driveway toward the house and I started walking down the road to go talk with Mr. Pitts about Thanksgiving, like he had asked. As I looked down the road, I could see his buggy turning the corner and heading up Cardner Road, riding full trot. I stopped on the side of the road and waited for his wagon.

He said, "Whoa!" and Nellie came to a stop, bouncing her head up and down a few times, enjoying the run in the brisk air. Holding the leather reins in his left hand, he reached down to the floorboard, lifted a wicker basket filled with eggs, and handed it out to me.

I could tell in his smile, he knew the trouble I may be in.

I took it and stepped back from the buggy.

"Hold on, son," he said. He leaned down again and picked up a burlap bag with a bailing twine bow tying it closed. He handed it out to me and said, "I'll do it. I'm thinking this Sunday is good to bring your friends by. I'm too old to get in too much trouble. Merry Christmas, son."

He didn't say another word. He winked a smile at me and told his horse, "Giddyap!" then turned the wagon into our alfalfa field so he could pull around and head back down Cardner Road.

I shouted: "Thanks, Mr. Pitts."

He waved his arm, turning around, tilted the visor of his wool cap, smiled, and said, "It's Charlie, son. Call me Charlie. Merry Christmas."

He clicked a *ktch, ktch* with his mouth, slapped the reins down gently on Nellie's behind, and off she trotted.

When I got into the house and put the eggs in the kitchen, Mom asked, "Does Mr. Pitts need more chicken feed?"

She was assuming the lack of eggs last night was a nutritional thing.

"Maybe," I said. I went to my room and looked at the bag. It had a tag made from the back of a piece of an old wall calendar he had cut out. On it he had written "To Gerry, from Charlie."

I knew he'd spelled my name wrong from the Christmas card my folks sent out once where the printer spelled my name wrong on it. It wasn't Thanksgiving yet, much less Christmas, but I decided to open the bag. I was amazed. Charlie gave me a hunting knife and holster, two long turkey feathers, and a World War I water canteen with cook pot attached. There was a lantern in the bag, a bottle of kerosene, and a box of stick matches. These great gifts that once belonged to Charlie put me in the Christmas spirit right away. I sat at my desk, wrote him a thank you letter, walked out, and put it in the mailbox.

CHAPTER SIXTEEN

A PEEK AT DEATH

Late Friday night I was restless. I didn't know why. I couldn't sleep, I couldn't read, and I didn't feel like listening to the radio.

I got up off my bed, grabbed my knapsack and the bedroll from my closet shelf, and snuck down the hall in the dark and out the front door. There was no wind. The air wasn't cold. I decided to go up to my camp on top of the cliff across the creek. I walked out to the swings and sat in one of them, thinking. Should I walk down through the alfalfa field and up to my camp the back way and keep dry, or should I cross the creek here and climb the cliff, the shortcut way up by the big white rock? Or should I just go back to bed?

I remembered the lantern Charlie gave me, ran in, got it, lit it, and made my decision.

The icy cold creek water on my legs reminded me I hadn't filled my canteen at the house. I stopped in the middle of the creek, took it out of my knapsack, unscrewed its cap, bent down, and dunked it under the water in the brook until I could hear the air bubbles as it was filled. I screwed the top back on, slid it into my knapsack, and put it on my back for the climb up the cliff.

At my camp I laid out my bedroll and hung the knapsack and lantern on a tree limb. I walked around gathering branches, twigs, and leaves, and started a fire. I stacked some larger logs, to keep it stoked all night. I blew out the lantern. Sitting by the fire and watching the warm glow of my camp was one of my favorite things to do now that I was getting used to the woods.

I leaned back on my bedroll covered up, and looked up at the stars through the trees.

I fell asleep.

I woke at dawn and sat up, stirred what was left of the fire with a stick, listened to the birds, and watched a chipmunk running around the base of a tree and keeping a careful eye on me. I drank some water.

I put my hands together to blow a mourning dove call.

"Whoo ... eee ... who ... who ... who ..."

"Whoo ... eee ... who ... who ... who ..."

It wasn't long before a dove landed close to me and walked about, looking for where the sound had come from, listening for another call.

"Whoo ... eee ... who ... who ... who ..."

"Whoo ... eee ... who ... who ... who ..."

I hadn't brought eggs. I had my can of Spam but I didn't want to open and waste half of it. I decided I'd just drink my water now and go walking along the top of the cliff by the upper waterfall. I'd watch for animals, and eat when I went back down to the house. I walked and finished off my canteen of water.

Back at camp, I put handfuls of dirt over the fire, smothering it out before I left. I packed up and headed back down to the house the way I'd come up last night, down the cliff hillside. I got down as far as the white rock and rested on it a minute. I wasn't feeling good all of a sudden. Something wasn't right. Sweat beaded on my forehead, and I never sweated like that. I slid further down the cliff, to the edge of the creek, and stood up straight. All of a sudden, something slammed me, and I had a sharp cramp that felt like I'd been punched in the stomach. I bent over and braced my hands on my knees a second before I could straighten up again.

When I looked at the stream, I noticed dead fish floating by in some foam. My first thought was that they'd been killed by an animal, maybe a muskrat. I had never seen anything like that before. I started to wade across; in the middle, two more dead fish floated by, and then six more, all floating downstream in the foam. I crossed quickly, threw my knapsack up on the bank, and crawled up, looking back over my shoulder at the water.

From the top of the bank, I watched hundreds of dead fish floating downstream in the foam. I doubled over with another sharp stomach cramp.

"Ayiiieee!"

This time, I ran into the house as fast as I could.

"Mom, Dad, come quick, you have to see this!"

Dad was gone to work, but Mom walked out from the kitchen. Mike ran out of his room.

"Hurry!"

I opened the back door and led them to the side of the creek.

"Oh, my Lord!" said Mom.

"Something's killing them!" yelled Mike. "Some chemical."

There were dead fish floating down the creek everywhere you looked. Then I had another stabbing stomach cramp, and bent forward almost to my knees, nearly knocking the wind out of me. This time I was holding my stomach.

"Ayiiieee!"

"What's wrong, Jerry?" Mom asked.

Mike thought quickly and shouted, "Jerry, did you drink from the creek!?"

Still bent over, I told him, "Last night I'd filled the canteen from the creek and drank it all this morning instead of eating."

"Mike," said Mom, "you get in the car right this minute and drive Jerry to Dr. Morrow in Cazenovia. Drive carefully, but hurry. I'll call him right now and tell him you are on your way and why you're coming."

Then she said, "Jerry's been poisoned—hurry!"

Mike and I didn't say anything the whole trip to the doctor's. I could see his worried eyes. I kept thinking about the dead fish.

When we got to Dr. Morrow's house, Mike stopped short and parked by the side nearest the door to his office and jumped out. The doctor was waiting by the door and took me right into his examining room, telling us that after Mom called him, he called the sheriff, who told him that a new employee at the dairy in New Woodstock had accidentally spilled the cleaning chemicals and ammonia they used to clean their dairy equipment into the creek. He asked me how much I drank, and if it was from last night's water or this morning's. He said last night's would have been very dangerous. He said that last night's water would have had more chemicals and ammonia in it, and I needed to try to get it out of my system. When I told him it was from last night, but I only drank it this morning, he broke three eggs into a glass and made me drink them down, raw.

"This will help you throw up," he said. "Throwing up will help get the poison out."

I threw up right away. I threw up two times, in fact. His phone rang, and someone told him the ammonia in the stream was killing all the fish. He told the caller they should quickly warn the farmers along the creek for at least twenty miles, tell them to keep their livestock away from the stream, and families, too. He told Mike that I would be very sick, but I should be okay since I drank it this morning and it hadn't had a chance to work through my whole system yet.

"Keep an eye on him, and make him rest twenty-four hours. Most of the fish probably died closer to the dairy, which was a mile or so above the lower falls."

Mike drove me home, and Mom made me lie on the couch.

I kept throwing up in a pot all day and early into the night. I wondered if I was going to die, like the fish.

Dad sat up tall in the chair near the couch all night, making sure I was okay.

I woke up while it was still dark out and ate some cereal. I felt good. Dad had already gone to work.

Later in the morning, Dick and I were on the ground by the barn garage tossing acorns and talking about the dairy and the trouble they were in for killing all the fish. Dick was lying on his back, one foot on the ground with his knee bent, the other leg resting across that knee. He was throwing acorns into the air and watching where they landed, studying their trajectory, he would say.

Dad's car pulled through the gate, up the drive, and around behind the swings. He got out, took some things from the back-seat, and started towards the house.

"How you feeling Jerry, me boy?" he shouted. "Who wants to go fishing, and then to Carthage and stay all night?" Dad's bakery had opened another bakery up in Carthage, in northern New York, near Watertown, where the plane had flown me that time.

He didn't wait for an answer. With Dad, this was known as a warning shout, like an enemy ship that shoots a cannonball over the bow of your ship to get your attention. Dad wanted to give us the *lure* of fishing, and then the proper amount of time to think about it. His strategy was to let us get all the thinking out of the way, so there wouldn't be a lot of wasted time talking on the subject. True adventures were best done on impulse, with very little thought and planning, he would say. Those are the most fun and appreciated—because everything would be a surprise.

Dick said, "I can't go, I have to work."

I looked forward to any adventure with Dad and ran into the house to pack my knapsack. I went to tell Mom, who was in the book den talking to him. Mom was reading about colleges for Mike's master's after he graduated from college, which I didn't understand. She called me over and asked, "How are you feeling, Jerry?"

"I'm good. It's all out of me. I ate a lot of cereal this morning."

She felt my forehead while she asked me to open my knapsack, so she could see what I'd packed.

"Where's the toothbrush and comb?" she prodded. "And put a pair of underwear in there. And some socks. Where's your Baby Brownie camera? And don't forget some film for your camera—I have some in my purse. Take a roll."

Mom was so good at packing.

She told me to have fun in Carthage.

Dad and I walked to the car. Dick was still lying on the ground, throwing acorns in the air, but he managed a wave good-bye.

"We're going to Sandy Pond to catch some sunfish for our supper, maybe a bass or two."

We would get to ride in a wooden rowboat at Sandy Pond, and he always let me row. We traded off like that. I would row, while he sat and untangled the lines of four fishing poles so we could actually fish.

What was great about Dad was he wouldn't just say something like, "We're going fishing," he would say, "We're going to catch our supper!"

What could be more fun than knowing what we were going to accomplish?

"Thanks for sitting up with me, Dad," I said.

Dad looked over at me. "Welcome, Jerry, me boy. Things happen in life. You weren't hurt, that's the important thing. We just have to say our blessings, get past it, and move on—be strong. What say we get past your swallowing down half a creek and getting sick by catching some fish for supper?"

Dad had his work suit on, so I knew that meant we might stop at a few stores along the way. He could see if the bread was fresh and straight on the shelves; and when we went to Carthage, he might have to go into the bakery there to meet someone. In the meantime, though, Dad knew how much I loved rowing, so he started to sing at the top of his voice:

Row—row—row your boat
Gently down the stream
Merrily—merrily—merrily—merrily
Life is but a dream.

I sang along with him a few times, just to get in the adventure mood.

Row—row—row your boat
Gently down the stream
Merrily—merrily—merrily—merrily
Life is but a dream.

When we got to Sandy Pond, he pulled the car around behind the fishing lodge and asked me if I wanted a soda pop.

"No thanks." I told him I would meet him by the boats.

"Pick out a good one," he said.

A good boat was pretty simple to pick out. One with no water in it, which meant it didn't leak; one with two oars that were in good shape; and one with an anchor. Whenever I picked the boat, I always pretended I was the new captain getting aboard. I would introduce myself: "Hello, boat; hello, oar; hello, other oar; hello, anchor; hello, anchor rope; hello, little dragonfly, looking for some food."

It was fun. Of course, if Dick was here, I wouldn't do this ritual—at least not out loud, anyway.

Dad bought coffee and worms in the lodge, came out tucking his tie between two buttons of his shirt, to protect it from getting worm guts on it. I had turned the boat around. He handed me things to put in the back where he would sit: four fishing poles, a tackle box, and a bag of sandwiches.

"Put the sandwiches in front, by you," he said.

One time someone asked him why he always had four, sometimes six fishing poles. "I have kids, they have friends," he said. "With kids and their friends, you need a lot of fishing poles."

Now most people would think that was very thoughtful and generous of him to be prepared, but there was really a smarter reason. Kids drop things, and he needed more poles just to replace the ones we dropped in the lake by accident. Catching fish was never interrupted by a lost fishing pole or two. It was a matter of efficiency.

I rowed us out to a place Dad said was far enough. He dropped anchor and tied the rope to the oar hinge once it hit the bottom. I always liked knowing we were connected to the bottom of the lake. It was like having our world of adventure get bigger somehow.

Dad put a bobber on the lines. That was a ball of cork or a red and white plastic ball, which floated on top of the water, attached to the fishing line. When a fish nibbled on the worm, the bobber would bounce down under. That was when you reeled in the fish. Dad was very good at knowing just when to reel in. Sometimes he would tell me when I had a bite and should reel in.

While we waited for nibbles, Dad talked about Charlie Pitts and how sick he was. He told me the doctors were trying to do everything they could, but he could use our prayers. I said an "Our Father" and a "Hail Mary" to myself while Dad talked, and I promised myself to say a rosary for Charlie when we got back home.

Between the two of us, we caught fourteen sunfish, some perch, and one bigmouth bass, and kept them all for our supper. I asked how we were going to cook them. He explained that the owner of the Imperial Hotel, in Carthage, was a friend of his.

He would cook them for us in the hotel kitchen and eat with us. Every time Dad had to stay overnight on business in Carthage, he stayed at the Imperial Hotel.

Now you would think, by the name, that the Imperial Hotel was a royal palace or something, but it wasn't. It was dark when we got to the street it was on, so it wasn't easy to see it clearly. The streetlamps were lit, so that helped. It was a wood-planked hotel, like a big old haunted mansion, and it looked gray in the dark and had a lot of windows. It was built on a corner, where two streets came to a V, and the front of the hotel came to a V, too.

It had four spooky-looking floors, with sitting porches along two of the floors. One side of the porch, by the front door, had eight wooden rocking chairs. Across the street was a train terminal, with about ten sets of train tracks. Four trains of box cars were parked, waiting for something or someone. I couldn't see any engines, just box cars.

Two old men were sitting on the side porch, rocking away. One was lighting a pipe, and the other was pointing at something and telling the other a story.

When we got to the hotel's front desk, a man took our fish and gave Dad a hotel room key.

"Usual, Mike?"

"The usual," Dad answered. "Mr. Franks, meet me boy, Jerry. Jerry, meet Mr. Franks, the owner of this fine establishment."

"Chief cook and bottle washer is more like it," said Mr. Franks. He shook my hand, and Dad and I went up the stairs in the front of the lobby.

"The usual" meant room number six, on the second floor, with a small porch. Dad told me he liked that room because if the hotel caught on fire, he could shimmy from the porch down the tall white column to the sidewalk below.

"How would *I* get down?" I asked.

"On my back, of course," he answered without a second's hesitation.

Sometimes I could ask some really dumb questions.

Inside number six were two rooms—one was a big room with his bed, and a sink on the wall. The other was a smaller room, with just an old iron bed on a hardwood floor. It was perfect—a first—my own hotel room. We had to share the sink in Dad's room and the bathroom out in the hall. I had a window at both ends of my room. I put the knapsack on my bed, and we went downstairs to the hotel restaurant.

Well, it was more like a bar, but it had tables. In the corner stood a tall cooler, which looked exactly like an aluminum pop bottle with a glass door. It was filled with pop bottles and beer bottles. The top of the cooler came to a point and had a big bottle cap top.

Dad and I pulled up barstools, and Mr. Franks brought out a big platter filled with our fish he had cleaned and pan fried. He gave us plates, forks, knives, and napkins. He stood on the other side of the bar with his plate. The fish was so good. There was a stack of sliced bread on a plate, and Dad told me if I accidentally swallowed a fish bone, I should eat a piece of bread, fast. Swallowing the bread would get the bone down my throat safely.

Knowing we'd caught our supper that very day, at Sandy Pond, was almost as much fun as camping out.

After supper, Dad told me to thank Mr. Franks for cooking up our fish and to get to bed. He said we would get up early and head for home. I told Mr. Franks the fish were great, and thanked him for cooking them, and for the orange pop. He told me we could bring fish any old time, and it would be his personal honor and privilege to get to share them with us. Dad had nice friends, everywhere.

In the night I woke up—just trying to remember where I was—and could hear Dad snoring loudly in the other room. I lay in my bed awhile with my eyes half open, staring out the window at the street lamp and all the moths circling around it to get warm, and thinking what a great adventure I had been on today … and then I fell asleep again.

KAAA-BLAMMMM! KUNK! KUNK! KUNK!

I thought I was having a heart attack. In the dark my whole body flinched—my arms and legs jerked out and grabbed the sides of the mattress. I opened my eyes, looking at the ceiling, to see the ceiling lamp had moved somehow. It had actually moved from where it was. I thought maybe someone crashed a truck, or a train, into the hotel. Dad was snoring, so I knew he was still in his room.

KAAA-BLAMMMM! KUNK! KUNK! KUNK!

This time I knew the ceiling lamp had moved. I could see it. *This can't be good.*

There was not a question in my mind … we were definitely being attacked, from Mars, and monsters, from Mars, were landing on the hotel. I'd heard on radio where it happened in New Jersey once.

KAAA-BLAMMMM! KUNK! KUNK! KUNK!

Now the ceiling lamp looked like it had turned around cock-eyed so the space creatures could crawl through it. I was doomed for sure … I was going to die. I'm going to die, I thought. Please, God, don't let me die.

I could feel the sweat on my face and hands.

Dad was still snoring, so it must have been the people from Mars were afraid of snoring noise … I knew Mom sometimes slept on the couch because of Dad's snoring.

I waited for the final attack—for the ceiling to come crashing in—for the final breath of life I would take when a monster from Mars put me on a giant fish hook and asked Mr. Franks to pan fry me for supper. That's all I remember.

In the morning, I could hear Dad brushing his teeth and gargling at the sink. I first thought about not opening my eyes, in case I was surrounded by Martians. I heard his door open and close. I grabbed both sides of the mattress for safety, opened my eyes, and looked up at the ceiling … then at one wall … then another wall … then the floor. The only thing that had moved during the night was my bed. It had rolled, clear across the floor—with me in it—almost to the other side of the room, and almost completely around in a circle. I got dressed in nine seconds flat, darted out the door and down the stairs two steps at a time. Dad was just starting up the stairs, with a cup of hot chocolate.

"Oh, good, you're up," he said as I came loping down. "Go sit on the porch and drink this while I make some calls, and then we will head home and have a nice breakfast in Watertown, on the way."

It amazed me how loud snoring could save a man's life! I certainly hoped that when I got older, I could snore as loudly as my dad, to keep the aliens from attacking my room in the future.

I took my hot chocolate out to the side porch where the rocking chairs were. The same old man, with the pipe, was in the same rocker he was in last night, and his friend was in the one beside him.

I sat next to him.

"Morning, son."

"Morning, sir."

"Sleep well, son?"

KAAA-BLAMMMM! KUNK! KUNK! KUNK!

"Wha-wha-wha-what was that?" I stuttered, my arm jerking my hot chocolate cup and nearly spilling it.

"Son … it's a train yard over there, and that was a train … see? Look—there's one moving, right now."

KAAA-BLAMMMM! KUNK! KUNK! KUNK!

"So *that's* what I heard all night?"

"Son, I'm only going to say this once, because no one is around to listen. A train yard has trains in it, see, and they're supposed to move around, and connect with each other … and yes, when they have a lot of cars attached, they make banging noises."

He smiled at me with a sparkle in his eyes while he started lighting his pipe again. I could see all the empty rocking chairs on both sides of us were rocking, back and forth, back and forth, because of the last train's connections—*ka-blammm!*

The old man watched my eyes looking at the chairs rocking, and he leaned toward me, like he was going to tell me a big secret, and whispered, "Ghosts."

He leaned back in his chair, puffed on his pipe, began to rock, and with a twinkling in his eyes, he winked.

We got through downtown and were driving out of Carthage on Route 11 to Watertown to have breakfast before we headed home. We were listening to Arthur Godfrey talking about Lipton's soup on the radio. I was thinking of the rocking chairs at the hotel.

Dad kept looking over at me, with something on his mind (I could tell), and then he would look back at the road. He reached for the radio knob, turned it off, and said, "Son, Charlie Pitts died this morning. I know he was your friend, so I thought you should know. The sheriff called me at the bakery."

He stopped talking and looked over at me.

I stared up at him, stunned in disbelief. I let what he said sink in, and turned my head straight forward again when it finally hit me. I stared down at the floor of the car. Tears flowed on their own from my eyes. My cheeks grimaced as my lips tightened.

"They found his cow loose on the road, took it back to his place, and found him on the ground at the gate to his field."

"Bessie," I whimpered.

Dad looked at me and said, "We'll drive straight home, okay, son?"

I couldn't stop the tears. My mouth hurt now. I couldn't see through my eyes.

"He had a heart attack. Just keeled over."

Dad touched my hand with a folded handkerchief. I took it.

I looked up. "Did it hurt?

"I don't think so, son. God took him quick."

My voice cracked and wobbled. "Charlie was my friend, Dad."

"I know, son. I know. The sheriff said there were some things in a sack in his house. Charlie had written your name on it, so they are holding it for you."

"He did?" I asked.

"Charlie thought the world of you. He thought of you as a son. He lost his own boy in the First World War. You reminded him of his son."

He added, "They're boxing up the chickens, geese, and ducks and taking them to our place and putting the feed in the small barn. You want to help take care of them?"

"Charlie told me how."

"Should we build a coop for them?" asked Dad.

"No." But I didn't want to talk for a while so I didn't say any more.

Neither did Dad.

He didn't say any more until I was ready.

I thought of old Charlie and his old barn that always made me think of Christmas because it had bright golden straw everywhere that glowed like a Christmas card. He had one cow, one horse, and not much else. I remember it shined even brighter at night if he hung a kerosene lantern on a post when he had to milk his one cow or do some work.

Then I thought—Charlie knew he was going to die. That's why he kept saying "Merry Christmas."

When we got to Tully and turned onto Route 80 towards home, I said, "We can range them, Dad. I know how."

As we drove through the gate, Mom and Dick were throwing chicken feed around by the small barn, and the chickens were getting used to the place. The geese ran right at the car and chased us up the driveway and around behind the swings.

I wanted to be alone so I went to my room. On my bed was a burlap bag with bailing twine around the top. It had a scissor-cut back of a calendar page attached to it, like the last one, where Charlie had written "Gerry."

I opened the bag and found another lantern from his house. In a paper sack was a bottle of kerosene, four wicks, and two large boxes of safety kitchen matches. In a small box was a framed picture of Charlie in his soldier uniform in 1891. I put everything on my desk. That night I kept my promise and said a rosary for Charlie.

Every morning after that, I would get up earlier than anyone else and go gather the eggs from all the spots where the hens would nest in the early morning to lay their eggs. It took me a few days to find them all. Once I had, getting eggs in the morning was easy. I would always tell all the chickens, geese, and ducks, "Charlie says hello."

CHAPTER SEVENTEEN

A NEW PLAN

About the time I got comfortable with the chickens and geese, I went into Mom and Dad's room, picked up the phone, and asked Myrtie to get me Barber.

"Isn't it sad about Charlie?" Myrtie asked. "He was such a nice man. He didn't have a phone, but I would see him in church up on the hill sometimes."

"Yes, ma'am," I said. "He was my friend, too."

"Here's Dale, hon. Say hi to your mom."

"Hello?"

"Dale, I need to set up a meeting—the sooner the better. Charlie Pitts died and we need a new plan now."

"Too late for the weekend," Barber said. "How about at lunch tomorrow at school?"

"Yeah. That'll work. Thanks."

"I'll set it up. First one to the cafeteria, save the table," he added and then we hung up.

We all wound up together in the cafeteria line so we met there while we slid our trays.

"They're all at my house now," I told them.

"The coop, too?" asked Barber, picking up his daily tomato soup and Jell-O.

"Nah, they're all free ranged, all over the place," I answered.

"We just have to catch them all and hide them somewhere until after Thanksgiving," said Mary. "That's all we have to do."

"Right!" said Bases, Vaas, Barber, Holbrook, and now the Mayor, who had joined us in line. They all got chili and beans, chocolate pudding, and chocolate milk.

End of meeting.

For nearly two weeks Holbrook, Bases, Barber, Vaas, Crane, the Mayor, and I sat at the same table every day in the school cafeteria, planning how we were going to get all thirty chickens into the barn without anyone seeing us or knowing anything about it.

We decided that Monday night was the right time to do it. We would wait up on the cliff by the big white rock, across the creek from my house, until after dark, for when the time was right, when all the lights in the house went off and everyone had gone to bed and fallen asleep.

I taught them what Charlie had taught me about chickens. We didn't have a chicken coop, but we knew chickens roosted on fences or higher on tree branches at night when they slept; so we decided it would be best to catch them while they were dozing and just carry them one at a time into the barn.

Mary said, "Once they're in there, you'll have to go in every day, Jerry, and see they have plenty of chicken feed and water."

Barber thought Mary was sounding like a mother hen. "Yes, dear," he said with a giggle. Just as soon as he said it, though, he said, "Oh geez," realizing full well he had crossed the line with our president.

Mary reached in front of Bases, picked up Barber's little dessert bowl of Jell-O, and dumped it into his bowl of tomato soup. He got the message.

"The geese are going to be another problem," said Holbrook. "They sleep on the ground at night, but they're too mean to catch by hand. The ducks would pretty much follow you anywhere."

"The only thing we haven't thought of is how everyone is going to get to Jerry's house that Monday night without being seen and then how we get back home," said Randy.

Bases must have been dozing or engrossed in protecting his chili bowl from Mary because he repeated exactly what Randy had just said.

My brother Dick walked past our lunch table.

"Dick!" I shouted, trying to get his attention.

He paused, gave me a look like didn't I know it wasn't cool for older kids in school to talk to younger kids? "What?" he growled as if this better be good.

"This isn't an SOS or anything like that, but we're doing something secret next Monday night and everyone here needs a ride to our alfalfa field after dark for a couple of hours and then a ride back home. Can you get that done?"

"Two shakes," said Dick, and he walked away and over to the lunch table where Duba, Minneapolis Moline Conway, and Dwyer were sitting with some girls. Dick leaned down to their table and talked with them. Each of them, in turn, raised their head up and stared over at us, one at a time, and then lowered it back into conversation. Dick stood back up, turned, and walked over to our table. "We can arrange it," he said, "but you'll have to rake leaves."

I knew this was Dick's chore for Thanksgiving, to rake the leaves, so I said, "No problem, I'll rake the leaves."

"No way," said Dick, "you'll *all* rake leaves. The leaves in Duba's yard, the leaves in Conway's yard, and the ones in Dwyer's yard—all this Saturday—so we can go to Suburban Park before they close it for the winter."

We looked at each other.

"You'll bring us there and wait as long as it takes and bring us all home?" Mary asked.

"Yes."

"Deal," said Holbrook.

"Hold on," said Barber. "We don't want your dad to get suspicious since Mr. Pitts died. The Dubas have chickens. You have to tell your dad you heard Duba is going to help Jerry and Holbrook butcher the chickens and geese."

Dick didn't have a problem with that. Actually he thought it was pretty clever. He said okay and walked away.

Dick and his friends were all fourteen and still didn't have driver's licenses, but their word was their bond. If they said they would do it, they would do it.

On Monday night I closed my bedroom door and went to bed early, opened my window, crawled out, and made my way along the edge of the hill leading up to the woods until I was at the gate. I ran down to the alfalfa field. Duba's dad's big long Lincoln was there already, in the middle of the field, with Dick and Duba in front. I wasn't sure who was in the backseat.

As I walked down into the field, Minneapolis Moline Conway drove in with his dad's 1948 Dodge, with Conway and Dwyer in front. It drove up around next to the Lincoln, stopped, and turned its lights off. Car doors opened all at once. Vaas, Crane, Holbrook, Barber, the Mayor, and Bases stepped out.

"Take off," said Dick. "We'll be here when you get back."

We all ran back to the edge of the hill behind the alfalfa field and climbed up the back way. We moved like a pack of wolves. We were on a mission that could not be denied. We made it up the hill in the dark, pulling each other along when we had to. We made it to the top and then over to just above the white rock on the cliff by my house to rest and plan.

Looking down from the top of the cliff we could see the white rock halfway down and the creek below, and the barns and house across the creek. We made it down to the rock and sat on it and all around it to form a strategy.

"How far do they go from the barn?" asked Dale.

"Maybe twenty feet. Front, sides, and back," I told him. "A lot inside the barn garage are on the suspension wires."

"If they're already in the barn garage, why do we have to catch them?" asked Mary.

"The big barn garage has no doors in front. We have to take them to the small green barn next to it," I said.

"We need catchers and runners, then, or we'll waste a lot of time," said Mary.

"Explain," said Holbrook.

Mary stood up in front of us and lectured. "We need to start with the chickens. Once we start grabbing them, they may get smart and scatter. Half of us need to be catching and handing them off to a runner, who will hold two at a time and run them into the barn."

"I gotta pee," said Bases.

"Well, turn around and do it!" barked Mary. "Don't interrupt."

"I agree with Mary," said Randy. "We should pair up a catcher and runner on each team."

"Let's break the place into coordinates," said Barber. "Team one takes the left of the barn and the back. Team two the inside of the barn. Team three the right side and front."

"Runners, be sure to keep count. We need thirty-one catches," said Mary. "Chickens first, then the geese and ducks."

"Thirty," I said. "We have thirty chickens."

"Thirty-one," said Mary. "You have thirty chickens and one rooster. Thirty-one!"

"I wouldn't tick her off," whispered the Mayor.

He was aware of the cemetery "baseball" incident and the Jell-O flop. How right he was!

After the last light in the house went off, we waited thirty minutes for people to be asleep. As we passed the time, we teamed up, broke off in pairs, and planned our individual attack strategies.

I made the sacrifice: "After we get all the chickens, I volunteer to let the geese chase me into the barn. The ducks will follow them."

Holbrook volunteered to close the door quickly behind me after they were all in.

The time was right. We wished each other good luck and made our way down the cliff to the edge of the creek.

"Oh, geez," whispered Barber. "My ma will shoot me for getting my school shoes wet."

No one much cared.

Mary stepped in first, Randy followed, and then everyone else ceremoniously hopped in and waded across, knowing the sacrifice of a "talking to" was outweighed by the importance of our mission of stopping fourteen murders.

Mary was the runner on her team inside the barn. In the dark she snagged the back of her dress on a nail poking out of a worktable and ripped it considerably. Making the best of the situation, she reached her hands around behind her and tore the dress all the way down through the bottom hem. Lifting it up from both sides and around front like an apron, this let her hold three or four chickens safely in it instead of one in each hand.

Humility had its own reward.

Aside from the black and blue marks I had on my butt and legs from goose bites, and the scratched knee and elbow from falling off a tree branch holding two chickens that were flapping their wings like crazy, I was okay. Holbrook tore the knee out of his jeans while doing a diving tackle on one of the hens at full speed. The hen won. The rooster threatened the lives of both Randy and the Mayor until Randy had the foresight to throw a burlap bag over it. Soon after that, a goose pecked Randy squarely in the behind, taking him a few inches off the ground, as a goose will do, sending him sliding headfirst in chicken and goose poop on the grassy side of the green barn. Holbrook's glasses did fall off in the dark when the rooster broke free from the burlap bag long enough to look him straight in the eye, caw once, and jump up and over him, flying into the barn on its own steam. Barber accidentally stepped on the glasses while sliding, tripped over Randy, and fell in goose poop himself. It pushed a lens out, but they weren't bent all that bad. He could still see out of one side if he held his head at a proper angle. After the geese chased me into the barn, forcing me to land in a wheelbarrow and tip it over, we made the count, closed and padlocked the door with a wooden peg, and hid behind the barn garage trying to catch our breath, looking to see if any blood was coming through our clothing and trying to calm down. Bases had found an empty cotton chicken feed sack in the small barn, pulled it from his belt, and handed it to Mary; she could wrap it around her torn dress with a string to restore her ladylike modesty.

Everything went pretty much as planned.

We spent half an hour in the dark, like chimpanzees, picking feathers off ourselves, our teammates, out of our hair, wondering if the smell would ever come out of our clothes.

"I smell so bad, Ma will never notice my shoes," mused Dale.

"Will you all come to my house the Monday after Thanksgiving and sled?" asked the Mayor. He thought the Pompey Hollow Book Club was inspiring. "Can I join your club?"

"Maybe—if there was snow," everyone affirmed, still flicking specks from their clothing. Randy had a stick and was scraping goose and chicken poop from his pant legs. We were all too busy to explain that joining didn't involve much more than just showing up. The plan for hiding the chickens and geese worked perfectly. Side by side, no one walking downwind, we walked down the drive onto Cardner Road and down to the alfalfa field—as *champions*. The two cars saw us, lights went on ... loaded up quickly with our troops and started to drive off. Just down the road about fifty feet, Duba's long black Lincoln jerked to a sudden stop, screeching its tires, rocking the front of the car up and down while the driver door blew open. David jumped out of the car choking and coughing and wheezing—squeezing his nose and hopping like he had a hot foot and screamed: "OPEN THE GOL-DANGED WINDOWS!"

Randy must have been in his car.

The windows all rolled down. He let it air out a few seconds and got back in and drove away.

I walked back home, climbed through my bedroom window, took all my clothes off, and dropped them out my window to air out on the ground outside.

By late that Monday night before Thanksgiving, there wasn't a chicken or goose to be seen or heard anywhere, thanks to the Pompey Hollow Book Club.

Mr. Hastings had the store-bought fowl right on time as he promised. Holbrook and I walked from the store to the house with them in three big sacks. We put all but two of the geese and five of the chickens in the icebox for when Mom and Dad got home, which would be any time. Holbrook used our telephone to call Tommy Kellish to ask his dad to come get him. Then we both went up the side hill and climbed into Dick's tree house and decided to hide out. We thought it best to stay out of sight in case there were questions. We hated questions, especially when we were guilty. I personally never knew what to say. I would just stand there with my mouth hanging open.

Holbrook would stand there and point at me.

CHAPTER EIGHTEEN

HAPPY THANKSGIVING

On Thanksgiving Day the house was filled with people, which was exciting because we knew Christmas and Santa were not very far away. I had almost completely forgotten about the geese and chickens and was enjoying my second piece of pumpkin pie when Dad called for me to come to the kitchen.

Gulp! My knees buckled.

To me, my dad always looked extremely tall when I thought I was in trouble. Whenever I was guilty, I always thought I was in trouble. He was standing in an apron, serving food to people as they came in for second helpings while Mom poured coffee all around. He stopped serving and turned.

"Jerry, this was a very nice Thanksgiving for everyone, and we all owe a lot of it to you and Holbrook for all the effort you both went through in getting us chickens and geese. Thank you, son."

"You're welcome, Dad," I stuttered.

Then he looked me straight in the eye, smiled a little, leaned down, took my hand, and put seven price tags in my palm—five chicken price tags and two goose price tags.

"Your prices seem reasonable, son—do I owe you for these, or do I owe someone else?"

My life passed before my eyes. Caught! I was caught! Holbrook had left the stupid price tags on. I knew I would get caught.

I fessed up: "We got them from Mr. Hastings."

"I already know, son—the store name is on the price tags, and now you are going to work for Mr. Hastings every Saturday after we come back from the bakery until they're paid for, aren't you?"

"Yes, sir," I replied.

"And Mr. Holbrook is seeing that Holbrook bakes four iced two-layer cakes for Mr. Hastings to sell, to make up for their chickens and geese.

I was so worried I was going to get killed and so bothered by my conscience for lying, I thanked Dad and promised him I would never let him down ever again.

"You didn't let me down, son. I'm proud that you took a stand for something. I suspect the Pompey Hollow Book Club did what they thought was right. You all protected what you thought was important to you. Next time, trust me. I would understand. Now, go let them all out of the barn so they can get some air."

"You knew they were in there, Dad?"

"Happy Thanksgiving, Jerry, me boy."

"Happy Thanksgiving, Dad."

CHAPTER NINETEEN

CHRISTMAS

Waiting for the classroom to quiet down, Mrs. Bredesen walked over to my desk and handed me a pass to go see Mr. Spinner, the band director, during recess. It meant Mom got me out of piano, but who knew what else she'd got me into.

"Good morning, class. It's that time of year again. Who's looking forward to celebrating the Christmas holiday with family or friends?"

Every hand in the classroom went up.

"Now class, what is it I want you all to try and remember? It's always better to …"

Every kid chorused: "It's always better to give than to receive."

"Very good."

That was the starting gun. This little talk was about all it took for every kid in the room to start thinking of Christmas, Santa, and receiving. None of us gave a whit if it was an eighty-nine-cent set of flying ace pilot goggles with the imitation lamb wool ear straps, a box of Lincoln Logs, a tube of Tinker Toys, some modeling clay, or even a book or a record. Christmas and the rustling of wrapping paper were on their way and this was the best time of the year, for any kid. Its diversions even helped us get through five years of a world at War.

Mrs. Bredesen continued, "Now class, the boys and girls who are seniors this year are doing something very special for the families of the boys and girls who graduated before them and lost their lives in the War—the men and women who fought or helped all around the world all through the War. Show of hands if you knew someone who was lost or wounded during the War. It could be a family member, a friend's family member, even someone you knew or just heard about."

Every hand in the room went up.

"As their legacy, the seniors want to have a bronze plaque engraved for the front hall wall of the school. It will be a plaque honoring past students killed or missing during the War. To pay for it, the senior class is going to have a roller skating party at the roller rink down in Cortland the Thursday before Christmas break. Who would like to help?"

Every hand went up. There were probably only two kids in the whole room who knew how to roller skate.

"Now class, the grade that encourages the most children to attend the roller skating party and raises the most money might get their picture in the paper. Let me have your ideas," she said.

One at a time, each idea volunteer stood up with a good idea on how we could get the most kids from our room to go. The ideas ranged from giving roller skating lessons during recess to the kids who wanted to go to the skating party, to guaranteeing anyone who went to the skating party an A in geography or arithmetic, their choice.

When it was my turn, I summoned all the creativity I could muster that early in the morning by thinking about things my dad had taught me riding with him in his car. I stood up. "It's a numbers game," I began. "We need to get the word out. We get us some really important-looking roller skating party identification cards printed—like the Buster Brown Shoe Club cards—advertising the skating party, and then everyone will want one to carry in their wallets and they'll show it off to their friends like they were important or valuable. You know, advertising."

It made sense to all the Pompey Hollow Book Club and some of the other kids. Bases dozed off, plopping his head down on his desk with a thump. I must have said it with such conviction that some of the others thought I knew what I was talking about—which of course I didn't.

"Congratulations, Jerry," Mrs. Bredesen said, "you are the official chairman of our grade's roller skating party attendance promotion for the Senior War Memorial plaque. Good luck. You may select anyone in the class to help you."

Of course, I would pick the Pompey Hollow Book Club—Barber, Crane, Holbrook, and Randy, and Bases if he woke up. I was thinking maybe Judy Finch, and Mary Margaret Cox, too, if teacher insisted I use a lot of kids. These two knew all the girls. I'd think of more if I had to.

By way of notes posted on the bulletin board, the whole class was invited to Mary Margaret's house for a holiday party. Her mother was a teacher. When invitations were posted on the bulletin board our mothers mostly made us go. After Mary Margaret's party there was a party at Mary Crane's to learn how to square dance to the new square dance record Mary got for her birthday.

Mrs. Bredesen turned to me. "Jerry, you may be excused to go to the band room."

Mr. Spinner, the band director, was a nice enough man and always had a smile on his face. He smelled of tobacco and his fingers were brownish yellow from smoking. He enjoyed making jokes, like the time in a band recital when he introduced a piece the band was going to play as "Locked in a Stable with the Sheep" when it was supposed to be called "Rocked in a Cradle of the Deep." Kids didn't always get his jokes, but he would squint his eyes in a grin, prune his lips in a smile, and turn around to conduct his band.

The band room was next to the furnace room on the ground floor. It had windows running the length of the side wall and one in the center of the back wall. There was a glare on Mr. Spinner's glasses at most angles, making him look like a friend of Little Orphan Annie or Daddy Warbucks in the Sunday comics, where they just had white circles for eyes. The band room was filled with rows of bent-wood chairs in a half circle around a conductor's podium in the center.

"Hello, Jerry," said Mr. Spinner, with a big smile. "Come in, take a seat. Your mother called. We'll get right down to business and have you on your way in no time."

We sat down on chairs facing each other.

"Jerry, I want you to tell me all your interests. I will then try to select an instrument to your liking and aptitude."

I assumed if he thought I had a musical "aptitude," he never saw me play piano.

"I like to camp in the woods, ride my bike. I like going to Dale Barber's or the Mayor's house and stacking hay. I like playing king of the mountain in their barns. I like to help Farmer Parker call in the cows. I want a horse. I like the Pompey Hollow Book Club. I like to play Pitch with Holbrook and swim. Swimming's fun ..."

Mr. Spinner hid a yawn with the back of his hand. "Music, do you like music, Jerry?"

"I like listening to it on the radio or at the picture show. Like 'She Wore a Yellow Ribbon,' and sometimes I sing in the car with my dad."

Mr. Spinner squinted his eyes, pruned his lips up in an approving smile, and nodded his head gently. He reached to his side and opened a black carrying case resting on the chair beside him and lifted two parts of a black clarinet from it. He carefully assembled them and asked, "Jerry, how about the woody, some-what dulcet tone of the clarinet?"

I shrugged my left shoulder. "Hokay."

He wasn't happy with my answer.

He pulled the clarinet apart, returned it to its case, and opened another case—this time lifting a trumpet like he was lift-ing a golden crown. He wriggled his eyebrows as if he were about to share a lewd secret and asked, "How about the brassier sharp-ness of the heralded trumpet?—French horn?—a more mellow trombone?"

Again, although this time from the right shoulder. "Hokay."

He was still not convinced, but he wouldn't give up. He wrin-kled his eyebrows, returned the trumpet to its case, placed his fist on his cheek, and tweaked his sideburn with his forefinger, thinking. With his other hand, he pointed to the drums in the back of the room and asked, "How about the simple beat of a drum?"

"Hokie-dokie."

The only musical talent I was aware I had was that I could make a dove call blowing through my hands that attracted doves, and sing some show tunes from movies at the Saturday picture show. To me, playing a musical instrument would be like me removing my own appendix. They were all just pianos in different shapes and sizes.

"Jerry, you're supposed to help me here. Certainly there is a preference in your mind that might stir your imagination. Certainly you have a sense of or feeling toward a particular sound—a spirit—of an instrument. The passion you feel might fit your personality and desire to express yourself through music."

I considered a short nap, sitting up.

"Jerry, hasn't there ever been that single moment in your life—one moment when you expressed yourself with a simple gesture that showed your feelings? You wanted to rejoice and relive it again and again, study it in your mind? You wanted to share it with the world? Certainly there must be one moment in time." Mr. Spinner bent his head, peering over his glasses, in hope. "Think Jerry, think! What was that one point of expression that comes to your mind?"

"When I kissed Linda Oats?"

There was silence.

Mr. Spinner's head dipped, it slumped in defeat, flopped down to his chest, bouncing loosely. Then he lifted his head and glared at me over the tops of his glasses for the longest time. The glare of his glasses sent a flickering of the sun onto my heart like a rifle scope.

Suddenly, magically, his eyes popped white like flashbulbs. He pruned his lips to a smile, thrust his right arm straight up, jumped off his chair, and stood tall as if he wanted to touch the ceiling light in joy. "The tuba!" he shouted.

It was as if he had discovered electricity.

He sat back down with a thunk, smiling and waving both of his hands in the air like he was conducting a full orchestra.

"Tuba wants exuberance, Jerry—tuba needs caring. To be held, and above all else, a tuba needs a great pucker to warm its cold curves, its corners and elegant bold crevices with the breath of warm life that will become a beautiful sound. A tuba needs to be kissed, Jerry! The tuba, it is!"

I was looking to see if the band room door was locked and did the math in my head on how long it would take me to get out it or through the open window.

Mr. Spinner jumped straight up again. This time his feet left the floor, like he'd won a raffle. He hurried to the back of the room through the maze of chairs, his arms conducting, tipping one music stand and letting it fall in his excitement. As it tipped over it took another two with it. At the back of the room he reached around the big sousaphone stand, pulled out the tuba's mouthpiece, and carried it delicately back as though he had retrieved the Holy Grail. He picked up the music stands as he passed them, backing into a chair and knocking it over in the process.

"Jerry, put your lips together—pucker and blow—like this—BblbBblbBblbBblbBblbBblbBblbBblbBblbBblb."

I tried: "Pfffffft?"

"Like this, Jerry—BblbBblbBblbBblbBblbBblbBblbBblbBblbBbl."

"BBBbbbppppffffttt?"

"BblbBblbBblbBblbBBblbBblbBblb, Jerry."

He pressed the cold metal mouthpiece into my palm. It was big enough to be used as a funnel in the kitchen.

"Jerry, take this mouthpiece home and practice; do your BbbBbb lip exercises and blowing techniques. You will begin your tuba lessons tomorrow. Be relentless, young man—purse your pucker … and … welcome to the band!"

I couldn't see through the white glare of his glasses, but it sounded like his discovery may have brought a tear to his eye. He had saved another youth.

I put the mouthpiece in my pocket, tried to hide it with my shirt tail, and went back to my school room.

The word spread through school like wild fire: "Jerry got stuck with the tuba."

When I got home I handed the tuba mouthpiece to Mom. She lifted it to her nose, smelled it. "I'll boil it."

At supper I announced my busy whirlwind Christmas calendar and social season ahead.

"Mrs. Bredesen made me official chairman. I'm in charge of the senior class Christmas roller skating party War Memorial money raiser for our grade. The grade that gets the most kids to go to the roller skating party, and collects the most money, will maybe get their picture in the newspaper. We're going to advertise, of course. We'll win easy—piece of cake. I'm thinking front-page headlines."

I could almost hear the crowd cheering.

Mom set her salad fork down. "Don't be fresh, dear. Speak like a gentleman, not like a big shot. Nobody likes a big shot."

Dad passed a platter of pork chops and looked down the table at Mom with a smile. "Remember our evenings at the roller rink, Mommy?"

Mom smiled back. "I loved the beautiful organ music ... and, my, but you were so graceful in skates," she blushed.

"We certainly could cut a rug, couldn't we?" Dad said. "When's the roller skating party, son? What's the money going to be used for?"

Delighted their walk down memory lane was over, I said, "It's Thursday before Christmas break. The seniors are raising money with a roller skating party so they can pay for a bronze plaque for the students from Fabius who were drafted and killed or lost during the War."

"Worthy cause," said Dad, bowing his head.

"Most worthy cause," repeated Mom quietly. "What thoughtful children; what a wonderful Christmas gift for all the families. What a delightful community spirit that school inspires."

"We're tacking a notice on the bulletin board in our room. You know, Dad, we're going to advertise?"

Dad smiled at my reference to advertising and said, "This is an important event, son. Maybe you should do more than advertise. Maybe you should sell tickets in advance so you'll know how many people are going and how much money you make even before the skating party. You might come up with a way to get store owners to lend a hand, as well."

"We don't have any tickets, Dad. I think kids just pay when they get off the school bus at the rink. But I did have an idea of getting something important-looking printed. Like the Buster Brown Shoe club membership card. Some advertising we could pass out and show everybody. I was thinking something that could fit in a kid's wallet or pocket, like that."

"Son, if you'll write down all the information a printer will need, I'll give it some thought and have something nice printed for your grade to use. We'll donate the printing so your class can do a good job getting kids to go to the roller skating party, won't we dear?"

Mom added, "Don't be a braggart, son. Be a gentleman."

"Gee, thanks, Dad. Thanks, Mom."

I got up from the table, ran to my room, got all the papers with the information about the roller skating party, and handed it all to Dad.

It was nearly three weeks before Christmas vacation. I was immersed in the spirit, woke early, and was sitting on the edge of my bed and looking out my window, thinking of the upcoming happy holiday. All I could see between our house and Farmer Parker's across the way was a brown lawn, wet mud, and patches of crusty, half-melted snow piles. I and every other kid on earth were hoping for fresh white snow soon, a lot of snow.

This Christmas was going to be spectacular, snow or no snow, if I had anything to do with it, I convinced myself. Every week all summer, I'd mowed Doc Webb's lawn, for a dollar fifty each time. He'd always throw in a bag of maple sugar candy.

I had Christmas shopping to do, and a dollar fifty a week added up to a lot more money than I'd seen in one place since the Pompey Hollow Book Club's Easter bunny kidnapping caper's reward money. I never counted what I had, but it stacked neatly on my closet shelf. I only took money from the pile once, to buy a tire patch kit for my bike, as I recall. Oh, then there was the time I bought two rolls of red, white, and blue striped crepe paper. I decorated the spokes on my bike with it so I could ride with the Pompey Hollow Book Club in the Memorial Day parade in Fabius.

I remember asking Mom one time if there was a Santa. She told me straight out, Santa only came for people who believed in him, so that was good enough for me. I still had money left and I was going to be the best Santa's helper ever. He could bring the good stuff, and I'd just pitch in, a little, and get presents for my friends, brothers, and aunts, and for Mom and Dad. I had a special present for Aunt Kate.

CHAPTER TWENTY

SO MANY TO THINK ABOUT

Every Saturday morning I rode to Homer with Dad. Every Saturday Dad took a shiny quarter out of his pocket, and with his thumb flipped it way up in the air so it blurred it spun so fast, high enough to nearly touch the ceiling.

"Call it, Bucky!" he shouted, not taking his eyes off the flying quarter.

"Heads!"

"Tails," reported Dad. Bucky put both his hands on the counter and jumped his legs up sideways, clicking his heels together in the air.

Dad slid the quarter over anyway. "How about an egg and olive sandwich for Jerry, me boy, here—so he has the strength to carry the mail this morning?"

Bucky clicked his fingers. "Gotcha!" and pointed at me with a wink.

My errand for Dad on Saturdays was getting the post office box key from the hook on his office wall, walking across the street, and fetching all the bakery mail back to him. While he opened and read it, I had time to walk to the General Store. This store had all kinds of things to buy, and a pretty decorated Christmas tree just for gazing inside, by the front door. On my first "planning trip" for Christmas, I mostly walked around the

store, looking and thinking about everyone I had to buy for. I
considered it more of a reconnaissance mission. I needed a plan.
I decided I would go home and make a list of names, and what
I wanted to get each. I picked up a roll of wrapping paper. It
had a likeable Santa all over it, with drawings of store-wrapped
presents and candy canes. I bought it and a roll of gold ribbon
to go along with it.

Driving back to Delphi Falls, I asked Dad, "For Christmas, if
I want to tell Aunt Kate I know she's my grandma, will I get in
trouble, Dad?"

"Jerry, that would be a generous, thoughtful, and wonderful
gift. You would never get in trouble for something like that. You
can share it with her, it would please her no end, but it would be
her secret to share with others, can you understand that?"

"Yes, sir."

"You're a good boy, Jerry, me boy!"

Dad happened to look down in my shopping bag, which was
set between us on the front seat.

"What else do you have in mind, son? Anything I can help
you with? I can keep Christmas secrets and I have personally met
Santa Clause three times … well, two times, I'm sure of. I can't
be positive about the third time."

He didn't say anything about the wrapping paper and ribbon
between us. I could tell he knew I was up to something very large.

"I want to help Holbrook have a nice Christmas, Dad. Do you
think Santa will go to his house?"

"I guarantee it, son. I can personally guarantee it."

I knew I could trust my dad, but I knew I needed tighter
security. I needed to get to my desk, make a secret Christmas
shopping list, and plan my shopping. I needed to think and be
organized.

In the matter of security and privacy, my room lacked one
important element—a doorknob. My privacy was at the mercy
of anyone just pushing my door open or closed. It was always
ajar. I think it was a War thing. During the War, people couldn't
buy many metal knobs and locks because of iron and steel short-
ages, and just before the War was when Dad and Mom decided
to remodel the old country dance hall into the house it was now.

We couldn't move from Cortland until after the War was over. It just took longer for the War to be over than anyone thought it would.

Thinking security, I had an inspiration.

I ran out to the barn, found the hammer, a nail, and a small scrap of wood, maybe three inches in length. Back in my room, I turned the radio on and the volume up, as loud as it could go, blasting the always arguing "Bickering Bickersons" radio show. I needed noise to camouflage my nail-pounding.

In this radio show, Mr. Bickerson was yelling at his wife, Mrs. Bickerson. My hammer pounded while the Bickersons bickered.

"Blanche, you've never appreciated me. You've never appreciated anything I do."

"Why should I? You said 'I do' and you haven't done anything to appreciate since."

"How can you say that, Blanche? Blanche, how about that time I came home from a whole day's fishing at the pier for our supper and you made me get the fish out of the house and take them to the garage? Blanche, I worked all day that day trying to catch those five trout and three smelt."

Blanche yelled back, "They all smelt. That's why I wanted them in the garage."

I had put the nail in the middle of the board, and pounded it into the door jam, right next to my door. The small stick of wood would now spin like the propeller on the DC-3 I'd flown on from Cortland to Watertown.

It was perfect. One turn and the piece of wood would hold the door closed. Another turn and it would let the door push open. My secret Christmas shopping list would now be safe. I sat at my desk and started writing names of friends, kids at home, kids away at college, and kids married and away, too.

For the Pompey Hollow Book Club I wrote Barber, Crane, and Holbrook on the list. I added Randy, Bases, and the Mayor.

For family, I wrote Dick, Mike, uncles and aunts, Dorothy, Mary, some cousins, Mom, Dad, Aunt Kate …

"Yikes."

It was a lot of names. I hoped I had enough money.

I started my list again, with Dad and Mom, and moved back-wards. Dad was my favorite person, besides Mom, so I wanted to get him something special. At the General Store in Homer I had seen some Sock-Mocs I thought he would like. They were half socks and half moccasins. The great thing about them was that they were only $2.14. The Sock-Moc—perfect for strolling about the house, in quiet comfort, with style and flair; just a hint of adventure. Dad would love them.

Mom was next. With Mom, I had to be careful. Anything I gave her would make her cry. Anything any of her kids gave her would make her cry. The trick was to find something that would just make her cry, not want to hold me on her lap for half an hour, hugging me and telling me what a good boy I was. I had lost whole pieces of dessert to my brothers during a hug like that. One time, Dick told Mom that I had told him how much I loved her, and that I'd said she was the best mom on earth—while all along, he was staring at my piece of lemon meringue pie. That hug cost me my pie and the last piece of meatloaf on my plate (although Dick denied it). It was simple: Mom would get a hand-kerchief. That way, when she opened the package and started crying, she could keep her hands busy wiping her eyes, and not hugging me. It was settled. Handkerchiefs it was, for both Mom and our grandma, Aunt Kate. Aunt Kate would also get my other special surprise.

My brother, Mike, was easy. Weren't no secret he was a gour-met. I still wasn't certain what a gourmet was, but I figured it meant he cooked and ate things nobody liked, without a dare—like snails, frogs, and really bad-smelling cheeses. I knew exactly what I was going to get him: some Limburger cheese. Mike Shea sold it at his store. It was so stinky you could smell it from the barbershop next door. Holbrook dared me to smell it up close once, and I nearly passed out. It smelled worse than rutabagas. Limburger cheese … perfect for Mike.

Dick was next. Dick was sometimes getting beaten up, mostly for flirting with other guys' girlfriends. I remember walking home from St. Mary's School in the first grade, back in Cortland, and seeing Dick lying on the sidewalk with a boy sit-ting on top of him, threatening to punch him for even talking to his girlfriend. Dick was lying there, denying everything, all the while never once loosening the grip he had on the books he was carrying home for the boy's girlfriend. I'd get Dick a box of Band-Aids.

The next few weeks would be busy catching rides with Mom or Dad, scouring stores to do my shopping. On a lunch break at school, Holbrook and I walked down to Mike Shea's store. With my nose pressed to the window of the butcher counter cabinet, I asked Mike how much Limburger cheese he thought a dollar twenty would buy. He asked, "Son, are you looking for cheese in a jar or a freshly cut wedge?"

I looked up over the counter and caught his eye. "Would a gourmet like it in a jar better or a cut wedge better?"

"Oh, definitely a fresh-cut wedge, a gourmet would know," he answered, without hesitation, appreciating I knew enough to ask. I wondered if Mike Shea could sense an air of importance about me, what with my new responsibilities as the official chairman of our grade for the senior class's Christmas roller skating party. I think it showed in my face.

I got a very nice-sized wedge of fresh Limburger cheese that Mike Shea wrapped carefully in the double sheets of butcher paper he tore from a big roll, and wrapped with string.

"Want me to keep it refrigerated for you, until you come and get it after school?" he asked.

Holbrook and I looked at each other like, What was he talking about? Why would we walk all the way back here after school just to get cheese I could easily put in my desk? Besides, I would be very busy with my numerous roller skating party official chairman responsibilities for our grade.

"No thanks," I said, "I'll take it with me. But thank you."

On the way out of the store, a stack of handkerchiefs on a shelf caught my eye.

"Mike Shea, are these girl's handkerchiefs or boy's handkerchiefs?"

"The girl's ones are on the left, boy's handkerchiefs are on the other aisle," he said.

This was too easy.

I bought two girl's handkerchiefs and now I had three of the presents done. I saw a box of Band-Aids behind the counter, but I figured Dick might see them back at school or on the bus, so I decided to get them in Homer when I went there with Dad on Saturday.

Holbrook agreed with a compliment: "Superior thinking."

After school, I locked myself in my room and wrapped my brother Mike's gourmet cheese, tied a bow around it nicely, tight like a shoelace. Mike Shea had given me two boxes—one for each of the handkerchiefs, so they were easier to wrap. I tied bows on them. There was only one safe hiding place near Christmas, next to the piano in the living room. People could put presents and packages there for Santa to leave under the tree, along with the ones he brought. The rule was nobody could look at or touch these presents, so I knew they would be safe there. That night I knelt and prayed that Santa would not forget Holbrook and his family.

It only took another Saturday to find my aunt's, uncle's, and cousin's presents. I bought five-dollar savings stamps for each of the Pompey Hollow Book Club members (they cost $2.50 each) and got them each a Christmas card to put it in. I would hand them the cards the last day of school before Christmas break. I had everything else wrapped and put over by the piano with the other presents.

When I got home from school the next day and went to my room, there, on my bed, was a big box with a lid on it. I lifted the lid slowly to look inside and slammed the lid back down quickly in disbelief. I needed to catch my breath. Maybe I saw it wrong. Maybe someone delivered someone else's printing. I lifted the lid up slowly and peered in. The box was filled with skating party tickets—not advertising fliers, not advertising cards, but expensive-looking, Oyster patterned, embossed and engraved skating party tickets, and one rubber stamp for imprinting "THANK YOU!" and an ink pad for the stamp. I dropped the box to the floor and began desperately counting the tickets. There were three hundred of them.

Both my hands raised and slapped up on my cheeks.

"Oh my God! THREE HUNDRED TICKETS!"

There were only twenty-eight kids in my grade. There weren't three hundred kids in the whole school old enough to even go to the roller skating party. Forget the school, there weren't three hundred townspeople in all of Fabius and Delphi Falls combined who could go. I think Dad had a ticket printed for every kid on the planet.

I was about to have a heart attack.

I put one of the tickets in my left jean pocket. I put the "THANK YOU!" rubber stamp in my other pocket and slid the box deep under my bed, kicking it with my foot to the wall, to hide the rest. I needed time to think.

I went out to the kitchen where Mom told me Mike was home from college for the weekend and was going to drive me up to Mary Margaret's tonight for a party.

"Go put a clean shirt on," she said. "I'll pick you up at ten-thirty."

I had completely forgotten the party.

The Pompey Hollow Book Club members plus a lot of other kids in our grade were there already. Holbrook, Crane, Barber, Bases, Randy, plus Mary Margaret, Smith, Kellish, Lowe, Finch, Sexton, Paddock, Fish, and the Mayor were there and others still coming.

Most everyone was talking about Christmas.

I motioned for Barber, Crane, and Holbrook to step outside for a second. On the way out, I caught Randy's and Bases's eye to come join us. Once outside I turned and pulled the printed ticket out of my left pocket, the "THANK YOU!" rubber stamp from my right pocket, held them both up, and got it over with: "I thought my dad and mom were going to get advertising fliers printed for the roller skating party. Just like the Buster Brown Shoe Club cards. That's what I asked for. I asked for a card for every kid in OUR grade," my voice cracked and whimpered, just on the verge of either tears or a possible nervous breakdown.

"Good idea, did he get fliers printed? Are they nice? Why are you so green?" asked Barber.

"They don't look like fliers," offered Holbrook.

"They got roller skating party TICKETS printed. Roller skating party tickets, which we have to sell." I held up the sample ticket again. "They threw in this 'THANK YOU!' rubber stamp and an ink pad." I held it up again as well.

Everyone stared at the ticket in my hand and tried to make sense out of my confusion. Mary thought the ticket was pretty and liked the oyster shell background.

"Kids will like these," said Holbrook. "Everyone will want one."

"But there's a slight problem," I added. "Dad got three hundred of them printed. He actually printed three hundred tickets, just like this one. He must have misunderstood me. We only needed twenty-eight advertising fliers. Now I have three hundred expensive oyster shell tickets hidden under my bed and a stamp ink pad. My Dad went nuts with his numbers! I'm a failure as the official chairman."

"Uh-oh," came from most of the kids.

Barber said, "You can't just throw them away. You're going to have to tell your dad about the mistake."

"Anyone got any better ideas?" I asked.

Randy threw us an anchor. "How do we get rid of the three hundred roller skating party tickets when there aren't three hundred kids in the school? Are we even allowed to have tickets to sell? I think we're sunk."

Mary Margaret happened to be listening at the screen door. Her mother was a school teacher so Mary Margaret looked at our problem through a different set of eyes. She suggested, "Why don't you give the tickets to my mom to give to the school principal to hand out to all the grades for them to sell in their own grade?"

It was a thought.

Mary Crane stepped up. "Why don't we just sell all the tickets ourselves? There's no rule says we can't. Then we will be sure to win and maybe get our picture in the paper."

The kids paused to reflect the concept.

"No rule says we can't," Holbrook said. "Is there a rule says we can? Wouldn't our printing tickets be counterfeiting?"

Mary Margaret stepped outside, closed the screen door behind her, and added some brilliance of her own: "Mary's right. The rule is the grade that gets the most to attend the roller skating party wins, isn't it? The rules never said anything about the kids we get to go have to be from the same grade or even from our grade for that matter. Why not each one of us take twenty tickets and we go ask everyone we know in school who wants one and we sell them that way and give all the money to the seniors? We can use the tickets as proof that it was our grade that got them to go."

That was such a brilliant idea I wanted to give Mary Margaret a big kiss, but her mom was sitting by the window, peering out. Her mom made me pound the chalkboard erasers one time during recess just for running in the halls. One kiss and she'd probably make me paint her house.

Holbrook said, "Jerry, call your mom and ask her to bring the tickets with her when she comes to pick you up so we can divide them here."

Mom arrived with the tickets and went inside for tea with Mrs. Cox.

The Pompey Hollow Book Club and Mary Margaret each got twenty tickets. I got nineteen. That was all we needed because that was the number of kids at school (176) who could go if they wanted to.

Mary Crane said, "At school Monday morning, tell anyone who wants a ticket to pay before the roller skating party or they can't get on the bus ... and to write down everyone's name."

This was genius. Here we were all worried about how to sell the tickets and she told us to trust everyone to pay ... that everyone wanted to go and nobody would cheat us. A brilliant idea.

And just about the time we were all realizing what a great idea that was, the Pompey Hollow Book Club's very own president, Mary Crane, came up with still another idea: "When you give each kid their ticket, instead of writing their name on the sheet of paper, have them sign their own name for it on a pad. Remember the rabbits, Jerry? This will be our written proof we were the ones to get them to go to the roller skating party."

It was because of these ideas I nominated both Mary Margaret and Mary Crane to be president of our grade. Holbrook and I voted for them both, using two separate ballot boxes.

We met in the school cafeteria for lunch on Monday. Not only had we sold all 176 tickets, we had rubber stamped the remaining 124 tickets with "THANK YOU" and given half of them to Mike Shea at his Fabius store and half to Mr. Hastings at his Delphi Falls store to give to people who dropped donation money in a jar for the bronze plaque. When we gave our completed lists of names to Mrs. Bredesen and explained what we had done, she told the class to sit and behave while she left the class to go speak with the principal to see if we had broken any rules.

She came back into the room with a big smile on her face.

Teacher congratulated the class for thinking "out of the box" and announced that the school Christmas roller skating party would raise more money than ever before. It would be a very nice Senior War Memorial plaque remembering those we had lost.

Even Mom and Dad were proud of us.

"How did you all sell so many so quickly?" asked Dad at the supper table.

"Well, we each had twenty—well me, nineteen—and we walked into every classroom and announced, 'I only have twenty tickets left for the roller skating party. Who would like them?' I guess everyone thought there were only twenty tickets left, and they didn't want to miss out. We sold them in minutes."

Dad and Mom smiled at each other.

"Your class is to be congratulated," said Mom.

"It was the other kids' ideas," I said.

Mom was most proud of her gentleman.

CHAPTER TWENTY-ONE

A BIG OOPS!

"Yikes!" I shouted, sitting up in bed, just waking up. "I forgot all about Santa."

I put my feet on the floor and looked out through my window, seeing it had snowed all night, and all that ran through my mind was that Christmas was coming, Santa was coming, and I hadn't even thought of a present for Santa. I'd thought about everyone but Santa.

I pulled on my clothes, bundled up, and ran out to the barn. I was trying to slide the small barn door open without letting the whole pile of fresh fallen snow that had drifted onto it nearly up to my waist tip over inside the barn. I knew it would have been smarter to shovel the snow away before trying to open the barn door, but it would have been even smarter than that not to have left the shovel in the barn, where it wasn't needed anyway, in the first place.

Sometimes being smart could be tricky in the country, and sometimes, like then, it could save you a lot of work you weren't particularly in the mood for—like shoveling snow.

It was also smart to buckle your galoshes so you wouldn't trip over them. It was way too late for me to think of that, because as soon as the door slid open, I raised one leg way up in the air to step into the barn over the snowdrift. The buckle of that boot in the air got caught somehow on the buckle of the boot still on the ground, and I began tripping forward, hopping on my left foot at least halfway through the room, ultimately losing my balance just in time to fall headfirst into an empty bucket Dick used for carrying chemicals to the water softener.

CLANG!

The noise of my head clanging into the empty bucket scared Ginger, our outdoor dog with her nubby tail. She ran out of the barn yipping, while my whole right boot came off, pulling my shoe with the knot in the lace and sock off with it.

This was not a good way to start a Christmas holiday, and I had now completely forgotten why I had gone to the barn in the first place. I knew it wouldn't be long before I remembered, but before I could do anything, anyway, I had to take the knot out of my shoelace, and put my sock, shoe, and boot back on, and this time, buckle the boots.

It was moments like these that gave me a better understanding of why Mom would always say, "Don't forget to buckle your galoshes, dear."

Oh, yeah … I remembered. Santa!

I had gone to the barn to look for something I could leave Santa's reindeers' harvest cow corn in, for when Santa Claus came. The harvest cow corn I would get from Farmer Parker's barn this afternoon.

I knew carrots were very popular with deer, but I thought corn would last longer, and maybe the crunching sounds would wake me up so I could at least see the reindeer. Santa always brought our Christmas tree and decorated it in the night, so I knew that task alone would take him a little more time than he'd take at houses that already had a Christmas tree. His reindeer would have more time to rest up and eat some refreshing cow corn. I even asked Charlie Pitts, before he died, if Santa's reindeer would like cow corn, and he said, "Oh ya, you betcha they do."

You couldn't get proof any better than that, so I knew I was doing the right thing. Charlie would have let me have as much as I wanted from the cow corn crib. He was a nice man who always reminded me of Christmas and I missed him, a lot. I considered him a best friend of mine, ever since he didn't laugh at me, or tell anyone about the time I dropped the eggs on the road.

I found a garbage can lid with the handle smashed flat down that somebody must have driven over with the car. It was perfect! I decided I would turn it upside down, fill it with cow corn, and leave it by our fireplace. For sure, Santa would see it when he came down the chimney, and know it was my present to him for the reindeer. I'd write a note for him. I also planned to leave an empty, rolled-up, paper potato sack, just in case Santa decided to take the harvest cow corn with him and feed the reindeer throughout the evening. This was some superior thinking, and bound to get me on very good terms with Santa Claus. He was exactly the one person all kids wanted to be on very good terms with. I could even imagine him coming down the hallway, to my room, and telling me a personal thank you for being so considerate, that is, if he had the time. Santa Claus was a very busy person.

Aunt Kate had come to stay until after New Year's. Mike had just driven in from Lemoyne until after Christmas.

During supper, the cold Wednesday evening before Christmas, he stacked wood and built a big nice warm fire in the fireplace before he sat down at the table.

For some reason Mom seemed uneasy, edgy. It wasn't like her. She kept making strange contorted faces, like she had something heavy on her mind, or had forgotten something really important and was trying hard to remember what it was. We were all eating and not making a lot of noise, so none of us paid much attention. She would lean out of her seat over to the left, turn her head around to one side, stick her nose up, and kind of sniff the air. Then she'd lean out the other way, turn her head to the other side, stick her nose up, and sniff again.

Befuddled, she looked forward, set her salad fork down, pushed her plate away, and declared in no uncertain terms: "What is that horrible stench?"

The only problem with that was that neither Dick nor I quite understood what the word "stench" meant or even implied. Mike knew it from his experience as a gourmet, but we weren't to know that. A gourmet would understand stench, I was later to find out.

Mom pushed her chair back.

"Children," she demanded, "everybody line up, over here, right now, please."

There was always trouble, regardless of our ages, when Mom referred to us as "children." What has she caught us doing now? was the first thing that would normally run through our heads, and what is a stench? was the second, hoping for a clue. With such a pained expression on her face, we weren't about to argue.

We all stood up and got in line. One by one we walked up to Mom, and she sniffed the air around us, and then asked the next one to step forward and get sniffed. After we were all properly sniffed, Mom told us to sit back down, and in one final act of desperation, she repeated in words we would understand, "What on earth is that horrible smell?"

"So that's what stench means," said Dick, like he'd discovered pasteurization.

We all began to sniff the air.

Boys in the late 1940s had fairly simple senses of smell. We could smell food being cooked; cabbage, the farthest away; various and assorted farm fragrances; and, of course, dirty socks. We could smell Christmas trees. Not much else.

"Smells like Jerry's room," Dick said. Aunt Kate cracked him on the knuckles with a wooden serving spoon.

Mom pushed her chair back again, stood up, and started sniffing the air—first, in a full circle around the dining room table, then in a short loop through the kitchen and out into the living room.

We followed her.

Not too close.

She made short, snorting, sniffing sounds with her wrinkled-up nose, using a wriggling upper lip as antennae. We could hear her in the other room, along the wall, around the corner, into the living room, moving closer and closer to the piano, and over to the floor by the wall, which was piled with Christmas presents. Her snorting vibrated the piano strings of the upright.

"Call Ginger in," she demanded.

Now, truth be known, calling Ginger in was probably the simplest chore there would ever be at our house. Ginger was our half-beagle, half-cocker spaniel. Although we only kept her outside, she only wanted to be an inside dog, so she never left the door. Ginger spent her entire life leaning on the door wanting to be let in.

Mike opened the door just enough to wake her from a nap without tipping her over and called her name, as a matter of courtesy. Ginger went nuts with joy and popped in at the tiniest opening of the door, like a kangaroo that didn't have to be asked twice. She never calmed down until she had jumped exactly three times, for each and every person she saw, and then she ran, at full speed, two times, throughout the entire house. Every time she turned a corner, her paws on the carpet sounded like she was sliding into third; she was just making certain nothing had changed, or she hadn't missed anyone.

Mom called her over, held her by the collar, pointed her at the pile to get her focused, and led her to one Christmas package at a time. At one point Ginger yipped, like something had bitten her. She tugged backwards on the collar, causing her normally tight furry skin to wrinkle over her eyes like a bloodhound, trying to back away from a pile of clues at any cost. Mom let go of her collar. With her thumbs and first fingers, she lifted the suspicious package up from the pile.

Ginger ran to the door begging to be let out.

Something began to ooze from the package.

"Someone bring me a dish," Mom demanded. "Hurry, please!"

Dick ran one over to her, chewing on my ear of corn that was on it, and handed the plate to her. She put the plate under the package, now leaking a gummy, gooey slime.

She turned and gave me a stern look. "Jerome, suppose you take this out to the garbage barrel, bring the plate back, and meet your mother in the kitchen. Mike and Dick, supper is being delayed, both of you please go into Dick's room and close the door."

This can't be good.

When I got back to the kitchen, all I could think of was there was trouble in the air, or in this case, a stench.

First off, she knew the Christmas package was mine, because the tag on the present said, "To Mike, from Jerry."

Second, when she called me Jerome, I was very likely to get beaned or lectured.

Third, anytime Mom called herself "Your Mother," rumor was she wanted no witnesses, just in case she accidentally drew blood, or murdered somebody.

"Jerry, I want the absolute truth."

Now this offended me. I almost always told Mom the truth, except for the time I kissed Linda Oats in the cider mill. I told her I'd tripped on a step and fallen into the cider tub, trying to help someone reach for a broom to sweep up the place. Or the time I told her I had eaten the disgusting rutabagas she'd served for dinner, which smelled like swamp water, when I really only hid them on a ledge under the supper table until after everybody went to bed, and then I got them from their hiding place, took them up into the woods next to the house, and properly stomped on them with my heel, eliminating even the slightest possibility they could ever go to seed and grow again.

"Jerry, do you have any other food wrapped and put over there as presents for anyone?"

"No, ma'am," I said.

"Just what was in that package, child?"

"Limburger cheese, for Mike, because he's a gourmet."

Mom smiled. I thought she was going to give me a hug; thank God, she didn't. This whole thing already cost me my corn, maybe even supper.

"I will give you fifty cents, dear. When you go back to the store, you can buy Limburger cheese in a jar that will be just as nice for your brother. It's such a thoughtful gift, Jerry."

"By the way," she added, "just where did you get the package of Limburger?"

"At Mike Shea's store, in Fabius," I replied.

"Son, didn't anyone there tell you the package should be refrigerated?"

"Mike Shea said that word, Mom, but Holbrook and I didn't know what he meant. I didn't have any more money, in case it— the *frigerate* thing—would cost me more, so we didn't pay any mind to it," I explained.

Mom stepped back and stared at me with eyes glazed over, the way she did when she thought I had a fever or some rare disease. Then she walked over to the ice box, pointed to it like a teacher pointing to a chalkboard, and said, "Jerry, this is a *refrigerator*. It keeps food cold, and fresh."

"Well, I'll be," I said. "I sure thought that was an *ice box*."

I reminded her, once again, that when we moved to the country, there were some things I just stopped learning.

"Mom, I swear, in Cortland, we called that thing an icebox, and nobody ever told me someone had gone and changed its name to refrigerator. Well, I'll be."

Mom didn't argue with me, because she knew I had her stumped.

"Go to bed, dear, and tell everyone to put their pajamas on and go to bed, too."

CHAPTER TWENTY-TWO

SKATING PARTY

I had never been at a roller skating party. It was more fun than a hayride ... well, it got to be after I stopped falling down and crashing into railings and poles and walls. The Mayor's t-shirt was blotched with orange drink because his hand holding his paper cup smashed against the wall. Holbrook's right lens fell out of his glasses.

He shrieked like a girl: "Nobody skate!"

It had no effect in the middle of a skating party with the organ player smiling and playing "Somewhere Over the Rainbow" and everybody holding hands just so they could keep from falling down.

Once most of us got past the part where our knees would wobble in and out and our arms made big circles backwards like windmills while we tried not losing our total balance, it started to be fun. It wasn't long before everybody could skate ... or at least thought they could, and holding hands was better, with much less hand cramping.

After I skated all night and finally took the skates off to go outside and look for a school bus, I bounced when I walked, as if the skates were still on. I almost had to learn how to walk again, taking steps and not sliding my feet. I'd heard of Navy sailors having sea legs when they first got off their ship; I guess this would have been called skate legs. I got on the closest bus, which was dark inside, stepped in, walked tenderly to the back where it was even darker, and sat down next to Mary Crane, whose reflection I could see in the bus window.

Well, now. Not only was Mary a really good roller skater, and we skated together this evening a bunch, while sitting on the bus she couldn't have been prettier, with her hair combed up in a ponytail and a yellow ribbon she must have put on while sitting there. It reminded me of the "yellow ribbon," and caused me great pause to be looking at Mary in a way I hadn't before. After all, she was the president of our club, the Pompey Hollow Book Club, and I had a deep and great respect for the office of what might possibly be, to my and the boys' very limited understanding of government and politics, the very first girl president in these United States of America.

At her party we'd square danced several times, but like ladies and gents in the movies, we didn't play spin-the-bottle with some of the other kids. The thought never entered my head. As the bus started backing around, right next to Bucky's Diner, to get on Route 11 and head north out of Cortland, I looked all over the bus every time we passed under a streetlamp that washed the inside with light as we drove by. The inexperienced, part-time, substitute night bus driver ground the gears like a coffee grinder. The bus jerked on up the highway. There was a full moon.

I told Mary how much fun the skating party was.

Tightening the yellow ribbon on her pony tail, she couldn't have agreed more.

On reflection, I wish she hadn't.

You see, I could see her reflection from time to time in the bus window. I could see the yellow ribbon, the same yellow ribbon Olivia Dandridge wore. I remembered how awkward my first kiss in the old mill was. I remembered Mary's frown of disappointment. Even Tom Sawyer had a better first kiss than I did, I thought, and I'm practically eleven … well, I would be in a year or so, anyway.

Sitting next to Mary, I slowly raised and stretched my arms up and out with a loud, obvious, cartoon-like noisy yawn, just as if to send a signaled message—*it sure is getting late and maybe I'll just take a short nap on the way back to school and not be kissing any girls*—and that was about the time I rested my right arm conveniently on the seat back, right behind Mary's neck and ponytail. What a coincidence, I thought. Perfect.

A lot of kids on the bus who never had a beer in their lives were singing, "Ninety-nine bottles of beer on the wall, ninety-nine bottles of beer … If one of the bottles happens to fall, ninety-eight bottles of beer on the wall … Ninety-eight bottles of beer on the wall, ninety-eight bottles of beer … If one of the bottles happens to fall, ninety-seven bottles of beer on the wall …"

My current situation caused me to gather some much needed thoughts. Faced with a yellow ribbon and pretty smile, I needed a strategy—president or not.

I reflected on the time Dick tried to explain boy and girl courting to me. He said courting, in a city like Cortland, was different than courting in Delphi Falls. He said city courting was a long, drawn-out series of visits to a girl's home, and then perhaps a supper or two with her parents, and then maybe a picture show with a chaperone sitting a row behind them. If it was going well after that, they could maybe hold hands or sit in the parlor or porch swing and talk, with the parents in the next room.

"Country courting was different," Dick and Duba both insisted.

"Kids in the country live miles from each other and have to court different than the city," Duba said. "It comes down from the pilgrims. Every minute counts in the country. No taxis, no trolleys, no city buses."

"And Indians," said Dick. "Don't forget country folk never knew when they would be attacked."

"How do people court in the country?" I pleaded.

"You kiss. In the country, courting is pretty much kissing, simple as that."

They were both emphatic.

"Yep … lots of kissing," Duba reinforced.

At "eighty-five bottles of beer on the wall," I saw the reflection of the yellow ribbon once again as we passed a lonely streetlamp somewhere in Homer. I closed my eyes, didn't even think about it, leaned like a B-17 bomber over Berlin, did a good ol' tuba purse-pucker with my lips that even Mr. Spinner would have been proud of. I planted a kiss on my president, Mary Crane, the likes of which she was not likely soon to forget—a kiss that might could be the envy in Hollywood—and held the kiss easy through "seventy-four bottles of beer on the wall."

Still kissing at "fifty-nine bottles of beer on the wall," I was considering forgetting about Olivia Dandridge and maybe painting my bike green.

It wasn't until fifty-six bottles, with what had to be an all-time record kiss for school bus number 23, when I opened my eyes in my bliss just to see if Mary maybe needed some oxygen and to possibly oblige her with a breathing spell. Doing so, my eyes looked up from our kiss and at our reflection in the window from the street light at Preble Crossing. In the bus window glass, Mary's eyes appeared to be wide open and staring straight up at the bus's ceiling. Her lips were all puckered up and waiting. It even appeared she had fresh lipstick on them. I never knew Mary to wear lipstick. The thought of how could her lips be puckered if I was kissing them crossed my mind.

"Forty-three bottles of beer on the wall" and now I was curious. I looked again—this time with my brain ...

Oh my God!

I was kissing her chin!

Holy Cobako! I thought.

I had planted a kiss on Mary's chin, just outside of Bucky's Diner in Cortland, with my best pursed-lip pucker, and stayed planted on her chin like a blithering idiot, absolutely convinced I was the next Errol Flynn all the way until the bus slowed down and jerked at the stoplight in Tully to turn right towards Fabius. The jar of the turn jostled us loose, lips and chin. I actually considered jumping off the bus and walking the ten miles home.

Mary didn't say a word and didn't laugh. Her thumb and finger wiggled her chin from side to side, trying to get the blood circulating again. She did rest her dreamy eyes on me like she understood I was under a lot of stress what with being official chairman and all and the skating party ticket sales and all that went with that. Presidents understood those things. When the bus stopped at the school, I started to stand up to run away. Mary said, "Hold on a minute," and she leaned over, took my cheeks in both her hands to control the aim, pulled my face toward hers, and gave me a good-night kiss which made me forget about Linda Oats. It was the best good-night kiss ever in history, I was certain. Mary smiled, pulled the ribbon from her ponytail, and handed it to me to keep.

I went home, crawled into bed with all my clothes and shoes on, and pulled the blanket up over my head. Smelling the perfume on the ribbon, now wrapped around my finger, I decided kissing was definitely very good, very hazardous but very good, and from now on I was more likely to hold hands or just have supper, and court like the people in Cortland court. Courting in the country could give a boy a heart attack.

CHAPTER TWENTY-THREE

O HOLY NIGHT!

On Christmas Eve, my aunts and uncles, Mike, and Mom and Dad were all in the living room around the fire. Aunts Mary and Dorothy played Christmas music on the phonograph while Mike played the piano. Everyone was having a good time, singing Christmas carols. I sat near Aunt Kate and listened as she read to our cousins "The Night Before Christmas," which was one of my favorite poems. I knew it by heart, but it was nice hearing someone read it, so I could imagine it. After a while, the little kids had to go to bed.

Little kids at our house were everyone in school or younger. Aunt Kate walked me to the bathroom to brush my teeth. Then she tucked me in and gave me a kiss good night. That was when I gave her my special Christmas surprise. I touched her cheek and whispered clearly, "Merry Christmas, Grammy. I love you. I'm happy you're my grandmother."

Her face trembled. I knew the secret. I could see a warm smile sparkle up in her eyes as the glare of the porch light reflected on a teardrop through her glasses. I could see it was a happy tear.

"Merry Christmas, my wonderful grandson, Merry Christmas. Thank you. Thank you."

She stood up, took her cane, and shuffled down the hall, wiping her eyes with a hanky.

The adults sang while all the kids were in bed, so Santa could come. But if Santa came during the night, everyone always promised to wake us up early, to see what he'd brought.

Half asleep I heard a low sudden noise outside my window. It seemed to shake the house.

THUMP! ... THUMP! ... THUMP! Jingle, jingle, jingle ...

THUMP! ... THUMP! ... THUMP! Jingle, jingle, jingle ...

I got up and ran down the hall in the dark and looked for the garbage can lid I'd left for Santa's deer.

"Look!" I said to myself in my loudest whisper. "The cow corn is gone ... the cow corn is gone!"

All of a sudden, the front door swung open loudly and hit the wall behind it, almost giving me a heart attack. Mike jumped in and yelled in a loud whisper, "Quick! Santa's still on the roof!"

He kneeled down so I could get on his shoulders. Outside we went in the dark to see Santa and the reindeer. He carried me out to the flagpole, just this side of the swings, for a good view of the roof, and turned around.

"Oh darn," said Mike as we turned full circle, "the reindeer finished the corn you left, Jerry, and they must have taken off."

He pointed to the left end of the roof. The trash can lid I had filled was up there, sure enough, but empty now, and nestled in some snow on the roof. There were two long deep ridges in the snow on the roof. Mike told me they were sleigh tracks.

It was amazing! We'd actually come to within seconds of seeing Santa and his reindeer. After we stared at the roof awhile, Mike took me back into the house and back to my room.

"Try to sleep, Jerry. Mom will be waking you soon. Merry Christmas."

It was almost impossible to get back to sleep, but I managed.

It was early Christmas morning, still dark, when Mom came into my room, woke me, and left. The hallway was aglow from all the Christmas tree light reflections, and from the decorations Santa had left in the living room. Every year it was such a big surprise to see the tree for the first time, early in the morning. The anticipation of it all made it seem to get bigger, with more lights, more beautiful shiny balls, more icicles on it than the year before. I still remember the candle lights that bubbled up magically. The presents were under and around the tree. Aunt Kate, Mom, Dad, Mike, and Dick were already in the living room, waiting.

Mom, Aunt Kate, and Dad were beaming smiles at me. It was still a secret, but I think Aunt Kate told them how happy she was that I knew she was my grandmother.

Aunt Mary sat down on the floor by the tree and handed out the presents. Everyone watched while the person opened it and told who it was from. Dad loved the Sock-Mocs and put them on right away. They fit perfectly and looked comfortable. He gave me a neck hug, thanked me, and whispered in my ear, "Jerry, me boy, your bike was pretty much your Christmas present this year. But here's a special Christmas present for you, directly from Santa. He arranged it personally. I met him twice, ya know. The owner of the Tully Bakery delivered a brand new hot water heater to Mr. and Mrs. Holbrook last night and had it hooked up for them—big enough for the entire family. Bob has it nearly half paid for, working part-time in the bakery after school or on weekends. Half his pay stub goes to paying it off. They can pour a hot tub starting this Christmas morning. I know he's your best friend and thought you'd like to know, young man. Merry Christmas, son."

I couldn't believe my ears.

Mom opened her handkerchief box, and started to tear up. To save myself a half-hour and my hot chocolate, I hurried over to her, gave her a kiss on the cheek, and said, "Merry Christmas, Mom."

"It's lovely, dear—thank you, so much."

Then Mom took my arm and pulled me close and whispered in my ear, "Jerry, your bike is your present from your dad and me, dear, but here's your aunt's and uncle's Christmas present for you. Dr. Porterfield from Syracuse University was your aunt's professor in college. He and several War veteran gentlemen, including some pilots who flew B-17s in the War, contacted some railroad union officials they knew from the service and were able to get Bob Holbrook's father, Mr. Holbrook, a full journeyman status with the railroad union. Their eleven children are from a combination of two families. They are such good people. God bless them. Now Mr. Holbrook will make more money, steady money, working full-time and qualify for their retirement pension, too. I know Bob is your best friend, Jerry. It's a present to him and you from us—Merry Christmas."

I stood there trying to take it all in. I was in awe. I thought that maybe now Holbrook could get a telephone.

Aunt Kate loved her handkerchief. She pulled me closer than she ever had and gave me a hug and whispered in my ear. It was almost as if it was in her young, motherly voice, her voice as it would have been back in 1906, when she was the mother of a four-year-old girl: "You're one wonderful leprechaun, my grandson. You're a very special young man."

Then she patted me on the cheek with a happy smile.

Mike winked over at me and cheered when he opened his Limburger cheese. He asked Mom if she had any crackers in the house. I couldn't believe he was going to eat the same stuff that made Ginger want to be an outdoor dog. I guess gourmets will eat anything. His present to me was showing me where Santa was on the roof last night. With that, I knew I could still believe one more time.

Dick opened his Band-Aid box and scratched his head.

"Don't you get it?" I asked. "It's for when you get beat up."

He stared at me, like he might want to get up and slug me, but the more he thought about it, the more sense it made. Dick was smart. He leaned over and whispered, "We need to talk."

"What's up?"

"Duba and I did something and we don't want you getting sore at us."

"What'd you do?!"

"I finally have enough money to buy the Nash convertible from Lindsey Pryor. Duba's got enough to get the roadster he wants. We heard about the hot water heater and the railroad union thing for the Holbrooks, so Duba and I decided to give the '38 to Holbrook so his mom could drive him to the Tully Bakery after school whenever he needed to go, so he wouldn't have to walk."

I began to tear up. "Why would I be sore? Holbrook is my best friend ever."

"Well, we were going to give it to you for Christmas. So in a way, it is for you—a Christmas present for your best friend."

Not only were all of the SOSs Dick and his friends had come through with huge for the Pompey Hollow Book Club, but this was the biggest gift he and Duba could ever think of doing. He told me they put the '38 in the Holbrooks' drive after midnight last night with a note tied to the steering wheel with its two keys.

My aunts loved the records I gave them, one of "Oh Come All Ye Faithful" with Bing Crosby, and one of "Rudolph the Red-Nosed Reindeer" with Gene Autry.

We sat around the tree for the longest time, opening presents, singing songs, and drinking hot chocolate. Then we all had to go back to bed and sleep late so all of Santa's helpers could get some rest. It was hard trying to fall asleep again, but I did.

It was a very nice Christmas—the best Christmas ever. I kept the secret about hearing the reindeer always in my memories. I kept the secrets about each of Santa's special visits to Holbrook always in my heart.

On the Monday after Christmas, Mom dropped me at the Mayor's farm to sled. Along with Mary, Holbrook, and Barber, Randy and Bases showed up. It had snowed all weekend, so it was a perfect Christmas vacation, with tons piled up for sledding all day and into the evening.

After the Mayor pulled the sled from inside the barn, Holbrook pulled me inside to talk. He gave me a neck hug and said nobody ever had a better friend ever in the history of the world. He told me he cried when he saw it all happen, for his mom, for his dad, for the family, and for him. Then he added, "But if you ever tell anyone I cried, I'll beat the crap out of you."

"Our secret," I promised.

"Ever tell anybody I hugged you, I'll pound you to a pulp."

We all took turns pulling the sled up the hill a million times. After dusk, we'd follow boot tracks up the sledding hill in the moonlight, so we wouldn't fall down the steep hill where the bull was, all the time hoping we were in a safe snow groove, sledding back down the sledding hill, for the very same reason.

The side porch light flicked on and off, on and off, on and off, and then back on. Bob said, "That's Mom, calling us in."

"My ears are frozen; all I can hear is a dog barking," I said.

The porch light flicked off and on again. This time we all saw it. We let the sled slide down the steep hill on its own and walked down the sledding hill. It flew past the bull and under the barbed wire fence and into their snowy driveway.

The Mayor said, "I'll put the sled in the barn." Farm kids had to pick toys and sleds up to keep tractors and farm equipment from rolling over them.

Holbrook walked ahead, slid the barn door open for him, and waited outside.

Inside the farmhouse, the Mayor's mom told us to close the door behind us, everyone stand on the mat, and take our boots and shoes off. She took our coats, scarves, hats, and mittens and threw them in a box by the door.

"My goodness," she said, "you're all soaked right through, and your boots are filled with snow."

Sergeant Preston of the Royal Mounties, and King, his sled dog, had been through worse than this, during every radio episode.

Not only could we take it, we were actually beginning to thaw out from being inside a warm house.

When I could open my eyes fully, I saw Bob's brother's Christmas present on top of their small kitchen table. It was a genuine red and silver American Flyer train set and train track, complete with whistle, transformer, and everything. Wow! It had an engine, with an engineer painted on the window steering the train; a coal tender behind that; a flat car behind that; a passenger car behind that, with people painted in the windows; and a caboose behind all those.

It was the first time I'd ever seen a train set that wasn't in a department store Christmas window decoration.

We all knelt on the floor around the kitchen table of this cozy little farmhouse, our cold cheeks resting sideways on the warm, light, blue and white checkered oil cloth covering the table. We watched the train go around and around and around on the track.

The Mayor's mom, Mrs. Penoyer, made grilled cheese sandwiches, neatly cut in half for each of us to share, and gave us some tomato soup. She put the plates and our soup cups on chairs between us, so we could eat and enjoy the train at the same time.

"Careful you don't spill," she told us.

We slurped our hot tomato soup and ate our grilled cheese sandwiches in the warm, lingering glow of a wonderful 1949 Christmas passing through our lives. Resting our cheeks on the warm oilcloth of a small friendly kitchen table on Penoyer Road, each imagining the conductor waving at us as the train engine steamed by, or passengers busy reading their newspapers, looking up at us from the Pullman car flying past, or whoever was sleeping in the caboose waking up just to wave.

"I put harvest cow corn out for Santa's reindeer, and they ate it all," I said confidently.

"Reindeer love cow corn," Barber said, beading his eye for better focus on the smoke puffs coming out of the train engine's smoke stack racing around the table.

Clickety-clackety, clickety-clackety ...

"Remember the ketchup soup in Groton, and Uncle Harry?" snickered Mary, warming her hands with her cup of soup.

Mary and I glanced at each other and smiled, remembering our kiss on the skating bus. Kneeling next to her with our cheeks on the warm oilcloth staring at the train racing by, I happened to look up at the lone light bulb wire hanging from the ceiling over the small kitchen table. There was a little sprig of Mistletoe scotch taped to the lamp pull chain. I tapped Mary's shoulder, pointed up to it, and kissed her happy smile, this time right on the lips. Her smile was my Christmas present.

"How about our hiding the chickens and geese?" asked Randy. "Boy did we ever stink!"

"Santa left me a new baseball," said Bases.

"I got new shoes," said Barber.

Clickety-clackety, clickety-clackety ...

"I wonder where it's going," whispered Mary.

Holbrook had contentment in his eyes we hadn't seen in some time. "Anywhere we want, I suppose," he said with a smile. "Anywhere we want."

Whoooo! Whoooooo! Whoooooooooooo!

Watching the train puff its smoke and all the eyes glued to a promise of a dream come true in every puff, I thought out loud: "I have to remember to tell Charlie Pitts thanks, when we go to the Delphi Falls cemetery for our next meeting. He was so right about reindeer liking harvest cow corn at Christmastime."

EPILOGUE

THREE YEARS LATER

It was March and spring was coming soon, but not today.

It was a cold harsh winter we were coming out of in 1953, a winter which brought with it more snow days than usual. The schools were closed on snow days.

Dick and I came home from school and stepped off the school bus to a fresh new midday blanket of powdery white snow covering a layer of this morning's melting crust which lingered from the thaw earlier in the week. We started walking the long driveway to the house when we saw a car we didn't recognize start driving from the house down the snowy drive toward us. We could tell by the stature of the silhouette we could make out that our dad was in the backseat, a passenger. Some stranger was driving and what appeared to be a hospital nurse was sitting on the passenger side of the front seat. We stopped walking as the car approached and bent down to look in through the closed car windows as best we could in the glare of the sun. Dad was waving at us. All the windows were closed tight. The car kept moving towards the gate. It didn't slow, it didn't stop. We turned around backward to watch as the car drove off.

Maybe he didn't open a window because there was snow on the ground and it was cold out. Maybe he wasn't feeling well—he'd been coughing a lot lately. Maybe they were going to the doctor to get him some penicillin.

We could see Dad turn around in the backseat and wave at us a gentle, sad wave. His eyes were squinting from the tears we saw glistening in the light. Dad was weeping and neither of us knew why or where he was going. We stood there and watched him out of love and respect, just in case he was still watching us, until the car turned down Cardner Road. It picked up speed and drove out of sight. I started to cry. Our dad looked so sad staring back at us. He had never left us like this before and neither of us had any idea why—or why he didn't stop to talk. We ran as fast as we could into the house to find Mom standing in the book den, staring out the front window with tears in her eyes.

"Where's Dad going?"

"Why wouldn't he talk to us?"

"Why was he crying?"

I never felt quite as alone as I did at that moment. Never. Without taking her eyes from the long driveway Mom told us to go get out of our school clothes and meet her at the table. She had made hot chocolate for when we got home so we could talk. After we changed, Mom told us to come into the kitchen and get our cups and take them to the table. Now seeing us she was smiling a little. I think it was because we were home and she wasn't alone anymore—Mom had not been separated from Dad since the day they met and fell in love in 1919.

She sat down at the end of the table. "Boys, I have something to tell you. I need you to be strong and to be my men of the house. We will get through this together," she started.

The phone started ringing. We let it ring.

"Your father and I chose not to tell you about what I am going to share until we were sure. We didn't want to worry you unnecessarily. Your father has tuberculosis, and it's a very bad disease. When he passed you on the driveway, the hospital nurses were driving him to the TB sanitarium, where he will have to stay until he gets better."

"Is that why he was coughing so much, Mom?" Dick asked.

"Yes, dear. Tuberculosis attacks the lungs and it affects people's breathing."

I started to tear up. "Is that why he wouldn't talk to us or say good-bye?" I asked.

"Oh no, son, and I don't want either of you to think that. Please don't think that for a minute. It's just that they don't know a lot about tuberculosis. They think it may be highly contagious in the early stages, like polio, but they're not sure. Once the people from the sanitarium came today and told your father they confirmed he had TB, he couldn't and wouldn't risk exposing you to it. That's why he could only wave to you. He loves you both so very much—he would never not want to say good-bye to his children. Your dad even asked the driver to wait until he saw the school bus come so he could at least wave good-bye."

At least our minds could get around this a little better, but the air was still tense—Dick and I couldn't conceive not being with our dad again.

"When can we go see him?" asked Dick.

Mom looked down at her hands to gather her thoughts.

"I'm so sorry, boys, but you can't—not until he's better—not until they know it's safe for you to see him and for them to confirm that he isn't contagious. Just pray for your father every single day. Pray that he will be safe and come back to us healthy and strong."

"How long will Dad be gone?" I asked.

Mom looked at each of us. "It could be a year—it could be …"

Knowing the statistics, that TB was the number one killer in America, Mom started weeping; she was a strong woman, but her face dropped into her hands. Dick jumped up and ran into her and Dad's bedroom and came back with the handkerchief I had given her for Christmas years earlier.

"Thank you, dear," she mumbled.

She looked down at the tabletop as she kept wiping her eyes to avoid eye contact that would start her tears all over. We stood up, quietly pushed our chairs in, and walked around by Mom. We each put our hand on her shoulder as we walked by and went to our own rooms. I lay down on my bed and stared at the ceiling. I kept thinking of Dad looking around in the rear window of the car, crying as he waved. I turned over and buried my face in the pillow so no one could hear me cry.

The next morning was Friday. When the school bus came, we weren't out at the gate. Mr. Skelton honked the horn a few times, and then drove off. None of us, including Mom, got out of bed until later in the morning. Mom didn't say a word about our missing school. She felt that this was the right time for us all to be together and wanted us close to her in case any of us had any questions. The house was quiet all day. Dick was sitting on the floor looking in the encyclopedia to learn about tuberculosis. When it was time to get ready for supper, we went into the kitchen and fed ourselves. Most of the afternoon and even now, Mom was on the phone talking to our aunts and cousins about Dad going to the sanitarium and about the TB. Dick made a salad for Mom and warmed up two meatballs he found in the refrigerator and put them on a plate, in case she was hungry. Neither of us said a word to each other all day. We just walked around in a trance and looked out windows and teared up when we walked by a picture of Dad on the piano or the one of him on the wall in the hallway.

After dark we went to bed again. I knelt down by my bed and said prayers so my dad would get better, not be in pain, and be home for my birthday or for Christmas or anytime. Just so he came home.

The next morning, Saturday, Mom woke us up smiling. She had made breakfast and asked us to come as she had it all on the table. It was like she was a new person. Mom told us that God would answer our prayers. It was Saturday, but she got us out of bed and told us now was the time for us all to be strong and that our dad had been through worse than this in his life. With the Lord's help and our prayers, he would get through this, too.

"What was worse than this, Mom?" I asked.

Mom looked around at each of us and told us something we had never heard before. She asked us never to bring it up unless our dad did first.

"It was a very difficult time for your dad when his daddy fell off a barn roof in Minnesota and died when your dad was just a boy like you," she said. "Your father was the youngest of seven and so hurt by losing his father that he could never bring himself to talk about it or think about it."

"Is Dad going to die, Mom?" I asked.

"All your dad would want now is for you all to do the best you can, in everything you do, and to go on with your lives just as he taught you. If you do that for him, it will give him the strength he needs to get well again."

We promised we would. I asked her if we could write him.

She said, "It would be better to tell me things for him. I'm allowed to visit him, and I would relay the things you want him to know and any other news from us to him. That way, we can talk longer during my visits, and I could keep his spirits up. I could keep his mind busy with all the things we want to tell him. It's important we make sure he keeps positive and wants to get better and come back home."

We all understood this.

I told Mom I was going camping.

"In the snow?" asked Dick.

I got up from the table, went to my room to get dressed, and grabbed my knapsack and Charlie's lantern.

It felt like I was a grownup, all of a sudden, and not a kid anymore. I couldn't explain it. It was just not the same as before, somehow. I grabbed my knapsack and bedroll and headed out to the barn. Our two horses were standing close to each other, getting warm, soaking in the morning sun, but not moving or eating their broken bales of hay lying on the ground before them. Horses could sleep standing up, so I wasn't sure if they were asleep. I slid the stable barn door open and went in, stuffed my knapsack with as much hay as I could stuff in it, and then got Jack's—my horse's—saddle down off the rack. I brought it to the opened doorway and put it on the floor. I went back to get the saddle blanket.

Then I paused and walked back to the door and looked out at Jack. Jack was a tall gray gelding who loved a ride and a climb up our hills. His winter coat was still thick and feathery even though it was March. He lifted his head up and looked at me like he was waiting for me to make up my mind as to whether we were going with a saddle today or going bareback. It made no difference to him.

"Bareback," I said out loud. I put the saddle back on the rack and threw the saddle blanket over the stall door where it belonged.

I adjusted the straps on my knapsack, hooking the lantern to them, and put it on my back and stepped out of the barn stable, sliding the door closed. I put Jack's bridle on and led him away from Major's side—Major was Dick's horse—so I could get enough space to jump on his back with the help of a cinder block.

We rode the long driveway and down Cardner Road, across the small bridge at the creek and into the snow-covered alfalfa field that Molly, the workhorse, used to call home. The lumber people took Molly with them for other work, but they told us that someday soon they would bring her back. Jack raised his head high, his nostrils flaring puffs of morning air. He shook his head as though he were waking himself up. He knew we were going to climb the steep hill to go to my campsite. He liked to go camping with me. He also knew his footing wouldn't be as sure as he would like on snow-covered ground. We got to the back edge of the field. I decided to hold on and ride him up to see if I could stay on while he climbed the hill. Jack's thick coat helped my legs get traction, and the bare leafless trees let me see well. I squeezed tight with my legs and held a piece of his mane. Jack's nostrils snorted steam every time his legs sprung forward like claw hammers, pulling us up, while his hind legs pushed up like springs, kicking snow until we reached our trail at the top that was more level to our campsite. Steam was pounding from his nostrils like a steam engine.

We got to the site and I slid off his back, dropping the reins to the ground. I took off my knapsack and looked about in the snow near my fire hole for where I wanted to sleep. The hole was all covered in snow. I dragged my knapsack around a small square patch of ground to move the snow away. Once clear, I packed the snow solid to the ground with my feet. I hung my knapsack on a tree branch and started to gather logs, building the fire bigger than usual so there was more heat glowing off for both Jack and me. When it was going good I gathered and stacked up enough wood to take us through the night.

I mounted Jack again and told him we were going for a ride. When I was on his back, I realized that, for the first time, I'd mounted him with no help of any kind.

We headed back deeper into the woods by the upper water-falls, which were frozen over. A little water was trickling over the falls, dripping down the massive icicles melting slowly in the morning sun. I rode through the woods to the back fence of our property line and turned left to go north as far as we could—a ride I had never done on horseback. It was a longer ride than I had planned. When we came out of the woods into a clearing, we were across from Charlie Pitts's old place. I rode Jack to the edge of the field that faced across the road to Charlie's property and we stopped. We just stood there. Jack snorted puffs of steam. I remembered my friend Charlie—I thought about all the good times he and I'd had together. How he let me play in his barn. How nice he was to us all the time. I remembered how he got sick and how Dad would come back from work to drive him to a hospital in Rochester, so he wouldn't be alone for treatments before he died. I wondered if Charlie had had tuberculosis.

A tear blurred my vision—thinking of Charlie and wondering what I would ever do if my dad died. I pursed my lips in frustration, wishing both he and Dad could be here right now so we could all go ice fishing up at Pleasant Lake.

A breeze kicked up, so Jack and I turned and followed our tracks back to the camp. I took his bridle off and hung it with the knapsack. I stacked more firewood. I had two blankets so, with the fire, they were all I needed. I unbuckled the knapsack and pulled out almost a quarter of a bale of hay I had stuffed in it. I knew I wouldn't want to eat so I didn't pack any food for me. Jack leaned his head down, smelled the hay—then lifted his head up and turned towards me to thank me. He started munching on it. His back leg sprung as he relaxed. Horses can lock their knee joints. They will balance on three legs, resting one in case they have to move suddenly in the night. The horse's natural predator is the wolf. Their defense is speed.

I didn't need the lantern. I sat on a log by the fire and made some mourning dove calls for a while, trying to warm my hands.

"Whoo ... eee ... who ... who ... who ..."

"Whoo ... eee ... who ... who ... who ..."

"Whoo ... eee ... who ... who ... who ..."

I watched a squirrel carrying an acorn up the side of a tree and wondered where he had them all buried for the winter.

As the darkness came I unrolled my blankets and, lying back, watched the stars over the creek side of the cliff and listened to Jack munching on his hay.

I looked at the silhouette of a single dead leaf hanging from a branch surrounded by a full moon above, twisting in the wind. I wondered what my dad was doing.

I wondered if he was coughing a lot.

I wondered if he was losing any more weight.

I wondered if we would ever go fishing again.

I made the decision I wasn't going to talk about this with anyone at school other than Holbrook, Barber, or Crane. I knew my friends. Mary and I had never kissed again after that Christmas. We still smiled at each other remembering it, but she had a new boyfriend and we would just see each other whenever the club met, which had been awhile. They wouldn't bring it up unless I told them I wanted to talk about it. We knew each other like that—that was why we were such good friends. We were like brothers and sisters. Holbrook loved my dad, too.

I fell asleep knowing that the rest of school that year and next fall wouldn't be the same. School would never be the same again.

On Monday I was walking down the school hall pulling my jacket off. I noticed a girl I had never seen before. She was walking in my direction looking like she was lost. She was tall and slender and had curly hair. She had a plaid pleated skirt on and a green sweater over a white starched blouse. She had a pretty sparkling smile, and I could see a smile in her eyes. I told her my name and asked for hers. She told me she was Judy Blessing, new here from Baltimore, Maryland, and she was staying until next November while her parents were doing something—traveling or something, I don't remember.

She was staying with her uncle, Ted Dwyer, who lived across from Minneapolis Moline Conway.

I asked her if she had a locker.

"Not yet," she said.

"Use mine," I offered. "I never put a lock on it, if that's okay."

"I don't need locks," she said as she placed two books on the top shelf and hung her green sweater on one of the hooks, closing the door. "Thanks, Jerry—nice to meet you," she said. She smiled, turned, and walked away.

That same day, when I got home, a letter from my brother Mike was lying on my bed. In it he wrote that every week he was going to send me a new word to look up in the dictionary to learn and use in a sentence. His first word to me was "pedantic." I didn't know what it was, so I got the dictionary and looked it up. His second was "copious." His third was "prevaricate." This was fun. Every week his letter and word would take my mind off worrying about Dad, a little, and I got to learn a new word.

On Saturday I saddled Jack and rode down past Doc Webb's place to the end of the road and up the back hill to the big corner. Just across the road was Ted Dwyer's place, where Judy was living until she had to go back to Baltimore.

I rode across and up on their snowy front yard, dismounted, and knocked on the door. Judy came out and I asked, "Want to go for a ride?"

"Hold on while I put something warm on. Want to come in?"

"Nah, I'll wait out here."

When she came out, I mounted Jack, took my foot out of the left stirrup, and offered her a hand so Judy could use it to climb up. Now she was just behind the saddle with her arms around me, holding on. I knew Judy was older and in the eleventh grade, but it didn't matter, I liked her. Right now, we were on my horse riding back down the hill to my house for some hot chocolate. We passed the Reynolds' place, the Shaffers', the Butlers', and then Doc Webb's. Doc waved and shouted for me to check out his new syrup cabin when I had a chance. I waved back that I would as we rode on past.

Mom was at home when we got there. She said hello to Judy and they talked about Baltimore while I warmed up some milk. I had put Jack in the barn garage, still saddled, with some hay so he would be okay for a little while.

We drank hot chocolate and Judy and Mom talked.

Later I walked Judy out back to see the waterfalls, even though they were frozen over. We walked back down to the barn garage and I brought Jack out so I could take Judy home. Before we mounted, Jack moved his head around and nuzzled Judy like he liked her and wanted to say hello. Judy put one hand under his chin and with the other patted his nose and then the side of his neck. They became fast friends.

On the way back to the Dwyers', Judy rested her head on my back. I could hear her humming a song I couldn't make out but I liked hearing her voice. We didn't talk the whole ride back. She held me and kept her head on my shoulder.

When we got to her house Judy slid over to where she could reach her foot into the stirrup I had taken my foot out of. She held onto the back of the saddle and swung around slowly. I turned to help her and she paused, looked me in the eyes, and kissed me. She kissed me a wonderful long warm kiss. Then her head moved back and she looked in my eyes again and said, "I had fun, Jerry. Thank you for thinking of me." She lowered herself to the ground, rubbed Jack's nose good-bye, and ran into the house, waving at me just before she closed the door.

If it weren't for Dad being at the TB sanitarium, this growing up could be a good thing, I thought.

When I got home my world was shaken again. Mom was packing a small suitcase. She told me that the sanitarium had called while I was out riding and that Dad may need surgery. They wanted to remove a part of his lung. She had to go stay near him for a couple of days while he went through some tests and they talked it over with the doctors.

Mom kept packing and told me to tell Dick to please be mature and behave while she was gone, and that she would be back in a few days.

After she drove out I walked behind the swings and opened the door of Dad's Oldsmobile. I sat in the driver's seat. I thought of him sitting there. I grabbed the steering wheel like it was him driving and could smell him in the car. I thought about wanting him to meet Judy.

I went inside and heated up a tuna fish and noodle casserole for Dick and me for when he got home.

I told Dick about Dad and the operation he might have to have—taking some of his lung out.

Dick said he didn't think someone could live without both lungs.

I bolted around in a blind rage, running towards him, and pushed him back up against the wall so hard his head bounced off it. "You take that back!" I screamed. "You take that back!"

Dick stared at my fists, my jaw clenched, tears in my eyes. I just gave him a cold stare. He apologized.

We went to our rooms to calm down.

Judy and I went riding as often as we could and liked each other. I didn't know what love was so we didn't talk about that—I just knew that when we were together we were very happy, and when we weren't together we couldn't wait to be together again.

One time when Mom visited Dad, he told her how to get me a job if I wanted one. I said yes; Dick, too, if he wanted a summer job away from the Lincklean House. She told us at supper. Dick was all for it so Mom said she would take us to the place on Saturday, introduce us to the owner, and see if it all worked out. She said Dad wanted it to be a surprise, so she would tell us about it when we got there. It would be for the whole summer, from Memorial Day to Labor Day.

On Friday night I went to a school dance with Judy. We danced every slow dance. We even square danced when they played one that sounded easier than most. We would pair up with Mary Crane and her boyfriend.

I told Judy that in the morning I would be looking at a summer job my dad had arranged. I knew nothing about it yet, as he wanted it to be a surprise. Judy told me she was praying for Dad every day to get better. She was nice like that.

On Saturday Mom drove us all to a place called Snook's Pond near Manlius. It was part of a spring-fed lake that was used as a swimming hole in the summer. It had a building with men's lockers and changing areas on one side of the pond and another with ladies' lockers on the other side. At the end of the pond was a concrete walkway with chairs on all three sides and a diving board. Just at the entrance to Snook's Pond, after the parking area, were two small square huts that had big wood-flap shutters that, when lifted and held up with wooden poles, showed the counters on the front three sides. One shack was where people paid to get in and rent lockers. The other was a snack bar. You could get hot dogs, popcorn, and soda pop—all you wanted, in that one.

Mom introduced us to Mr. Snook, who walked us around the property and gave us the tour. He told us that if we wanted the jobs, it meant running the snack bar and three times a day going around the grounds, picking up empty bottles and papers and raking up cigarette butts. He said both of us could work—but it was seven days a week from Memorial Day, when they opened for summer, to Labor Day, when they closed for the winter.

Then he said, "Do you want to think about it, boys?"

Dick asked, "What does it pay?"

"Nothing," said Mr. Snook, "but you run the snack bar as your own and you keep any profits you make. How does that sound?"

Dick said, "We'll take it."

On the way home Dick asked Mom to ask Dad if he could make a list of what he thought we should buy to stock it, where to buy it, and how to pay for it.

The summer flew by. We got to take turns and swim whenever we wanted. We got to drive the orange Allis Chalmers tractor and wagon from our shop to the storage room down the driveway to get cases of soda pop for the snack bar. The day after Labor Day, summer was over. I walked all around the place doing a final pickup, knowing that I would probably never see it again, and I would miss it. I thanked the place for helping us all pass the time so we didn't mope around worrying about our dad and missing him.

When the car pulled up to the house, I ran out, saddled Jack, and slow-galloped down to the Reynolds' hill and up to Judy's. As soon as she opened the door I took her by the hand, didn't say a word, and led her out to Jack. I started to mount and she said, "Hold on a second, mister."

She took my face in her hands and gave me a kiss.

"I missed you this summer. Did you have fun?"

We rode for a couple of hours around the Conway and Dwyer farms. We never stopped talking. I was telling her about all the crazy people we saw at Snook's Pond and how to make twenty hot dogs at once so they were always hot and fresh. She told me about the books she read and that she was getting sad because she would have to leave soon. I didn't want to talk about that so we just rode. She held me close.

School started the next day.

Mom had arranged for me to go visit Mike at Lemoyne. It was his senior year. I had grown almost seven inches since spring.

Mike had invited me to come up for a weekend and stay at his fraternity house. I packed a bag. Mom drove me to Syracuse and dropped me off. The next week was Thanksgiving so he told Mom he would drive me home.

The weekend went by quickly.

As soon as we got home and walked in the door, Mom asked us to join Dick at the table, as she had some news.

"Your father and I thought it best not to worry you so we kept it from you that he had his surgery last Friday. I'm happy to tell you that your father is doing fine, and with prayers and hope, he could very well be home by Christmas if he heals well and has no complications."

I remember looking at Mom to see if her eyes were comfortable with what she was telling us or if they were nervous eyes and maybe hiding some bad news. She was smiling.

"The doctors make him cough several times a day to keep his lungs clear. It is very painful for him—but he knows he has to so he does his very best."

Dick asked, "Does he still have two lungs?"

"Yes, they only had to take the top portion of one of his lungs—so he still has two lungs."

We were so happy and now we couldn't wait to see our dad again, after almost a year. There was a holiday dance at the school that night. Mom drove me and stopped to pick up Judy. She and I danced all night. This might be the last time we get to dance, we thought, since she might have to move back to Baltimore any day.

We got busy during Thanksgiving with family. Then I started to get letters from Judy. She had moved back. Her parents had come during the school break and got her with no warning and gave her no time to say good-bye. She wrote me a letter that I held all night. We wrote back and forth for months. I missed her—but I missed my dad, too.

It was the morning of Christmas Eve, but the house didn't feel like Christmas at all. There was a lot of snow on the ground. We usually hoped for snow at Christmastime, and it was still snowing, but the house seemed cold now, still and quiet.

I got out of bed and went to the kitchen in my pajama bottoms and t-shirt. Dick was already there.

Mom said, "I'm making your favorite."

I knew it was poached eggs. Mom knew I loved poached eggs. I would put one on a slice of buttered toast and eat it like an open-faced sandwich.

Mom asked if we could help fold the clothes right after breakfast so we could get ready for Christmas. She told us Don and Mary were coming today from Harrisburg with our four cousins, Tommy, Timmy, Teddy, and Terry. Dorothy and Norman were coming in from Washington with their daughter, Karen. Mike would be here.

Mom made no mention of Dad. We were afraid to bring it up so early. We didn't want to make her cry. If Dad wasn't here, we thought, this would be the first Christmas without him. We felt the same—there wouldn't be a Christmas without Dad.

We moped around the kitchen, eating, talking, and folding our clothes as Mom piled them on the counter. It was almost two o'clock and I was still barefoot and in my pajama bottoms and t-shirt. Dick was looking at the pile of presents lying by the piano. Mike had come and was sitting on the piano bench playing "Volga Boatman," most of which he had memorized.

I went in my room and fell asleep.

The next thing I knew, Mom was pulling on my toe. "Jerry, get up, get up—your dad is coming home! Your father's coming home!"

I sat up and rubbed my eyes. It was dark outside. Mom had a big smile on her face. I wasn't sure if I was dreaming or really awake.

"Mike Shea just called and told me that the man who is driving him home stopped at the store and went in to buy your dad a newspaper. Mike Shea went out to the car and said hello to him.

He said your dad looks good, but he thought it would be nice to call us and let us know they were on their way—the man and your dad!"

I stood up. I could hear Dorothy and Norm laughing and talking with Dick and Mike in the living room. I brushed by Mom and went to the bathroom.

When I came out I looked from the hall through my bedroom window. Mary and Don were driving in with their lights on and had a big Christmas tree tied on their car roof. I didn't think we were going to have a tree this year. I started walking down the hall to get dressed when the telephone in Dad and Mom's room rang. I rushed in and picked it up.

"Hello?"

"Hello, is Jerry there?"

"This is Jerry."

"Jerry, this is Doctor Webb. Merry Christmas, young fella. I just thought you would like to know that your dad just drove past my place on his way home. I thought you would like to know, what it being Christmas and all."

"How did you know he was coming?" I asked.

"Us old fogies have our own SOS system, too, don't ya know," he laughed. "We invented it. Have a BULLY GOOD Merry Christmas, son! Mike Shea called me with the news."

I dropped the phone on the floor and ran out through the dining room past Dorothy and Norm to the front door and opened it.

Mom shouted for me to put something on but I was already out the door.

I jumped off the front step barefoot and started walking quickly through the snow toward the gate, not taking my eyes off the top of the road up by Farmer Parker's hill, looking for headlights from the car Dad would be in. I knew the car Dad was in would be coming over that hill any minute now.

Mary opened the window of her car as I scurried past and shouted, "Jerry, you will catch your death, go put something on."

I just kept walking as fast as I could, keeping my eye on the top of the hill.

Finally, almost to the gate, I saw the lights and a car come slowly over the hill, inching down around the curve. The road was unplowed and very slick so they were taking their time. I hopped out on Cardner Road. The car turned into the driveway and paused a moment. The back window opened down halfway and a hand came out for a shake.

It was my dad.

IT WAS MY DAD!

I grabbed his hand and squeezed it, walking alongside.

"Jerry?" he asked.

"Yes," I started to cry. I'd grown almost seven inches since he saw me last and I wasn't sure he could recognize me. It frightened me to think he may not remember me.

"Remember fishing at Little York Lake, Dad? Remember I rowed us out in the boat at Sandy Pond, Dad? Remember when you beat my airplane to Watertown, Dad? Remember teaching me how to make desserts, Dad? Can you remember me, Dad?"

We were at the house now and the family was all on the porch waving and cheering. Dad squeezed my hand and I heard him say, "You caught croppies we cooked at the Imperial House, remember, son?"

"Room number six, Dad."

"Room number six," he answered.

He remembered me.

The car stopped and Dad got out slowly. He was still tender and healing from his lung operation. When he stood straight up he looked at me and how tall I was. He ran his hand back and forth over my brush cut.

"You sure have grown, Jerry, me boy—you sure have grown."

I stared in his eyes. "I'm still the same, Dad—just like you're still the same."

He shook my hand, put his arm around my shoulder, and we walked into the house with everyone cheering, laughing, crying, and all happy again.

Mom barked at me: "Go take a warm shower so you don't get frostbite."

"No! I'm not leaving my dad!" I barked back.

"Well, at least go put some pants and shoes on."

I did do that, got a sweater, and came out and sat on the chair next to the couch where Dad was resting, smiling, watching everyone all talking at once.

Don, Norm, and Mike were putting up the Christmas tree and Mary, Dorothy, and Mom were bringing out boxes of decorations and lights.

Dad asked Dorothy for some writing paper and a pen or pencil. He wanted to write a friend in the TB sanitarium and wish him a Merry Christmas.

I remembered when I lay on that same couch, the day I was poisoned. I remembered Dad sitting where I was sitting now—sitting tall, watching over me all night long, his silhouette crested by moon glow.

I sat up taller in the chair.

When I woke it was still dark outside. The house was quiet and all the lights were out except for the tree. The Christmas tree was a spectacular glow of lights and colors and shiny, sparkling decorations. The presents were all stacked underneath. Dad was still on the couch with a blanket over him. He had the pen in his limp hand and paper on his lap—but he was asleep.

I got up and took the pen and paper off him and put them on my chair arm.

His eyes opened and he smiled. "Can I have some water, son?"

I got him a glass of water from the kitchen.

"Want a fire, Dad? I know how to build a good one."

"That would be nice, son."

I moved his papers to the seat of my chair and built a big fire with the largest logs, remembering the time I left ears of harvest cow corn right there by the fireplace, for Santa.

I stacked up some wood, enough that would take us through most of the night. I wasn't sure what time it was but I knew everyone would be getting up soon to celebrate Christmas.

I walked back to the chair. Dad was asleep again. I picked up the paper and pen and sat down.

I didn't read Dad's entire letter but I did read one paragraph:

I'm sleeping on the sofa, the first night home, just to be in the thick of things for Christmas in the morning. My boy, Jerry, is roughing it

on a less comfortable chair right beside me while he and I catch up.
He doesn't seem to mind. Watching him there makes me recall the
many nights he would sleep in a bed roll over the falls here at Delphi.
The horses would come around grazing or just snooping far into the
night. Jerry didn't mind horses, woodchucks, squirrels, rabbits, foxes,
deer, some bears, and a load of wild birds that roamed the upper falls
some of the time.

I remember looking up at the glowing tree.
Looking over at the burning fireplace.
Watching my dad sleeping.
Feeling a tear roll down my cheek.
"There is a Santa Claus," I said. "He came tonight."

CPSIA information can be obtained at www.ICGtesting.com
Printed in the USA
LVOW08s1910100615

441956LV00001B/121/P